What PRAYER Can Do

EDITORS of GUIDEPOSTS

Guideposts

Guideposts.org

Published by Guideposts Books & Inspirational Media
110 William Street
New York, New York 10038
Guideposts.org

This book is intended to be a spiritual reference volume only, not a medical manual. The presented information is meant to help you make informed decisions about your physical, emotional, and spiritual health. It is not intended to be a substitute for any treatment prescribed by your doctor. If you are experiencing symptoms or suspect that you have a medical problem, please seek medical help.

Acknowledgments

Every attempt has been made to credit the sources of copyrighted material used in this book. If any such acknowledgment has been inadvertently omitted or miscredited, receipt of such information would be appreciated.

Scripture quotations marked (AMP) are taken from *The Amplified Bible, Old Testament*. Copyright © 1965, 1987 by The Zondervan Corporation. *The Amplified New Testament*. Copyright © 1954, 1958, 1987 by The Lockman Foundation. Used by permission.

Scripture quotations marked (CEB) are taken from the *Common English Bible*. Copyright © 2011 by Common English Bible.

Scripture quotations marked (CJB) are taken from the *Complete Jewish Bible*. Copyright © 1998 by David H. Stern. All rights reserved.

Scripture quotations marked (ERV) are taken from the *Easy-to-Read Version*. Copyright © 2006 by Bible League International.

Scripture quotations marked (ESV) are taken from the *Holy Bible, English Standard Version*. Copyright © 2001 by Crossway Bibles, a division of Good News Publishers. Used by permission. All rights reserved.

Scripture quotations marked (ISV) are taken from the *International Standard Version of the Bible*. Copyright © 1995-2014 by ISV Foundation. All rights reserved internationally. Used by permission of Davidson Press, Inc.

Scripture quotations marked (KJV) are taken from *The King James Version of The Holy Bible*.

Scripture quotations marked (MEV) are taken from the *Modern English Version of The Holy Bible*. Copyright © 2014 by Military Bible Association. Used by permission. All rights reserved.

Scripture quotations marked (NASB) are taken from the *New American Standard Bible*. Copyright © 1960, 1962, 1963, 1968, 1971, 1972, 1973, 1975, 1977, 1995 by The Lockman Foundation. Used by permission. www.Lockman.org

Scripture quotations marked (NCV) are from the *New Century Version*®. Copyright © 2005 by Thomas Nelson, Inc. Used by permission. All rights reserved.

Scripture quotations marked (NIV) are taken from the *New International Version of The Holy Bible*. Copyright © 1973, 1978, 1984, 2011 by Biblica. Used by permission of Zondervan. All rights reserved worldwide. www.zondervan.com

Scripture quotations marked (NKJV) are taken from the *New King James Version of The Holy Bible*. Copyright © 1979, 1980, 1982, 1983, 1985, 1990, 1997 by Thomas Nelson, Inc. Used by permission. All rights reserved.

Scripture quotations marked (NLT) are taken from *The Holy Bible, New Living Translation*. Copyright © 1996. Used by permission of Tyndale House Publishers, Inc., Wheaton, Illinois 60189. All rights reserved.

Scripture quotations marked (NRSV) are taken from the *New Revised Standard Version Bible*. Copyright © 1989 by the Division of Christian Education of the National Council of the Churches of Christ in the U.S.A. Used by permission. All rights reserved.

Scripture quotations marked (PHILLIPS) are from *The New Testament in Modern English*, revised edition–J. B. Phillips, translator. © J.B. Phillips 1958, 1960, 1972. Used by permission of Macmillan Publishing Co., Inc.

Scripture quotations marked (RSV) are taken from the *Revised Standard Version of the Bible*. Copyright © 1946, 1952, 1971 by the Division of Christian Education of the National Council of the Churches of Christ in the U.S.A. Used by permission. All rights reserved.

Scripture quotations marked (TLB) are taken from *The Living Bible*. Copyright © 1971 by Tyndale House Foundation. Used by permission of Tyndale House Publishers, Inc., Carol Stream, Illinois 60188. All rights reserved.

Cover design by W Design Studio
Cover photo by Victoria Shibut from Dreamstime.com
Interior design and typesetting by Müllerhaus
Indexed by Maria A. Sullivan

Printed and bound in the United States of America

10 9 8 7 6 5 4 3 2 1

Prayer, properly utilized, can revolutionize our lives. It can help us to meet our difficulties, solve our problems, heal our diseases, overcome our weaknesses. It can bring us to a new plane of life.

—Norman Vincent Peale

Guideposts
New York

Inspiring the world to believe anything is possible
with hope, faith, and prayer.

Table of Contents

Introduction x

SECTION 1
What Prayer Can Do 1

An Intimate Look at Prayer 2

Why Pray? 6

How to Pray 10

SECTION 2
When God Answers Prayer 13

Prayer Works Wonders 14

God's Intrusion 16

Face-to-Face with Jesus 19

The Voice of My Maker 23

He Opened My Eyes 26

The Mysterious Comforter 31

The Healer She Could Only Imagine 35

The Angel Holdup 38

An Angel Named Grace 41

My Only True Security 45

Three Days to Live 50

Against All Odds 54

A Return to Sanity 58

Loving My Soldier 62

The Two-Percent Life Experience 67

He Gives His Angels Charge over Us 71

My Emmanuel Moment 74

An Unexpected Gift 77

My Dream Husband 80

A Heavenly Code Blue 83

The Prayer Stone 86

Breaking Selfish Pride 91

The Final Authority 95

Home Is Where the Heart Is 100

No More Headaches 104

Father Knows Best 108

Shortest, Biggest Prayer 112

A Race to the Bottom 115

Before the Snow Flies 119

Dad, Let's Pray! 122

An Earthquake Full of Blessings 125

The Message from Heaven 130

The Nativity Baby 133

The Miraculous Ride 136

Nowhere to Call Home 141

Leaving the God of Money 145

Paper Angels 148

A Bright New World 152

Miracle Boy 157

A Sparkling Miracle 161

A Precise Prayer for Healing 166

SECTION 3

A Guide for Prayer

A Guide for Prayer 171

Learn, Grow, Practice Prayer 172

The Prayer Effect

How to Use the Bible as a Guide to Effective Prayer 175

How to Be Moved to Pray 178

When You Can't Find the Words 183

How to Hear God 185

What God Says when He Talks to You 188

How Does God Talk to You? 191

When God Talks to You 193

Common Barriers to Prayer 195

Praying in the Middle of Life for You and Others

How to Pray with Longing while
Trying to Discover God's Will 199

How to Pray in a Group 202

How to Pray with Determination
during Suffering or Persecution 205

How to Pray with Power while
Wrestling with Temptation 207

How to Pray with Peace after Losing a Job 209

How to Pray with Insight about Time Management 211

How to Pray with Endurance while Raising Children 213

How to Pray in Grief while Facing Infertility 217

How to Pray with Confidence
concerning Military Service 219

How to Pray with Focus when Starting a New Job 221

How to Pray with Expectation when Getting Married ... 223

How to Pray with Excitement when Graduating 225

How to Pray in Sympathy when Someone Has Died 227

How to Pray when You Are Afraid 230

How to Pray when You Are Angry 232

How to Pray when You Are Depressed 234

How to Pray when You Doubt God 236

How to Pray when You Are Jealous 240

How to Pray when You Feel Exhausted 242

How to Pray during Illness 244

How to Pray when under Financial Distress 247

How to Pray in the Midst of Family Strife 249

How to Pray when You Are Worried 251

Practical Matters of Prayer

How to Pray Aloud 254

Holding Hands for Mealtime Prayers 256

Kneeling for Bedtime Prayers 258

"How Do I Know God Listens to Me?" 261

"How Do I Pray to God when He Knows Everything?" . . 263

"The Situation Is Impossible, How Do I Begin to Pray?" . . 264

The Prayers of the Bible

Jesus's Prayer for All Believers—How to Find Unity 267

Paul's Prayers for the Churches—How to Grow in Faith . . . 270

Nehemiah's Prayer Project—
"Have Mercy and Answer My Prayer" 273

Elijah's Prayer—"God, Reveal Yourself to Me" 275

David's Prayer of Protection—"Hide Me" 277

Solomon's Humility—"Grant Me Wisdom" 279

Jude's Praise—Worshipping through Prayer 282

Hannah's Heart—He's My Child 284

Stephen's Final Prayer—What to Pray at Life's End 286

Lord, Teach Us to Pray the Lord's Prayer

"Our Father in Heaven" 289

"Hallowed Be Your Name" 291

"Your Kingdom Come" 293

"Your Will Be Done on Earth as It Is in Heaven" 295

"Give Us This Day Our Daily Bread" 297

"Forgive Us Our Debts, as We Forgive Our Debtors" . . . 300

"Do Not Lead Us into Temptation,
but Deliver Us from the Evil One" 302

"For Yours Is the Kingdom and the
Power and the Glory Forever" 305

The Importance of Prayer

Praying for Wisdom 308

The Prayer of Saint Francis of Assisi—Praying for Peace 311

Praying for God's Protection 313

Praying for Forgiveness 315

Finding Words when You Have None 317

Contributors 320

Scripture Reference Index 325

Topical Index 329

Note from the Editors 338

Introduction

$\mathcal{P}$ause to consider this amazing gift called prayer. No pass needed, no ID required, no signature necessary—simply full, unearned access to the Creator of the universe to petition for all of our needs and wants, a direct and ever-open line to God Almighty, the greatest ear to talk to, the strongest shoulder to lean on, the friend of all friends Who hears our prayers and commands the earth to comply for our joy and His glory, according to His will. Anywhere, at any time, for any reason, we have a connection to the ultimate Healer, Deliverer, Restorer, Promise-keeper, the One Who says, *"Therefore I tell you, whatever you ask for in prayer, believe that you have received it, and it will be yours"* (Mark 11:24 NIV). We show up with nothing to offer but a believing heart and God is there. How incredible is that?

What Prayer Can Do explores and celebrates the power of this divine communication through biblical examples and gripping contemporary stories of people who prayed in dire situations and received God's answers. It also offers guidance on how to pray, helping us claim the promises of Scripture for ourselves and for others.

This book resonated with me for many reasons, chief among them its focus on what the Word says about prayer. I have long marveled at the reward gained through prayer in the Bible. Hannah, who had no children, prayed sincerely for a child and God granted

her desire (1 Samuel 1:16–17). Daniel committed to prayer several times a day and God faithfully turned events in his favor (Daniel 6:10). Elijah prayed for the life of a young child to be revived and God granted his request (1 Kings 17:21–22 NIV).

Nobly Jesus prayed to the Father despite His own will that God's will be done. *"Going a little farther, he fell with his face to the ground and prayed, 'My Father, if it is possible, may this cup be taken from me. Yet not as I will, but as you will'"* (Matthew 26:39 NIV). If prayer was a priority for Jesus, it surely needs to be a priority for all who follow Him.

Jesus set the model of prayer for my childhood home. In my earliest memories, I'm sitting beside Mom, who's on her knees during hours-long services at the Greater Refuge

Temple in Harlem, New York. On work days, she'd wake up extra early to spend time on her knees praying before heading off to her job as a technician at a hospital. And anytime before leaving the house, standing at the door, she'd lift up a prayer for divine protection, "Father, in the name of Jesus, thank You for this day and Your gift of life. Watch over us and keep Your angels encamped around us, keeping us from all hurt, harm, or danger. May our lives glorify You this day in all that we do, in Jesus's name, Amen." She encouraged me to pray the same. It's been a maturing journey.

I recall talking to God many times as a little girl, but as I reached my teenage years, the consistency and enthusiasm of my prayers grew faint. I became distracted with television and extracurricular activities. It wasn't until college, when I found myself confronting real-world issues and struggling to figure out who I wanted to be, that prayer became a central part of my life. I recognized that regardless of the number of friends I have or family members who support me, there are some things no one can understand or help me with but God.

What Prayer Can Do is filled with stories of people who have come to the same realization. In one story, *My Emmanuel Moment*, Holly Blevins writes, "During faith-defining moments, the Holy Spirit is right there covering us with grace and mercy, leading us and guiding us toward Him."

That line describes something I've experienced so often in my own life. Reading it brought to mind the time when, as a divinity student at New York Theological Seminary, I was invited on a mission trip to Istanbul to help refugees from Syria and Africa. To go, I needed to come up with three thousand dollars in less than a month. The program sponsored me for one thousand. Raising the balance seemed nearly impossible with such short notice. But I knew that if God wanted me to go, He would work out the finances. One morning I prayed, "Lord, I want to go to Turkey. If it's meant for me to go, please show me a sign."

A few minutes later, I was walking down the street when a bus rolled by with a big advertisement on its side: Visit Turkey. Really, Lord? An actual sign? I asked God to confirm it. That evening, I saw a bus with the same advertisement. Without having the money yet, I committed to going. Miraculously, while attending a seminary class, I told the other students about the mission and two people each gave me a thousand dollars. My trip was covered, all because I prayed and believed.

The power of prayer followed me to Turkey. Our group worked with a Christian community help center in Istanbul. There, we served the refugees any way we could, assisting doctors with getting prescription medicine, reading stories to and playing games with children, cooking and preparing food. One day, I was sitting in the center talking with a man who began telling me how he had to leave his home country and family because of his faith in God or else he would have been killed. As he talked, people began to gather around and listen. His story encouraged others—refugees and missionaries alike—to open up and share their stories. We all sensed the divine energy of God's presence. Hearts were open. I suggested we lift up a prayer for everyone. At this point, about fifteen of us were gathered. By the end of the prayer, we were all in tears. They were tears of hope, love, and peace shared in a community of strangers by name but spiritual siblings by faith.

Not everyone spoke English. We connected through the universal language of prayer. That moment, we all believed and God became tangible—*"For where two or three gather in my name, there am I with them"* (Matthew 18:20 NIV).

So pray always—in your style, your voice, your sincerity. Through it all, know that God hears your prayers and will answer them. And wherever you are in your prayer journey, I'm confident that, like me, after reading *What Prayer Can Do*, you'll hear your soul joyfully exclaiming, "What *can't* prayer do!"

—*P*astor Ty'Ann A. Brown, M.Div.

1

What Prayer Can Do

An Intimate Look at Prayer
Bob Hostetler

I have not always enjoyed prayer. That may seem odd given that I was born into a devout Christian family, grew up in the church, began my faith journey at a young age, and became a pastor at twenty-two. In my early forties, I even planted a church, which thrived and continues to grow. Still, I was not a person who relied consistently on prayer. I preached and taught on the subject, and from time to time summoned the will to carve out space in my schedule to pray every day. But it never lasted.

Then my son happened. When he entered high school, he began to struggle severely, not only with his grades but with life in general. He grew depressed and started to rebel. My wife and I could see that he was in pain, which led to dangerous choices, which led to more pain. He started wearing all black, reflecting the inner darkness he battled, and hanging around with a new group of friends (one of whom was an avowed Satanist). My son became distant. He stopped talking to his mother and me, except during painful conversations when we confronted him about skipping school, smoking heavily, and dating people who clearly did not have his best interests at heart. We tried hard to keep him close. We reinforced that we loved him and would be there for him, but our efforts seemed to have no effect. We felt desperate and helpless.

I searched for answers. I booked a weekend at a retreat center near our home. Though I am a voracious reader, I packed only my Bible. I'm also a music lover, but I took none of my favorite music. My plan was to achieve a state of "constructive boredom," in which I had nothing to do but pray for my son. It worked. I sat and I prayed. I walked and I prayed. I thumbed through my Bible and prayed its words. I prayed through meals. I prayed myself to sleep.

And my prayers were answered. I returned home a different man. I was still anxious, but no longer felt helpless. I had found a refuge from my worries and fears for my son. And to this day, I wholeheartedly believe that God worked through my prayers to transform first me, and then him.

Over the few years following that trip, my son gradually changed for the better. It was as if his heart had been renewed.

The steps forward were small but noticeable. Gone were the black clothes. His darkened spirit grew lighter. He buckled down in school and graduated. Then he went on to earn a college degree, growing into his manhood enough to confidently marry his "dream woman," and become a devoted husband to her. His long-dormant faith in God was not only revived; it saw him through an evolution into a devoted Christian father and church worship leader.

Prayer helped me survive the stress and anxiety—even depression—of those years. And I shudder to imagine what paths my son could have taken if he had not been surrounded and supported by my prayers and the prayers of many others. There is, of course, no objective way to measure what prayer accomplished. It's enough to know that God answered my desperate pleas. Some He answered beyond my wildest dreams. Others He answered differently than I might have liked, but still better than I might have hoped. And, as He often does, God did things for me and in me as a result of prayer that I could never have put into words in the first place. And my prayer retreat, which became the first of many, produced in me a dependence on God through prayer that I am convinced pays rich and lasting dividends to this day.

What prayer has done for me, I have seen it do for many others. And I am a grateful witness to the glorious possibilities the come with prayer.

The Biblical Promises of Prayer

"Prayer is the root, the fountain, the mother of a thousand blessings." Those words written by South African pastor, writer, and teacher Andrew Murray came after he experienced a personal crisis. At the age of fifty, after many years of successful ministry, he became sick and lost his ability to speak. This malady continued for more than two years. Seeking a way to cope, he traveled to London. There, he studied and prayed with William E. Boardman, another minister and author, for three weeks. When Murray left London, he was completely healed, and able to resume preaching and writing for another forty years.

Murray's experience affirms the promises of God found throughout the Bible. Scripture tells us that those who pray will release for themselves and others a flowing stream of blessings and benefits. They include:

The beauty and security of God's presence. "Whoever dwells in the shelter of the Most High"—which may be understood to be the place of prayer— "will rest in the shadow of the Almighty. I will say of the Lord, 'He is my refuge and my fortress, my God, in whom I trust'" (Psalm 91:1–2 NIV). The beauty and security of God's presence are accessible to all who pray; as the early church leader James wrote, "Come near to God and He will come near to you" (James 4:8 NIV).

Mercy and grace. Prayer opens the windows of heaven to the soul. "Let us come boldly to the throne of our gracious God. There we will receive his mercy, and we will find grace to help us when we need it most" (Hebrews 4:16 NLT).

Perfect peace. In the Bible, God invites us to "Cast all your anxiety on him because he cares for you" (1 Peter 5:7 NIV). Prayer is the way we can get to that promised peace: "Do not be anxious about anything, but in every situation, by prayer and petition, with thanksgiving, present your requests to God. And the peace of God, which transcends all understanding, will guard your hearts and your minds in Christ Jesus" (Philippians 4:6–7 NIV).

Wisdom. The Bible tells us that through prayer you can gain wise counsel: "If any of you lacks wisdom, you should ask God, who gives generously to all without finding fault, and it will be given to you" (James 1:5–6 NIV). And God promised something even beyond wisdom to those who pray: "Call on me in prayer and I will answer you. I will show you great and mysterious things which you still do not know about" (Jeremiah 33:3 NET).

Healing. Prayer puts God's healing mercies on display in wondrous ways. The New Testament book of James says, "Are any of you sick? You should call for the elders of the church to come and pray over you, anointing you with oil in the name of the Lord. Such a prayer offered in faith will heal the sick, and the Lord will make you well" (James 5:14–15 NLT).

Forgiveness and a clean conscience. Beyond physical healing, this passage also promises healing for the soul: "Such a prayer offered in faith will heal the sick, and the Lord will make you well. And if you have committed any sins, you will be forgiven. Confess your sins to each other and pray for each other so that you may be healed. The earnest prayer of a righteous person has great power and produces wonderful results" (James 5:15–16 NLT).

Safety, strength, and comfort. These are among the most enduring benefits of prayer, an embrace of God's presence and protection. In the words of Psalm 23: "Even when I walk through the darkest valley, I will not be afraid, for you are close beside me. Your rod and your staff protect and comfort me" (NLT).

Why Pray?

$\mathcal{P}$raying is by no means an uncommon practice. In fact, more than half of Americans say they pray every day, according to a recent Pew Research survey.[1] And around 45 percent of Americans say they rely heavily on prayer when making major life decisions.[2] But the pull of prayer seems to be strongest when we are at our most vulnerable. People who are confronting a serious illness almost universally turn to prayer—more than 85 percent of them, according to a University of Rochester study.[3] And Harvard University's Dr. Herbert Benson, author of *Timeless Healing: The Power and Biology of Belief,* routinely urges his patients to participate in their own treatment by choosing a word or phrase to repeat when they are stressed, afraid, or in pain. Dr. Benson says that more than 80 percent of those who follow his advice choose a prayer.[4]

Why?

Is it just a reflex? Or is it a habit—something ingrained in us from childhood? Do we pray simply because we don't know what else to do? Or do we pray because somewhere—down deep, perhaps—we suspect (or at least hope) that prayer accomplishes something, and that there are measurable benefits? And if so, what are those?

Centuries after the Bible proclaimed the physical, mental, and emotional benefits of prayer, medical researchers have begun testing these promises with scientific studies. While these studies are far from conclusive, their results suggest that, as Hamlet said, "There are more things in heaven and earth…than are dreamt of."[5] Researchers have found that people who pray experience some form of relief from many common ailments.

---

[1] http://www.pewforum.org/2015/11/03/chapter-2-religious-practices-and-experiences/#private-devotions
[2] http://www.people-press.org/2012/06/04/section-6-religion-and-social-values/
[3] "Many Cancer Patients Turn to Complementary Therapies for Healing," University of Rochester Medical Center, June 7, 2004 (https://www.urmc.rochester.edu/news/story/573/many-cancer-patients-turn-to-complementary-therapies-for-healing.aspx).
[4] Herbert Benson, MD, *Timeless Healing: The Power and Biology of Belief* (New York: Scribner, 1996), 152.
[5] William Shakespeare, *Hamlet*, Act I, Scene V, lines 919–920.

For example, while preparing his doctoral dissertation, S. P. Laird of the University of Kansas looked at the role of prayer when used as a coping technique for adult patients with arthritis. Laird found that having faith in prayer resulted in people displaying positive emotions and that praying more days per week correlated to fewer physical concerns.

High blood pressure was the focus of Duke University psychiatrist Harold Koenig, who conducted a six-year study of nearly four thousand older adults and discovered that individuals who prayed daily were 40 percent less likely to have the condition than those without a regular prayer practice.[6]

Another study centered on the often-debilitating affliction of migraine headaches. Dr. Kenneth Pargament of Bowling Green State University[7] conducted research in which he separated eighty-three migraine sufferers into four groups. One group practiced twenty minutes a day of prayerful meditation for one month. Another group used "internal secular meditation" (repeating a phrase such as "I am content" or "I am happy"). A third group followed "external secular meditation" (focusing on phrases such as "Grass is green" or "Sand is soft"). A fourth group was taught to use relaxation techniques rather than meditation. At the end of the month, those using prayerful meditation reported a greater decline in the number of headaches—and a greater increase in pain tolerance—than those in the other three groups.

Multiple studies have shown that prayer can also have a substantial effect on depression and anxiety. Lisa Miller, professor of clinical psychology and director of the Spirituality Mind Body Institute at Teachers College, Columbia University, studied people whose family history put them at a high risk of depression. Professor Miller found that people who prayed regularly possessed thicker cortices—the thin layer covering the brain—than those who did not regularly practice prayer. A thinning cortex can indicate poor health, and even depression. The study also suggests that prayer can not only help prevent the onset of depression but also reduce its severity.[8] The *British Journal of Health Psychology* published another study that backed Professor Miller's findings. It showed that praying can reduce a

[6] Koenig H.G, et al. 1998. "The relationship between religious activities and blood pressure in older adults," *International Journal of Psychiatry in Medicine* 28: 189–213.
[7] Wachholtz, A. B. and Pargament, K. I. "Migraines and meditation: Does spirituality matter?" *Journal of Behavioral Medicine* 31, no. 4 (August 2008): 351–366.
[8] Lisa Miller, Ravi Bansal, Priya Wickramaratne, Xuejun Hao, Craig E. Tenke, Myrna M. Weissman, Bradley S. Peterson. "Neuroanatomical Correlates of Religiosity and Spirituality," *JAMA Psychiatry*, 2013; 1 DOI: 10.1001/jamapsychiatry.2013.3067

person's risk of developing depression as well as anxiety.[9] And a Baylor University study of 1,714 individuals[10] found that people who pray and embrace a loving and protective concept of God experience a more pronounced reduction in anxiety compared to others who suffer.

In *Timeless Healing*, Dr. Benson cites scientific research, but also draws on his decades as a physician for anecdotal evidence of how prayer can help patients. He tells the story of Janet Frank, who suffered with insomnia:

"Mrs. Frank was lucky if she got to sleep by four or five a.m. even if she'd gone to bed by eleven the night before. Her sleeping troubles began in 1980 as a result of a very traumatic experience.… At first, Mrs. Frank just had trouble sleeping in strange places, at friends' homes or in hotels; gradually she stopped going places for fear of being unable to sleep. Unfortunately, the problem worsened. Eventually, she couldn't sleep even in her own house, so Mrs. Frank stayed up all night, listening to talk radio, making muffins, catching up on ironing, and walking around the house for hours at a time.… She came in to see Dr. Gregg D. Jacobs, my colleague, who specialized in insomnia treatment.

"Before she began [treatment], Mrs. Frank always needed the radio on to go to sleep, because the voices it broadcast overcame the voices in her head. But when she lay down and recited 'The Lord is my shepherd' or 'Give me peace' to herself, her heart stopped beating as hard as it used to and she could drop off to sleep. She explains, 'I would visualize God and I could almost see God watching over me. God would calm me down. I could almost reach out and touch Him, that's how real it was to me.'"[11]

Beyond battling specific ailments, research shows prayer can also help us lead happier and even longer lives.

Dr. Andrew Newberg, professor of psychiatry at the University of Pennsylvania, found that prayer can affect the nervous system, making a person feel happier and more optimistic. The research found people experienced a more long-term positive outlook, showing the true lasting impact of prayer.[12]

---

[9] Maltby, J., Lewis, C. A. and Day, L. (1999), Religious orientation and psychological well-being: The role of the frequency of personal prayer. *British Journal of Health Psychology*, 4: 363–378. doi:10.1348/135910799168704

[10] Ellison, C., Bradshaw, M., Flannelly, K., Galek. K. "Prayer, Attachment to God, and Symptoms of Anxiety-Related Disorders among U.S. Adults," *Sociology of Religion*, 2014, 75:2 208–233 doi:10.1093/socrel/srt079

[11] Dr. Herbert Benson, *Timeless Healing: The Power and Biology of Belief* (New York: Scribner, 1996), 129–130.

[12] Newberg, Andrew B. "The Neuroscientific Study of Spiritual Practices." *Frontiers in Psychology 5* (2014): 215. PMC. Web. 2 June 2017.

The Journals of Gerontology published findings[13, 14] of a study that considered the relationship between prayer and long life. For six years, researchers examined the role of prayer in the lives of more than a thousand older people. They began by asking participants, "How often do you spend time in private religious activities, such as prayer, meditation, or Bible study?" They were able to conclude that private spiritual practices such as prayer and regular attendance in public prayer and worship promoted not only better health, but longevity.

Some people believe prayer is where science meets God. How does prayer lead to healing? Ultimately, researchers may never be able to fully comprehend or quantify the effects of prayer. To grasp God's promises, we rely not on science, but on our faith in His Word. For those who have a desire to grab hold of all that prayer has to offer, we continue on this journey to explore how it's done.

[13] Hughes M. Helma, Judith C. Hays, Elizabeth P. Flint, Harold G. Koenig and Dan G. Blazera. 2000. Does Private Religious Activity Prolong Survival? A Six-Year Follow-up Study of 3,851 Older Adults. *The Journals of Gerontology* Series A: Biological Sciences and Medical Sciences 55: M400–M405.
[14] Koenig H.G., Hays J.C., Larson D.B., et al. 1999. Does religious attendance prolong survival? A six-year follow-up study of 3,968 older adults. *J Gerontol Med Sci.* 54A: M370–M377.

How to Pray

$\mathcal{P}$oet and hymnist James Montgomery wrote:

> Prayer is the simplest form of speech
> That infant lips can try;
> Prayer, the sublimest strains that reach
> The Majesty on high.[15]

It is easy to overcomplicate the act of praying, to worry that we aren't doing it "right." But prayer requires no special setting, no fancy formula. Even the most sophisticated prayer consists of just three basic steps: talking (offering praise, confession, and thanks to God, and asking for things from God), listening (reading or meditating), and "being" (silence, stillness, and awareness). Some of the most sincere prayers are the simplest: "Thanks," "I'm sorry," and "Help!"

The Bible demonstrates not only what prayer can do, but also how to practice prayer. Hannah, burdened by her childlessness, cried out in anguish, "Lord Almighty, if you will only look on your servant's misery and remember me, and not forget your servant but give her a son, then I will give him to the Lord for all the days of his life" (1 Samuel 1:11 NIV). King David, who had fallen into loathsome sin, poured out his confession in the words, "O God…Create in me a clean heart" (Psalm 51:1, 10 NIV). Another king, Jehoshaphat, addressed himself to "Lord, the God of our ancestors" (2 Chronicles 20:6 NIV). Daniel, the survivor of the lions' den and counselor to pagan kings, made his prayers to "Lord, the great and awesome God, who keeps his covenant of love with those who love him and keep his

[15] James Montgomery, "Prayer is the soul's sincere desire," public domain.

commandments" (Daniel 9:4 NIV). And, of course, Jesus taught His first followers to pray, "Our Father" (Matthew 6:9 NIV).

These biblical examples show that there are many ways to approach God in prayer. And apart from telling His followers not to be show-offs when they pray, as Jesus does in the book of Matthew, He doesn't discourage people from using various roads that lead to God. In fact, He encourages us to pray often and even offers guidance. This guidance doesn't involve rules or procedures; it's about the attitude of our hearts. Jesus said:

Pray relationally. When His earliest followers asked Him to teach them more about prayer, Jesus said, "When you pray, say: 'Father'" (Luke 11:2 CEB). In other words, remember that we are not praying to some distant, unapproachable being, but to our loving Father. That relationship is important to establish because familiarity seems to make it easier to talk to Him.

Pray practically. Jesus also instructed us to pray, "Give us each day our daily bread" (Luke 11:3 ESV). What could be more practical than bread? Those seven words symbolize our everyday concerns and needs. And God cares that our needs are met: children, health, job, home, car, food. We can indeed take all of this and more to Him in prayer

Pray humbly. Jesus noted that we should pray, "Forgive us our sins, for we also forgive everyone who sins against us" (Luke 11:4 NIV). It takes humility to admit our sins and forgive those who sin against us, but those are among the most fruitful prayers we will ever pray.

Pray expectantly. Jesus concluded His signature prayer by saying: "And lead us not into temptation, but deliver us from evil" (Matthew 6:13 ESV). The more we pray, the more we can expect victory over temptation and deliverance from evil—that which surrounds us and that which too often erupts from within us. What seems impossible without prayer is attainable through prayer.

Pray persistently. After giving His followers what has come to be called "The Lord's Prayer," Jesus told a story about a man who called on a friend late one night to ask a favor. The friend had already gone to bed and didn't want to be bothered. But the man continued to knock, until his friend finally gave in and granted his request. So, Jesus said, "Ask and it will be given to you; seek and you will find; knock and the door will be opened to you. For everyone who asks receives; the one who seeks finds; and to the one who knocks, the door will be opened" (Luke 11:9–10 NIV). God encourages us to keep the prayer conversation going.

Later in this book, you'll find detailed instructions for how to pray when dealing with daily challenges and when facing life-changing events. They're not meant as a set of regulations, but as a path laid out by Scripture and the experiences of people who have encountered similar struggles.

Underlying it all is the conviction that prayer is our seed of hope. We are encouraged to "always pray and not give up" (Luke 18:1 NIV), knowing that God hears us and will intervene and fill our lives with the promise of "a thousand blessings" that can only come through prayer.

2

When God Answers Prayer

Prayer Works Wonders

❧

"*I* want to do that."

I said those words to my wife recently as we watched an acquaintance play the ukulele with beauty and brilliance. As he played, he smiled. His face glowed. He seemed as though he could lift off the ground and float on air. He did more than make it look easy; he showed it to be rewarding. We talked, but each of us intuited what the other was thinking: We wanted what he had. We signed up for lessons. We each bought a ukulele. We're not yet proficient, but we saw what music—specifically ukulele music—did for him. He inspired us to believe we could claim some of what he enjoyed.

I think something similar happened when Jesus walked the earth. Sometime after His first followers had coalesced into a group of twelve and watched how Jesus operated, they came to him and asked, "Lord, teach us to pray" (Luke 11:1 NIV). Those twelve men weren't saying they had never prayed before; they had prayed every day, all their lives. They had grown up seeing their parents pray. They had heard priests and rabbis pray. But they saw and heard something different when Jesus prayed. I think, in Jesus, they witnessed a different way of praying. And I think the effects of Jesus's prayers actually showed in His life. They saw that His enjoyment of life, command of the elements, authority over sickness and Satan, and more, were somehow connected not only to Who He was but also to how He prayed. They saw His prayers being answered. They watched

Him give thanks for a meager lunch of bread and fish and then turn it into a meal for thousands. They heard Him pray at the tomb of Lazarus and then call the man back from the dead. And they wanted what He had. They signed up for lessons. He inspired them to believe that they could claim some of what He enjoyed.

That is the purpose of these next few chapters. To show what prayer has done in the lives of a few otherwise ordinary people and stir a hunger for what they have and a hope that will inspire you to believe that you, too, can claim some of the blessings they have experienced. This collection shares the real-life stories of people who are not celebrities or scholars. They were not experts when they started, but they prayed, and their prayers were answered. Their prayers produced results. Their prayers worked wonders. Their prayers should give us every reason to believe, for ourselves, in what prayer can do.

God's Intrusion
Brenda Dillon

*W*hether it was shock, relief, or unexplainable awe that put me in a state of speech-lessness, I'll never know. I do know, however, that while my tongue was silent, my mind and heart were having a very serious emotional conversation with the Lord Jesus.

Seven years had passed since I was diagnosed with an abnormal tricuspid heart valve. The doctor explained that a normal tricuspid valve was round and had three flaps, making it look like a peace sign. Mine, however, was an oval with two flaps, making it look like an egg with a smile.

At the time, I thought, *No big deal—it works*. But the doctor told me I needed to have it checked every year—which, of course, went directly to the bottom of my to-do list.

Moving ahead seven years, I went to see my family doctor for a checkup, and he asked how the tricuspid was doing. When I told him I'd never had it checked, he imme-diately sent me to the other side of the building to see the heart doctor—who imme-diately sent me downstairs to radiology for an ultrasound.

It was a little unnerving when a technician asked to witness my test because she had never seen such an abnormality in real life.

Why not—bring in the whole crew!

I had second thoughts about that as more technicians began to hover over me, and the test seemed to go on and on. I remembered the earlier procedure only taking ten to fifteen minutes. I lay there watching the hands on the wall clock tick off the minutes while the confused technicians took turns looking at the ultrasound screen connected to my heart and checking it against my previous films.

I'm sure they must have seen a slight jolt on the monitor as I remembered the doctor holding up my films, pointing to the "smiling egg," and explaining to me that the flaps on a bicuspid valve were more apt to wear out than the flaps on a normal tricuspid valve.

I began to think about all the time I had spent hiking the peaks and canyons of our friend's ranch in the Big Horn Mountains. With every remembered step I thought, *I was wearing out my flappers…I was wearing out my flappers!*

Being one week away from my next trip to the ranch, I felt a foreboding melancholy coming over me. There would be no hiking this fall—maybe never again. As I lay there, feeling darker and darker, I heard a technician use the word *suspicious*, and, in my mind, that sealed my fate. Heart surgery was surely going to keep me from my annual adventure—perhaps permanently.

No, Lord, please! You know how much I love the mountains—You put that love in me. You and I have had wonderful times together scaling the peaks and creeping through the canyons. I feel so close to You when I stand on those rocky heights. Besides, I already have my plane ticket purchased. You know that I dearly love You and that my faith in You has a strong foundation. I believe that Your heart always desires the best for me. So if this is what You want to use in my life for continued growth and blessing, I surrender it to You. But please let me go to the mountains one last time.

I was finally told they were finished, but that I needed to see the doctor before I left. I said a quick prayer and stepped into his office.

He stood there with all my films hanging on the examination wall. He slowly pointed out the "smiling egg" of seven years ago—I remembered it well. Then, with a shaking hand, he pointed to the perfectly shaped "peace sign" they had recorded that day.

He must have said a dozen times, "I can't understand this! I've never seen anything like this."

I asked if I had somehow grown another "flap," and with irritation in his voice he said, "No! You're born with these things, you don't grow them."

If I hadn't seen the tests with my own eyes, I might have thought the films had gotten mixed up. But those were all my films—with my name, my birth date, and the calendar date of each test printed on the corners.

There was only one answer to the mystery. For whatever reason, God had chosen to turn my bicuspid heart valve into a perfectly working tricuspid valve.

The doctor said, "You don't have to come back," and I couldn't get out of the building fast enough.

When I reached my car, the tears cut loose. Not just tears of joy over the new miracle valve, but tears that came from the recognition that my God had chosen to lovingly intervene in my life in such a way that I couldn't doubt the source. One week later, I was worshipping God on top of a red-rock ridge in the Big Horn Mountains of Wyoming.

This miraculous intrusion by my Father God was a faith-building tool that He used to strengthen my spiritual foundation and increase my ability to trust Him in any situation.

Eleven years have passed since God performed a miraculous surgery on a heart that has been Christ's home for many years. His welcomed intrusions and constant presence have continued to build my faith and make Him very dear to me.

James 4:2 says we have not because we ask not. Matthew 13:57–58 says Jesus did few miracles in His hometown because of the people's unbelief. My desire is to never limit God by not asking or by not believing He can do something if He so chooses.

Each time He and I go hiking in the mountains, we have long discussions about how He renovated His home—both spiritually and physically.

Face-to-Face with Jesus
Delores E. Topliff

"If I only had a few days' rest, I could get back on top of things," my husband's youngest sister, Valerie, said. Her husband, Richard, was out West on a business trip. She sighed. "As darling as our kids are, it's hard taking care of two little girls and a five-month-old boy by myself."

"At least Doug's a good-natured baby."

"Yes, he is." She squeezed him.

I studied his sturdy limbs, his adorable wispy curls above dark brown eyes. "When does Richard get back?"

"Monday night."

"Doug drinks from a bottle now, doesn't he?"

"That's right. I couldn't manage otherwise." Valerie sank against the soft sofa cushions, looking exhausted.

I sat beside her. "Here, let me hold him." As I lifted him, he snuggled without fussing. This was Friday evening. I didn't have classes again until Monday. My husband, Jerome, and I exchanged glances. My eyes asked the question. His eyes answered.

"Valerie, my homework's caught up—no classes until Monday. If you think…" I swallowed. "I mean, if you'd be willing to trust me, we'd love to have him for the weekend."

When I patted Doug's cheek, he cooed.

Relief flooded her face. "Are you serious?"

"Yes," I said with more confidence than I may have felt. "I've watched you care for him. I helped lots with my younger brother when he was little, and he survived. Is there anything special I'd need to know?"

"Not really—not that I can think of. Phone if anything comes up."

Jerome chucked Doug under his chin; he grinned.

I shifted the baby's weight in my arms, and his smile grew. "Look, he understands. He's OK with us." My confidence grew.

"It looks that way. Wow. If you're sure, that would be amazing." Valerie gathered a few items in a diaper bag. "He's a good little guy. Here's lots of diapers, one prepared bottle, and plenty of formula."

She slid the diaper bag strap over my shoulder and kissed Doug's sweet forehead. "I love you, Dougie." He waved and cooed.

"Thanks so much," she said with a sigh. "A few days of rest will make me as good as new."

"It'll be fun. We're glad to help." It was after ten o'clock on a warm summer night in Richmond Hill, north of Toronto. We drove south on Highway 404, slowing to the posted forty-five miles per hour as we entered the residential area, though few houses were visible yet. The highway was well lit with little traffic. Road conditions were perfect.

Doug slept, wrapped in a blanket across my lap in those days before infant car seats. When he stirred minutes later, I felt impressed to give him his bottle immediately, before he woke up. Shifting him into the well-anchored football position, I placed the bottle in his mouth. I'd no sooner gripped him securely than something very large, loud, and fast crashed into us from behind.

Brakes squealed and torn metal screamed as our car crumpled and the violent impact propelled us forward. The steering wheel held Jerome upright, but his driver's door was torn off the frame and left behind on the highway.

Everything happened so fast. The magnetic flashlight on the front of our dash broke free and circled in the air. Though baby Doug's bottle was torn from my hand and joined the spinning flashlight, he stayed secure. Whatever hit us had such force it snapped the substantial solid steel rod across our car's front seat that released it to a complete fold-down bed. I was thrown into the backseat, still clutching baby Doug tight.

Until then, I hadn't believed people who said their whole lives flashed before them when they faced possible death, but mine did now.

As Doug and I flew to the backseat, with our car careening crazily forward, out of control, I asked the Lord, *Is this it? Are You taking us home?*

Badly shaken, with objects flying everywhere, my husband managed to steer the car to the shoulder, finally stopping.

I scrambled out with Doug. That's when I heard and saw Jesus—face-to-face.

"What did He look like?" people ask.

"Like you would expect," I answer. He appears in ways familiar to us, I think, so that we'll recognize Him.

Back in Sunday school days, I'd always loved the Sallman *Head of Christ* portrait, so that's how Jesus appeared to me. Calm. Solid. Smiling. Real. With honey-brown hair curling to His shoulders, warm brown eyes, and wearing a long, simple homespun robe. He stood so near in the twilight, I could have reached out and touched Him. But it was enough to bask in His presence.

Clutching Doug close, I felt cocooned in peace. Jesus was there with us, only three or four feet away.

"Your time is not yet," love and peace emanating from His warm gaze. *"I have more for you to do."* I heard His soft, reassuring voice. Comforting.

I felt safe, surrounded by great peace. I knew no serious harm could reach us.

I turned to Jerome. "The Lord is here. Do you see Him?"

He answered, "No, but I believe you. I feel the peace."

Several things happened very fast. A car driving the opposite direction squealed to a stop as the driver ran to us, carrying a black leather bag. "I'm a news photographer with the *Toronto Globe and Mail*." He hauled out a huge camera and started clicking away. "I saw the whole thing, so I'm taking these pictures and can be your witness. The driver didn't hit his brakes at all. It's almost like he hit you on purpose."

The police came. The seventeen-year-old driver who'd crashed his father's heavy car into us was going nearly eighty in a forty-five-mile-per-hour zone. He didn't have his headlights on and didn't engage his brakes.

The young man was unhurt, since his car was so large and heavy. But he tested positive for drugs, lost his license, and faced serious charges.

Our car was totaled and missing a door, but we could drive home very slowly. Severe whiplash troubled me for years but eventually subsided. Best of all, clutched safe and secure in my tight football hold, since I'd given baby Doug his bottle as soon as he stirred, he suffered no harm at all. Several doctors said if the steel rod controlling the release of our car's front seat hadn't broken completely, throwing Doug and me into the backseat, my neck would have snapped, paralyzing or killing me.

What I recall most about that unforgettable night is Jesus's loving presence reassuring me that He had a plan and purpose for our lives through every circumstance. Although we've faced tests since then, He's always kept His word.

The Voice of My Maker
Cassie Harris

According to the neurologists, I am an unsolvable mystery. My apparently incurable epilepsy is a prime example of why even the wisest doctors say they only *practice* medicine.

Neurologists loved gazing at the statistics of my young life, seeming to hope their next perusal would give a cure. The doctors never received their wish. It seemed as if all they truly knew were the two most basic things about my case: my name and the disease that rocked my body without mercy.

At sixteen years old, I had undergone two brain surgeries and tried hundreds of medications to find relief from the disease that had become my identity. Regardless of the doctors' relentless efforts, I experienced nearly thirty seizures a day with no light at the end of the tunnel. I was in survival mode.

I lived in a paradox. Understandably, I hated the seizures that took my mind and body captive. With my type of epilepsy, if anyone tried to help me during a seizure, they ran the risk of causing permanent brain damage.

I hated the loneliness I was forced to endure because of the disease. However, as a born-again Christian, I found that within the seizures I was granted an unfathomable audience with my Lord and Savior, Jesus Christ. My loved ones couldn't touch or talk to me without causing me harm, but Jesus could.

As anyone who bears a chronic disorder will tell you, trusting God's love gets more difficult the longer you wait on answers. I knew God loved me. I knew the Scripture verses to prove that God is Who He says He is and He will do what He says He will do. I had the head knowledge.

But the head knowledge often broke my heart when I faced baffled confusion. *God is good? If God is good, why won't He heal me?*

If I wasn't faced with questions of God's goodness, His mere existence was often questioned when people looked at my life.

I begged God to reveal His love for me in undeniable ways. I had accepted the reality that I might not be healed this side of heaven. Whether healing would be a part of my story or not, I was desperate for proof that I was not the only human being God's mercy hadn't reached. I longed to have a story of miraculous healing to tell my children and grandchildren for years to come. What would be better than telling a story of a faithful God who took a child at death's door and restored her to full health?

Over time, God revealed the beauty of *not* healing me. In firm yet merciful ways, He showed me how my life spoke of His miraculous grace and mercy *because* He didn't heal me. I was made to glorify Him; who was I to tell Him He'd messed up so badly He couldn't use my diseased body? Who was I to declare that God's deity was not strong enough to supersede my disabilities, to work within them, not in spite of them?

"You may not understand how I'm using your trials," He seemed to whisper. *"Start looking for ways I intervene to spare your life. Look for the small miracles, child. There are so many things I have given you to shout My love for you from the rooftops. The problem is you're too busy looking for what I haven't given you. Look for My glory in My interventions and the ways I have stayed by your side. You will find Me there."*

One day stands out in my mind when I remember Jesus's miraculous intervention in my life. On average, my seizures would last only a few minutes, though each second felt like a torturous eternity. We had been told that seizures more than ten minutes could cause permanent brain damage.

On this particular day, the seizure lasted almost seven minutes. My mother stood near the bed I was lying on, trying to be supportive in a silent, inactive way.

Epileptics are taught how to test their own brain function during a seizure. It is not uncommon to hear an epileptic come out of a seizure muttering simple facts such as his or her name, birthday, and the country's current president. During bouts of mental lucidity, I formed the one-syllable question I could manage with my disobedient tongue.

"Name?" I couldn't comprehend what such a word meant, let alone the answer. I simply clung to the fact that somewhere in my mind, an answer to that question would gain my mind's freedom.

"Name!" I shouted louder, pounding the bed with my jolting fists. Only silence met my inquiry. Panic filled every fiber of my being.

"Jesus! Jesus! *Name?*" I screamed desperately.

Somewhere in the dark, tortured recesses of my mind, I heard a man's voice singing, *"I am your Maker. I know your name."*

As the seizure continued, hope rushed to the forefront of my mind. I knew that voice. It was the voice of my Maker.

"Child! My name. My name is Child of God," I forced out between the violent jolts of my muscles. "Child of God! I'm a child of God!"

Instantly, the seizure stopped. I was free!

Quietly, I joined the voice of my Maker God in the familiar song He was singing over me. "He knows my name…."

I made eye contact with my mother. Tears sprang to our eyes as we looked at a clock. The seizure had lasted nine minutes and forty-five seconds. God had relieved my body of its temporary torture with only seconds to spare.

During that seizure, I grasped an even deeper understanding of God's miraculous love. His greatest desire for us is that we learn to lean into the power and security we are given as His children. Every other blessing pales in comparison. Because of His miraculous love, I am not a mere survivor of epilepsy. He intervened in my life, and because of my faith in Him, He made me a victor over death.

He Opened My Eyes

Jeff Adams

Bam!

My eye seemed to explode into waves of pain as I crumpled to the floor.

I'd only turned my head for a moment to look at my racquetball opponent, Phil. But meanwhile, he had hit the ball, and it slammed into my left eye, breaking my glasses, cutting my eyebrow, and knocking me off my feet with the unexpected force.

The owner of the club looked at my injury. "You should get a couple of stitches," he advised. Reluctantly, I went to the ER, where a doctor assessed, "Two stitches." Someone came in with a sewing kit.

Afterward, with the outside of my eye clean and ready for a bandage, I asked, "When will I be able to see again?"

The physician assistant froze. "What do you mean?"

"I can't see."

"Open your eye." I did. No one had asked me to do that previously. They didn't think to, because they could see the obvious problem. I thought somehow blood from the cut had covered the outside of my eyeball, making it impossible for me to see. *If you just wash it out, I'll be fine.*

"Stay right here," the PA said. "Don't go anywhere. Don't move."

"OK."

The ophthalmologist joined the Worry Club that the PA chartered on my behalf. My cheery demeanor could easily be mistaken as a mask for panic. But I was not in shock, because I simply didn't know the seriousness of my injury. Dr. Shaw did.

"What do you see?"

Not much. "I can tell if the lights are on or off."

"Open your eye, slowly." Presumably, she gave that direction to avoid further trauma to my eye. The light I detected from the ceiling suddenly became gray. I asked what she did. "I blocked the light. Do you know how I did that?"

I had no clue. "Did you stand in front of me?" She said nothing. "Did you turn off the light?"

"Neither. I moved my hand in front of your face."

I had no sense of how near or far her hand had been in proximity to my face. I couldn't tell how big her hand was or how many fingers she held up or whether her hand was balled up in a fist or her palm was open. I couldn't see anything.

"Look up. No, no. Don't move your head. Just your eyes."

No change.

"Look down."

Still the same.

"Left."

I complied. "Now right."

I shook my head.

She already knew. "You have a hyphema." I must have looked puzzled. "The blood isn't on the outside. It's inside."

That doesn't sound good.

Had the accident happened two weeks earlier, I don't know what would have been done for me. Fortunately, Dr. Shaw had moved to our little town, giving us something we didn't have before—an ophthalmologist who could diagnose a hyphema.

"A hyphema is blood inside the anterior chamber of the eye, the space between the cornea and the iris. The blood is covering everything—the iris and the pupil. The white part of your eye is all red. That blood in the eye chamber is blocking your vision completely."

Such an injury is typically painful. My eye ached, but the pain didn't leave me in agony. I remained calm throughout her examination. That might have also contributed to her decision to keep me overnight for observation.

Before an aid took me upstairs, Dr. Shaw gave the good news and the bad news.

"There's nothing I can do. There's no surgery or medication."

I signed some forms and climbed off the table into the waiting wheelchair. "We'll keep you sitting up tonight and I'll see you in the morning."

You'll see me, but will I see you? I thought.

"The blood may drain a bit, but you still won't be able to see." Then she added, "You'll be legally blind."

Yeah, but I still have my right eye. I'll manage.

"There's a 70 percent chance you'll develop glaucoma in the other eye. If the blood in the left eye doesn't drain, over time the intraocular pressure could cause glaucoma."

I learned later that the injury to my left eye might produce trauma in my good eye that would result in irreversible optic nerve damage in both eyes.

She might as well have told me, "Get a dog and learn braille. You'll need both."

I thought that but quickly dismissed it. "We prayed. God will come through."

Anyone could summarize the extent of my friend Phil's and my knowledge of God in less than one minute: "Two Testaments. Four gospels. Some incredible stories. An apple. A flood. A guy swallowed by a whale. Two tablets with Ten Commandments that we seemed unable to keep. Jesus. Born to Mary, a virgin. Crucified. Dead. Buried. Rose from the dead on a Sunday. Our sins were forgiven."

We were too young in the faith not to believe God still works miracles. And I couldn't comprehend how much I needed one. So we just believed. Along with others.

Our pastor, Allen, and assistant pastor, Carl, came to the hospital. They prayed. They asked God to do the impossible. I believed anything was possible.

Although I'd grown up in church, I'd only come to faith in Jesus within the past year. Ordained as a deacon in a mainline denominational church, I heard the gospel. I could recite the Apostles' Creed, but I had no relationship with Jesus. Instead, I tried to keep God's rules, because if I didn't, well, there'd be hell to pay.

I did bad things for so many years, and I rarely did what I knew I should do. But no matter how hard I tried, nothing ever changed. I was in an impossible situation, and I needed a miracle.

That miracle came when I surrendered my life to God.

I can't fix me. I'm too broken, I'd prayed. I'd asked God to help me because I couldn't help myself.

Now, unable to see, I knew I once again faced an impossible situation. But that night one thing was different—I had hope. "Faith shows the reality of what we hope for; it is the evidence of things we cannot see" (Hebrews 11:1 NLT).

I'll just trust God. There's nothing else I can do.

The elders in our church anointed me with oil. They prayed. Nothing changed.

Upstairs, alone in a brightly lit room, I could see with only one eye. I sat propped up in the bed. Rather than being depressed or worrying about what my life would be like as a thirty-one-year-old blind man, I peeked. I lifted the bandage that covered my left eye. Nothing. *Not yet.*

The Bible talks about the gift of faith. It's something extra, something above and beyond what all of us are given—a measure of faith. God doesn't give it because we want it; He bestows it because we need it, when we need it.

Midnight had passed, and I couldn't sleep. I was too excited. I expected to see. That's why I kept peeking from beneath the bandage. That's why I describe the initial answer to my prayer as a gift of faith. Years of diligent study did not produce that faith. Faithful attendance and service didn't generate it. Sacrificial giving didn't purchase it. Years of prayer didn't build up my faith to supernatural proportions. I believed. Like a child, I trusted my Dad. I knew He loved me. I believed He wanted me to see again. I didn't doubt. Not because I possessed faith greater than other people, but because I believed just enough.

Moreover, it wasn't what I believed but Who I trusted that made the difference. I believed God would keep His promise. "Your Father knows the things you need before you ask him" (Matthew 6:8 NCV)! I peeked. Still no change. Nevertheless, I'd ask, just to make sure. "You don't get what you want because you don't ask God for it" (James 4:2 PHILLIPS).

God, please. I lifted the bandage. It was still night. "Everything good comes from God" (James 1:17 ERV). I believed God would do what I asked Him to do because He loved me, not because I'd been a good boy.

I peeked a few more times. Not because I wanted proof. I had that. But because I'd been assured. I prayed once more before I drifted off into a blissful sleep. *Thank You.*

What might have happened if I hadn't prayed? What if others hadn't prayed? My pastors? The church elders? It's not easy to speculate about what doesn't happen because a miracle does. All I know is that I was blind and now I see. I went to bed unable to distinguish anything except whether a light was on, and that only so long as no one played a trick on me and blocked the light from my eyes.

The next morning, Dr. Shaw's exam room was dark. My wife handed me my prescription sunglasses. Dr. Shaw lifted the bandage away from my injured eye. She covered my good eye.

"Take your time and try to focus. Tell me if you can see anything."

I smiled. I saw my wife, Rosemary.

"Can you read anything on the chart?"

I read the jumbled letters, line after line, until I got to DEFPOTEC, and kept reading—20/15, 20/12, 20/10. There was nothing else to read. But the doctor had more to say.

I'd read the chart. God answered my prayer and the prayers of others. He gave me a miracle. But she wasn't convinced.

"Just remember, there's still a 70 percent chance of glaucoma in the other eye."

"Doctor, with all due respect," and I meant that, "Jesus didn't heal me now so I could get glaucoma later."

A subsequent exam, and others in the following years, confirmed God's goodness. It's been more than thirty-three years since that accident. There's no sign of any problem. In fact, we eventually learned why my eyesight actually improved.

Examining me a week later for new glasses—because things didn't look right wearing my sunglasses—an optometrist listened to my story and confirmed my better eyesight. The force of the racquetball flattened my cornea, in much the way that Lasik surgery improves vision.

I prayed again. *You know I've hated wearing glasses since I was in grade school. Why didn't you fix my eyes so I don't have to wear glasses at all?* I waited a moment, then felt His whisper.

"You'd forget."

I understood. I remembered how Jacob limped after he wrestled with God. I doubt he forgot. I never have. Every time I clean my glasses, I remember that I was blind but now I see.

The Mysterious Comforter

Joshua F. Younce

$\mathscr{I}$ was driving south on Highway 23 in rural eastern Kentucky on August 19, 1999. I had driven that highway a thousand times to and from school, to football practice, and to court my fiancée. Our homes were about twenty minutes apart, and this would be one of the last times I would make this drive to pick her up while she was still using her maiden name—we were to be married in two days.

My fiancée and I had made the trip from the west suburbs of Chicago back home to Greenup, Kentucky, to be married in the church where she had grown up. A typical traditional wedding. Nothing fancy, nothing extraordinary, just a young man and woman ready to start their lives together.

I had met Cheri seven years before. She had attended a high school just fifteen minutes from mine, and we met at a combined high school function. I remember the first time I saw her—big brown eyes, dark hair, and a smile that lit up the room. She bubbled with personality and chatted with everyone. I, on the other hand, was "Mr. Cool Jock."

I was ready to enter my second year of chiropractic school in the fall. We had planned the wedding to coincide with one of my semester breaks. Cheri had just started a new job.

On the Thursday morning before our Saturday wedding, we were scheduled to meet with the minister and to pick up the marriage license at the courthouse. I was staying with my parents, and that morning I was driving my brother's '88 Nissan pickup truck to her parents' house. Nervous, excited, happy—I was experiencing all the emotions a man goes through days before his wedding.

When I turned onto the highway, I saw maybe two or three cars on the road and a tractor pulling a hay baler—a common sight in rural Kentucky. As I approached the tractor driving sixty miles per hour, I looked over my left shoulder to see if I could move to the left passing lane. As I turned back to look in front of me, I saw a giant green wall.

I slammed on the brakes with the baler just fifteen feet in front of me. I smashed into it with a force that should have thrown me over the hills surrounding the highway.

No seat belt, no airbag, a tin-can truck, sixty miles per hour, and a baler that weighed at least five thousand pounds. I honestly don't know how I survived.

I pulled myself up from the seat of the truck and looked in the mirror. My face was vibrating, my body was numb, and blood covered me and the truck cab. I glanced around and no one was in sight.

I dropped back down to the seat of the truck.

"Get up," a voice commanded. I wasn't sure whether it was in my head or coming from outside the truck, but I couldn't ignore it. I couldn't open the door, so I had to climb out the driver's window.

Stepping to the ground, I realized I couldn't put weight on my right leg, so I crawled to the side of the road, away from the smashed truck.

The tractor pulling the hay baler was five hundred yards up the road; the driver apparently had not realized what happened. Then I saw that the baler had broken loose from the tractor. That's why it collided with me so quickly.

I started to cry. My face was shaking, and my body hurt all over.

As anyone who has been hit in the face can tell you, the first thing you check is to see if any teeth are loose. No teeth were missing, but I was able to pull my left facial bone away from the rest of my skull. Then I started crying even more. I was to be married in two days and was badly hurt, and I was alone.

"You're going to be all right," a man's voice said into my left ear.

"You're a tough football player. I know you. You're Josh, right?" I continued to hear this voice in my left ear as an arm draped over my shoulder. *"Yeah, I know you. You'll be just fine. Say, what are you doing back here? I thought you lived in Chicago now."*

I continued to stare straight ahead and answered, "I am getting married in two days."

"Well, that's great. Congratulations!"

Still not looking directly at him, I could see him out of my peripheral vision. He was a medium-height, husky guy, African-American, which was strange, because most folks around my hometown were white. He seemed to know me, but I never asked his name.

"Say, what are you doing in Chicago?" he asked. I told him I was in chiropractic school, studying to be a doctor. He laughed and said he was going to need me one day when I graduated, but I was going to have to open an office back in Kentucky.

He was on one knee beside me hugging me, comforting me, talking to me.

"You're going to be just fine. Help is coming. I'm going to stay right here with you until they get here. Say, you still playing football?"

I laughed, and so did he. *"You've taken bigger hits in football than this one."*

Right then I heard another voice: "Hey, hey, are you OK?" A woman spoke into my right ear. I turned to look at her and saw that it was a local woman I knew named Tammy.

"The ambulance is coming," she said.

I could hear the sirens now. I told her I was hurt pretty bad and thought I'd broken my face and right leg.

The ambulance took me to the nearest hospital about thirty minutes away. I was rushed into the emergency room to a team of physicians surrounding my bed. I felt like I was on the TV show *ER*, except I couldn't change the channel. They stabilized me and moved me quickly to a room.

Soon my fiancée, Cheri, my brother, and our parents were all surrounding me in the ER. They knew I was badly hurt. Tammy, the woman at my side when the ambulance came, had come to the hospital to see how I was.

"What happened, Tammy?" I asked. She said she didn't see the accident. She'd come upon the site probably ten minutes after it happened. I told her and everyone in the room, "Ask the guy who was there when you came."

"Honey, I was the first one there," she said. "There was nobody else there when I came."

"No, no, the black guy, who was sitting beside me on the ground. He was to my left talking to me. He had his arm around me. He must have seen everything," I said.

"Josh, you were sitting on the side of the road by yourself when I got there," Tammy assured me.

"He was there!" I insisted.

Two days passed in the hospital, and I was hooked up to a morphine drip, with ice bags on my face and leg, and still days away from the needed surgeries. With all that loomed ahead of us—a continued hospital stay, surgery, healing, school, Cheri's job, we decided not to delay the wedding. We married on the day we had planned, Saturday, August 21, 1999.

We crowded twenty or so family and friends into that little hospital room, including the minister, who happened to be my Little League coach and a family friend. Cheri's best friend and maid of honor sang "Valentine" as Cheri and I sat on the hospital bed together. There was not a dry eye in the room. We said our marriage vows and kissed.

After a few minutes passed, everyone left the room. I told Cheri I was so sorry for what had happened. She looked up at me with those big brown eyes—into my swollen, bruised face—and said she loved me and we would get through this.

Then she closed her eyes and prayed, "God, we know You are still on the throne. I lift up Josh to you because You are the Great Physician. You are the Almighty God Who holds us in Your hands. Bring us safely through this and heal Josh's wounds, since we know You are the only One that is able. In Jesus's name. Amen."

The chances were great that I could have died in that accident. God saved me for Cheri, and He was there with me, comforting me the whole time on the side of the road with His angel of mercy. Cheri knew it, too, and gave me another kiss. That's when you know you've got a great God and a great woman. Thank God He loves me that much.

The Healer She Could Only Imagine

Charles Earl Harrel

The sun filtered through the alder trees on the hillside, causing our drenched lawn to glisten in the morning light. Saturated from an overnight storm, the ground still held small puddles.

We often had rain in Westport, Oregon. Sometimes it seemed like the towns along the lower Columbia River Basin experienced only two kinds of weather: wet and wetter. The night before had been one of the wetter ones. I decided to take advantage of the clear, dry conditions before the next storm moved in. My first project: trim back the wild blackberry forest that had spread out in every direction, crowding out the church's gravel parking lot.

After cutting blackberry vines for almost an hour, I heard the parsonage phone ring. I sprinted to the house, but by the time I got inside, the ringing had stopped. Out of breath, I paused a few minutes to see if my voice mail had recorded a message. The message indicator remained off.

"Hmm, I wonder who was calling this early." I sat at the kitchen counter, poured another cup of coffee, and waited to see if the phone would ring again. It did. The person on the other end told me her name was Marilyn.

A physician from a nearby hospital had suggested that Marilyn talk with a minister or personal counselor. She had tried calling several churches listed in the Clatskanie Yellow Pages, but no one answered their phones or returned her messages. Frustrated, she decided to run some errands in town, fill her gas tank, and pick up a prescription at Hi-School Pharmacy.

She told me she had arrived at the drugstore a few minutes after it opened. Fortunately, only a few shoppers were milling about. As the pharmacist filled her order, she had waited silently, her eyes fixed on the floor. Attempting to make conversation, Becky, the pharmacy technician, inquired, "So, how are we doing today?"

Marilyn had broken down in tears, telling Becky about her lousy Monday morning and being unable to find a minister to consult with. Becky suggested she try the Westport Assembly of God Church and gave her my home phone number.

My conversation with Marilyn was brief. She wanted to see me, the sooner the better. She would give me the reason in person.

The next morning, Tuesday, at ten o'clock, I met with her in the church office. Her story broke my heart. Marilyn's mother had been in a coma at Columbia Memorial Hospital in Astoria, Oregon, for weeks. Vital organs were shutting down. Feeding tubes and a ventilator were keeping her alive. The attending physician had told Marilyn he and the hospital staff could do nothing more. He recommended removing the life support and allowing her mother to pass on.

Marilyn told me she had never been a religious person. In fact, she wasn't sure if God even existed. However, to please the concerned hospital doctor, she agreed to consult with a minister before making any final decision concerning her mother.

As Marilyn talked, tears ran down her cheeks. She looked emotionally worn out. She did not want to lose her mother but didn't know how she could let her continue in a hopeless state.

"I only wish I had a little more time with Mom," she sighed.

I assumed Marilyn would ask me to go with her to the hospital, but she just wanted prayer to cope with her loss. Apparently, she had already made her decision based on the doctor's recommendation.

I didn't inquire about her mother's life story or ask for details about her illness. It didn't seem appropriate, considering the situation. I wept in my heart for her. Although I felt inadequate, I prayed for her to have strength and direction, and then added, "If a miracle is still possible, please give Marilyn her mother back." I ended with a quiet "Amen."

She only smiled a sad smile.

She arranged with the attending physician to disconnect her mom's life support on Thursday. Marilyn called me before leaving for the hospital to see if I could pray with her one more time. I asked her if she wanted me to accompany her, but she replied, "No, Reverend, this is something I have to do on my own."

So I offered another prayer, similar to the first, but this time Marilyn said "Amen" with me. She promised to call me back when it was over.

I waited for hours, but never heard back. Worry inundated my thoughts. I wondered if something had happened to Marilyn. As distraught as I knew she felt, the thought of her committing suicide crossed my mind. I had started looking up the phone number for the hospital when the phone rang. In haste, I almost dropped the receiver.

"Hello, Marilyn, is that you?"

I think she said yes, but someone nearby was talking with her, too, so I hesitated. After waiting a few more seconds, I continued with my rehearsed reply, "Marilyn, I am so sorry for your…" She cut me off mid-sentence.

"Reverend, you'll never guess what happened when they unplugged the life support equipment. My mom sat up in bed, looked around the room, and said, 'What the…!' I've been talking with Mom nonstop for two hours now. The staff already gave her some liquids and she's been eating gelatin and sipping chicken broth. She used the restroom, took a few steps around the hall, and now she's sitting in a chair. This is so wonderful! Her doctor thinks she can go home in a few days, after they figure out what happened. But I know what happened. It was a miracle, and the nursing staff believes it was a miracle, too. I am so happy! God is real after all. I have to go now. Just wanted to say thank you."

Overwhelmed, I thanked her for calling back and said something trivial like "You're welcome." However, I really don't think my efforts had anything to do with the outcome. Rather, it was a daughter's belief in a God she didn't know or understand, yet hoped would answer prayer and perform a miracle. All Marilyn desired was a little more time with her mother. In the end, God gave her more than she ever imagined.

I may not understand everything about divine intervention, miracles, or answered prayer. However, I have come to realize one thing: when we place our hope in God, the direst circumstances can become a springboard for the miraculous.

According to the apostle Paul, "[God] is able to do immeasurably more than all we ask or imagine, according to his power that is at work within us" (Ephesians 3:20 NIV).

Sometimes a simple *Amen* in faith is all that's needed.

The Angel Holdup

Susan Allen Panzica

"Those stairs. They worry me. I pray every day for your family on those stairs."

My husband's "crazy aunt Anna" was always praying for something. For her, prayer was like breathing. She never stopped until the day she died. She prayed for requests from local churches and over prayer lists from televangelists. She prayed for parking spaces, doctors' visits, and grocery orders. She prayed herself up and down the few steps in her small apartment.

Aunt Anna was our family's rock of faith. A widow with no children, she cared for her nieces and nephews, grandnieces and grandnephews, as if they were her own. When my children faced a pending test, audition, or big game, they'd ask Aunt Anna to pray for them, believing that she had a direct line to heaven. Of course, they knew that they could pray, too, but to them, Aunt Anna's prayers seemed more powerful.

In her younger years, she visited people in need of prayer. My husband was often sick as a child, and Aunt Anna came to his bedside and prayed for him. Years later, as she became more housebound, she increased her prayer time. Her kitchen table served as prayer headquarters, strewn with handwritten prayers, journals, Bibles, devotional books, and prayer requests—lots and lots of prayer requests.

And for some reason, Aunt Anna always reminded us that she prayed for safety on our basement staircase.

What was it about those stairs that scared her? With her one withered hand and two arthritic knees, Aunt Anna had three good reasons to fear them. But we didn't. We climbed up and down those stairs each time we left and returned home. The handrail on the left side did seem a bit awkward when descending. Could that be it? Or was it the hard concrete beneath the unpadded indoor/outdoor carpeting? Whatever it was, we didn't give the stairs a second thought.

Maybe we should have.

My four-year-old daughter's constant companion was her adorable talking doll, Katie. Lauren carried Katie everywhere she went, which was no small feat, as the doll was half Lauren's height. Lauren was a petite, quiet little girl with a mass of brown curls. Katie was a huge, blond doll that could robotically speak volumes.

One ordinary day, with our gathered belongings, we headed toward the stairs to the garage. My toddler son, A.J., rested heavily on my hip. Lauren carried Katie as she opened the basement door and started down the stairs.

What happened next took only a microsecond, yet it seemed to happen in slow motion. With the Katie doll in her left arm, Lauren stepped off the landing and made it to the second step before catapulting into the air. Her sneaker's thick rubber sole stuck on the carpet pile, propelling her headfirst down the hard flight of stairs. She rolled head over heels, gathering speed like a snowball in an avalanche.

Behind her, I was powerless to stop the unfolding nightmare as I envisioned my broken and bleeding little girl crumpled on the cement floor.

With teary eyes and pounding heart, I couldn't believe what I saw next. To this day, it seems like a film that's missing footage—as if several frames were lost on the cutting-room floor.

One second I saw Lauren flying. The next, I saw her twisted body at my feet lying diagonally on the stairs as if an angel had caught her in midair and gently laid her there. The rubber bottoms of her shoes faced up at me, her head a few steps down. The giant doll remained curled inside her left arm as her right hand somehow seized the railing on her left side.

Despite Lauren's wide-eyed terror, she didn't cry. She just waited calmly for me to gather her into my arms. As she nestled into my lap, her right hand—the one that held the banister—was balled in a fist. Prying her fingers open, I found a huge wad of contraband gummy-worm candies nesting inside. Unbelievable! It was impossible for her tiny fist to have grasped the railing without dropping the candies.

I knew I had just witnessed an angelic intervention.

Matthew 18:10 says of little ones, "Their angels in heaven continually see the face of My Father who is in heaven" (NASB). The psalmist wrote, "He will order His angels to protect you wherever you go. They will hold you up with their hands so you won't even hurt your foot on a stone" (Psalm 91:11–12 NLT).

I believe God directly answered Aunt Anna's prayers. Surely, He sent an invisible angel to keep Lauren from tumbling farther down the stairs.

That day changed our attitude toward prayer, toward the presence of angels, and toward Aunt Anna. She was so faithful, so *sure* God heard her prayers—for big things and little things.

Taking our cue from Aunt Anna, my family and I now share *all* our concerns in prayer, not just the "major" ones. After all, the Bible says to "Give *all* your worries and cares to God, for He cares about you" (1 Peter 5:7 NLT, emphasis added). I now know He cares so much He even sends angels in times of need.

When she heard about God's answer to her prayer, Aunt Anna simply nodded knowingly, as she lived with the expectation that God not only heard her prayers but was a trustworthy steward of those prayers, answering them in His perfect method and timing. And through her prayers and faithful devotion, my family's faith in God grew—which I think was an answer to Aunt Anna's greatest prayer.

An Angel Named Grace

Bill Shane, as told to Donna Lee (Shane) Loomis

*B*eep! *Whoosh! Hummm.*

I wanted to silence the monitors over my head. But if the noise ceased, would I stop breathing? Would this troublesome heart stop beating? Would my fragile lungs stop taking in good air and releasing the bad?

What if they did? This body no longer does what I want it to do.

The hospital was quiet—as quiet as a hospital gets. The door to my room was open, and I could hear the call bells from the other rooms. The chatter and laughter from the nurses' station seemed incessant.

God, what do You want from me? What am I supposed to do with this tired body? I don't even have the strength to pound a nail, let alone build a house, a cabinet, a dollhouse, or a cradle!

Picking up one of my grandchildren is more than I can handle. God, what kind of life is this?

I love my family. Betty is the best wife a man could ask for, and the girls and their families…I know they need me and love me. But they are all taking care of me instead of me taking care of them. I don't want to miss watching the grandkids grow up. I don't want to leave Betty alone, and what about my girls?

The battle raged in my mind. The ache in my back matched my pounding head. I wanted nothing more than to sleep, and yet sleep wouldn't come.

We'd made one more trip to the emergency room. I now had a stent in my chest to protect my lungs and a pacemaker to protect this troublesome heart.

Worries, fear, and discouragement were my constant companions. It appeared they'd be my only companions during this long, long night. At the nurse's insistence, Betty, the girls, and their families had all gone home. Supposedly, rest was the best thing for me. Didn't the nurses know my family was what helped me hold on when this tired body was telling me to just let go?

I knew from experience that the staff tried not to disturb patients during the night. They depended on all those monitors to alert them to anything wrong. The loneliness overwhelmed me, though, and increased the fear. I didn't want to be alone. I continued pleading with God.

As I listened to the rhythm of the heart machine, memories of another lonely, discouraging time surfaced.

After my open-heart surgery, bouts of depression began. Then a car accident left me battling insurance companies, stacking doctor visits, and enduring more pain and more depression. I finally had to give up building and refurbishing, which I loved doing. I'd meet the guys for a walk and coffee at the mall, and that would help for a while.

Betty kept busy with the house, the girls' families, selling Avon, and caring for me. She couldn't understand, try as she would, what I was going through, why I was so hard to get along with. We fought, and I'm afraid I made life pretty miserable for her.

Taking long drives soothed me. Sometimes I'd just take off and be gone a few hours. Other times I was gone for a few days. I didn't learn until later that Betty and the girls prayed for me every time I left.

I don't remember what brought it on, but on one particular day, I took off for the mountains. I didn't know where I was headed, but I knew I'd had enough of the struggles. At some point I pulled off near the top of a mountain pass. I looked over the mountainside. I stood there for some time, thinking, wondering, and praying…and in the quiet I heard my name.

"Bill."

I jumped and looked behind me—nothing. I leaned over the edge, searching. No one was there. Maybe behind the truck. I stooped to look under it.

Again—*"Bill."*

I dashed behind the truck, walked all the way around it. Nothing—no one was there.

It's just my imagination, I thought, *maybe the wind in the trees?*

"Bill!"

Was there a person down the road? Twisting and shielding my eyes from the sun, I looked for someone in the distance—but I knew the voice was right next to me.

"Where are you? Who are you? What do you want?" I asked.

"Bill, I'm not finished with you. I've still got work for you."

Deep inside, my heart knew what my head was still trying to figure out. His voice was strong and clear. I couldn't see Him, but I knew God was talking to me. He was right beside me. *Talking to me!*

I stood thinking for quite some time. I realized I had a wife who loved me. I had five beautiful girls who had husbands and children—all who loved me and relied on me.

We were a lucky family—with health, love for one another, and from time to time new babies. God wanted me to share that. We were blessed. He had plans for us, and I was in the middle of those plans, if only to tell the stories and remind others of God's blessings.

I couldn't get back in the truck and turn it toward home fast enough. I wanted to tell Betty and the girls, wondering if they'd believe me. It was hard to believe myself that I had heard the voice of God.

My mind returned to my hospital room. The mountain memory kept me going most of the time. But these constant visits to the hospital, each time leaving me weaker, seemed too much to handle.

Something warm and comforting touched my arm. "Hi, Bill. My name is Grace. I'm your nurse tonight. I just wanted to see how you are doing." She paused. "You seem to be restless. How can I help?"

She checked my temperature and read the monitors. Her hands smoothed the covers and the wrinkles from my sheets. Helping me raise my head, she fluffed my pillows. "Would you like another pillow or blanket?"

"I don't think so. My back hurts, and I can't seem to turn my mind off."

I was relieved to have her there. Her presence made me feel more comfortable.

"That's natural. You've been through a lot. I've got some time. Would you like a back rub?"

She helped me roll onto my side. She took out the lotion in my bedside table and talked as she rubbed it onto my tired, achy back.

"Would you like to tell me about your family?"

I told her about meeting Betty in grade school and how I used to torment her. "She wore her hair in pigtails, and I loved to tie them in knots."

I told her about how her parents felt about me as a result of those stories. "Later, they wouldn't let her go out with me. But love won out, and we have a great family and have been married nearly fifty years."

I told her about my girls and their families, explaining the twenty years between my oldest and youngest. I told stories about all the kids and how happy I was when they were around.

"It sounds like you have a lot of reasons to enjoy life," she said. The tenderness in her voice and the gentle rotating hands seemed to sense all the places that ached, inside and out. As I drifted off to sleep, my mind traveled back to that mountain and God calling my name.

The next morning, I woke up feeling better. I wanted to find Grace and thank her for calming me and helping me sleep. When they brought my breakfast tray, I asked, "Is Grace still here? I'd like to thank her for last night."

The young man gave me a puzzled look. "I don't remember a Grace," he said.

"She was my nurse last night, and she helped me to relax and get to sleep."

Again, he looked puzzled. "Maybe she just works different hours than I do. I'll check."

Later, when the morning nurse came in to check my vitals, I made the same inquiry. "We don't have a nurse here named Grace," she answered.

"Would you please check for sure? Someone gave me a back rub and made me feel so much better last night. She had light brown hair tucked under her cap. She wore a white uniform."

Amy, the morning nurse, looked at me and shook her head. Later she came back in. "Bill, there was not a nurse named Grace anywhere in this wing, not only last night, but on any of the staff lists. Besides, we haven't worn white caps and uniforms for nearly twenty years."

I was able to go home from the hospital a few days later. Even as I recovered and began to feel better, I was not able to stop thinking about Grace. She was the answer to my prayer on that dark, lonely, scary night.

My Only True Security

Anna M. Gregory

"*H*oney, they laid me off," Daniel said, a sheepish look on his face. "There's not enough work. I'll have to find another job."

I did not want to believe his words, but somehow I responded positively. "It will be all right. We'll manage." I hugged him and searched his face for assurance. Five precious boys to feed—we'd figure out a way to do this.

Day after day, Daniel came home after job-hunting, stomped into the living room, flipped on the television, and muttered, "Nothing, absolutely nothing."

Week after week, he searched. Jobs were scarce. The interviewer at one job declared Daniel overqualified. Another interviewer declared him underqualified.

I worked part-time, but my salary didn't pay all the bills. Each week after we squeezed out grocery money, very little was left.

One day, as we pondered what to do, frustration overwhelmed me. My sweet husband's eyes searched mine as I clenched my teeth.

"It won't help," he mumbled. "Anger won't solve this." He cleared his throat. "We need to sell some things."

"What could we sell?" I countered.

His eyes dropped.

"The expensive glassware your dad left you. We could sell the pictures on the walls." He motioned to them. "Some of the furniture, other stuff we can do without."

I cried as I realized we must sell our possessions so we could eat, so we could pay the light and water bills. It hurt, but I agreed.

Early the next morning, I started cleaning out cupboards, pulling out things we could do without, taking pictures from the walls. I set up tables outside, made a rummage sale sign, and prayed, "God, I don't want to part with my things, but we need to eat. Oh, God, what should I do?"

As though God wasn't listening, I saw car after car pull into my driveway. I could scarcely breathe as people bought my possessions, things I treasured.

I can live without these, I told myself.

I didn't cry until I sold my special picture of Jesus. As long as that picture sat on the small table beside me, I felt God's presence. After I sold that picture, I felt destitute. I knew God cared, but it felt like everything was being swept away.

At times, I couldn't see or feel God. Sometimes I grew angry because He didn't answer my tear-filled prayers. And yet, most of the time, I found myself praying more and leaning on God more. There simply was no one else to lean on, only God. Prayer was my lifeline. I cried out to God, hoping He would answer.

A week later, I discovered we did not have the money to pay the light bill. Thankfully, it was summertime, but no lights? And how would I wash our clothes? If I had enough money, I could go to the laundry, but how I hated that thought. Washing clothes for a family of seven was not easy. The thought of lugging those clothes somewhere filled me with dread.

That night, I dropped to my knees, praying desperately.

The next morning, I approached Daniel. "Honey, we don't have the money to pay the light bill. They'll shut our electricity off in a few days."

"It will be all right. We'll make do." Wrapping his arms around me, he held me tight as I cried.

That next day, I caught the first glimpse of God's wondrous, miraculous care. When I reached into the mailbox, I expected more bills I could not pay. Instead, I found a letter with a check.

"I felt compelled to send this to you. I hope it helps," the person had written.

I read the check amount twice. It was the exact amount of our light bill!

I cried with joy as I contemplated God's provision. Maybe things would get better.

The next day, I headed for the store to buy a few things for supper. As I walked, my mind whirled. We'd missed several house payments. Could we ever catch up? It would take a miracle to do so, but God did miracles, didn't He?

Gathering my purchases and rounding up the boys, I headed for home.

As I stepped into the house, I reached into my pocket and discovered three packages of Kool-Aid. I hadn't bought them, because I wasn't sure I had enough money. I realized one of my sons had placed them in my pocket—he had wanted Kool-Aid, and I'd told him no. If only I had paid attention! Now I would have to go back and pay for them, since we'd taken them out of the store. But how? We had no money left.

I dug around the house, searching for change. It was another miracle that I actually found enough change to pay for the Kool-Aid.

I cornered the son who'd taken them. "Son, I'm going back to the store to pay for these, and you're coming with me to apologize for stealing."

That night as I prepared supper, tears fell like rain. It broke my heart that my sons wanted simple things we couldn't afford.

At supper, Daniel took my hand in his. "Honey, we need to apply for public aid so we can feed the boys."

I dropped my head. It was the ultimate disgrace and humiliation to find you couldn't feed your children by your own hands.

Going to the public aid office was like visiting a foreign country. The woman at the reception desk was kind. The next woman I met, the one who would decide whether or not to help us, was horribly rude and uncaring. She informed me that my husband had not been wise to quit his job.

"My husband did not quit his job. He was laid off," I replied.

"No, it says here on this form that he quit."

"Well, he didn't," I insisted.

She rolled her eyes. Still, she processed my claim and approved us for food stamps. At the grocery store, people glared at me as I pulled out the food stamps. I wanted to run and hide, but I couldn't. My sons needed to eat.

For several months, we had been running on empty. The final straw came in a formal letter that announced, "Pay your back house payments or we will foreclose."

I surveyed our huge, lovely home, the large yard with the apple trees and beautiful giant pine. Tears filled my eyes at the thought of leaving, but I knew it was useless. We would have to leave.

We soon received another miraculous glimpse of God's abiding love. God was slowly moving mountains for us.

A week after the devastating foreclosure letter arrived, Daniel ran inside shouting, "I've found a job. It's fifty miles from here, so we will have to move." He stopped. "I know you want to stay, but we can't keep the house. We can't begin to catch up on the payments, and the job doesn't pay enough to drive the distance."

The town we moved to was nice enough. The house we rented was small, cramped, and not so nice—but it was affordable.

I hated the change and yearned to go home. Occasionally, we drove past the old house. It sat empty, abandoned. In my mind, I pictured the day we would move back. I was sure God could arrange that for us.

How surprised I was the day I drove by and the house was gone. It had burned to the ground. No pine tree, no apple trees, nothing. I was devastated. So much for my dreams and prayers to return there!

Time passed with lots of prayer before I saw the next miracle. I finally realized that God was pulling me from my comfort zone and turning my life around. He was giving me options. I could decide that I would survive and grow in grace or I could moan and cry over the past.

Even with Daniel's new job, it was still tough to make ends meet, so I looked for a job. Trusting that God knew what He was doing, I applied for a job at the local hardware store. It was a good match for my skills, so I hoped and prayed.

"I'm sorry, we don't have any openings," the owner said.

I fell to my knees that night and prayed again. "God, I need a job, any job."

Miraculously, two days later, the hardware store owner called and asked if I still wanted a job. One of their employees had decided to retire. I was ecstatic.

With both of us working, we settled into another house and found our lives coming back together.

Again, God gave me a miraculous glimpse of His love. Our sons settled in at school. Change had not been easy for them, either.

One of our sons deeply wanted to move back to our former town. He let us know how he felt time after time. But after many prayers and tears, all of the boys, even the one who wanted to go back home, finally made new friends.

Like mist clearing from a field, it took me a while to see what God was doing. God gave us each of the houses we lived in as a place to make cherished memories. Those homes were gifts to be enjoyed for certain seasons.

God showed me that no matter where we lived, He would be with us. With each move, He lifted me from my safe world and led me into the real world. I felt God's touch on my heart as He showed me that He, my God, is my only true security.

So far during my life, God has led me through numerous new paths. Some of them I scarcely endured. But if I look hard enough, and listen carefully and prayerfully, I can always see miraculous glimpses of God's ever-abiding love and care.

Three Days to Live

Virginia Rose Fairbrother

Thirty-seven years. That's how long my husband served as a pastor. But only a month after he left the pulpit, David had become deathly ill as a result of an autoimmune condition.

In the following months, he deteriorated to the point of barely being able to function. He couldn't remember how to spell the simplest words. His hand-eye coordination resulted in his writing becoming the tiniest scrawl. He shuffled from bed to the couch, bumping into walls, and dozed most of his days away in his favorite chair while we waited for the liver transplant team to let us know that a donor liver was available. The wait seemed endless!

Finally, we got the call from Vancouver General Hospital, letting us know it was time to fly there for the transplant. We were ecstatic!

In the intensive-care unit (ICU) after surgery, our family was overjoyed to see David pink-skinned instead of yellow. Hundreds of people had prayed for this day, and we received emails expressing joy and relief as we all thanked God for this precious gift of life.

Three weeks after the transplant, David was well enough to go "home" to our rented apartment in Vancouver, where we were to live for three months post-op, since our real home was too far away. David was on top of the world, but an even bigger test of our faith was right around the corner. Within twenty-four hours, David was rushed back to the hospital with bleeding and ended up in the same room he had just vacated. How demoralizing! He was released within a few days.

A week later, David was again taken to the hospital by ambulance, this time with massive internal bleeding. Health-care professionals performed multiple tests to determine what was wrong, but they could not find the cause and could not stop the bleeding.

David went into shock and was eventually put on life support. During the twenty-four hours before yet another surgery, he received twenty-seven units of blood—one and a half times the normal amount of blood in the body! The situation was critical. The social worker told me David was in danger of dying and to notify our family.

Once again, our three children flew in from out of town, arriving just in time to say their final, anguished good-byes to their unconscious father as he was wheeled away to the operating room. As we sat yet again in the ICU waiting room, we were very conscious of being held up by hundreds of prayers, and we were intensely aware of God's presence in the room with us.

When the doctor came out after the six-hour surgery to talk to us, he told us the main problem was that an aneurysm in the hepatic artery had burst, causing the massive bleeding. He informed us that the situation was tenuous at best.

David hovered between life and death in the ICU, so swollen from all the fluid pumped into him that he could not move any part of his body. And he couldn't talk because of the ventilator in his mouth.

"We are amazed he survived. It is quite incredible!" one doctor said with tears in her eyes. The hospital staff began to refer to him as the Miracle Man. Of course, we knew David had survived only because of the grace and power of God. He was the Great Physician Who alone could heal David if that was His plan.

Five days later, David was transferred to the solid organ transplant ward, but developed pneumonia and was taken back to the ICU, much to our discouragement.

Fifteen days after the second surgery, David woke with excruciating pain; his blood pressure was dropping—and the fight was on again to save his life!

Two months after the initial surgery, our youngest daughter and I were summoned to attend a conference with five doctors where we were told that 60 percent of David's new liver had died overnight from a lack of blood supply, likely from a clot in the artery. The only way he would survive was to get a new donor liver, and they estimated he had three days to live! David was immediately put on a Canada-wide urgent transplant list.

A couple of days later, David lay sleeping in the ICU while our oldest daughter sat by his bed. At 3:00 a.m., the nurse told them a second liver was available!

Our son and I had gone to the hotel late that evening for a rest, but I was lying awake, tossing and turning in bed, alternately praying but then despairing that a donor liver would not be found in time. I wept and begged God to spare David's life once more.

Suddenly, at 3:30 a.m., a lamp at the other end of the room switched on suddenly, flooding the room with light! Amazingly, I was not the least bit afraid. Instead, I thought, *There is light at the end of the tunnel.*

I felt as if God was saying to me that He would light the way and that David would survive. Feeling reassured, but still somewhat in disbelief, I got up, turned off the light, and immediately fell into a peaceful sleep, murmuring a prayer of heartfelt thanks to God.

Toward morning, when our daughter called with the tremendous news that a donor liver had been found, I was overjoyed! When I arrived at the hospital and told my husband what had happened with the light, he started to cry. He said that right after he was told about the liver at 3:00 a.m., he asked God for a sign that everything would be OK. It seemed clear to us that God was saying, "I will light the way before you, and I will bring you through this."

As David was wheeled to the operating room on November 11, just three days after his transplanted liver began to die, our family had an overwhelming sense of peace and confidence that he would live. When the doctor came out after the second six-hour surgery, he told us that David would not have survived much longer.

Unbelievably, David developed internal bleeding the next day, and on November 13, another six-hour surgery had to be done, although the cause of the bleeding was never found. It was David's fourth major surgery in forty-nine days!

Our youngest daughter and I were alone in the waiting room, waiting for the surgery to be finished, feeling lonely and overcome with emotion, when we both spontaneously started singing the same praise song.

God touched our hearts and filled us with His peace, reassuring us that He was in the room with us, and that He was with David in that operating room. Miraculously, the bleeding stopped on its own the following day.

While everyone was euphoric that David had survived this trauma, a difficult time lay ahead as his body struggled to heal. He had lost thirty pounds. Often it seemed there was little progress, but he was continually winning small battles just to stay alive. Everything was a struggle for David, but the nurses called him a fighter and constantly encouraged him. The occupational therapist said, "Think of this time as similar to learning to ride a bike. Right now you're using training wheels."

Our daughter quipped, "But you've been run over by the bike!"

Finally, after five long months in Vancouver, we drove back to our home six hours away. David had high hopes of a fast recovery in familiar territory.

It was a long, difficult year for us, however, with many ups and downs. At first, David was too weak to even step into the shower alone. He only weighed 108 pounds. He couldn't put his own socks on. He had no energy. Nothing tasted good. He only ate because he wanted to live. Sometimes God seemed far away.

As we, and countless others, continued to pray, the Lord worked His miraculous healing in David's body. David gradually regained his strength, and after some months he began to write his transplant story to encourage himself and others.

You cannot go through a journey like this without learning some profound spiritual lessons. I learned that nothing is too hard for God. When things seemed hopeless to me, God gave hope and whispered, *"Trust me."* When my strength was gone, God carried me.

Above all, I realized afresh that God is only a prayer away, and He delights in the cries of His children. David could not have survived the trauma had it not been for the grace of God in answer to all the prayers. He is truly a God of miracles!

Against All Odds

Marybeth Mitcham

$\mathscr{I}$was only seventeen when my husband and I learned something was very wrong with our unborn baby. The ultrasound revealed gastroschisis—a congenital disorder that keeps the unborn child's abdominal cavity from correctly closing, allowing for a large portion of the intestines and possibly other internal organs to protrude from the abdomen through a small hole.

When the doctors first told us about the deformity, they strongly encouraged us to end the pregnancy because the prognosis for our child's survival and quality of life was grim. They stressed that the child would probably have severe cognitive defects, which would cause developmental delays and a lack of adequate physical mobility—that is, if the baby survived birth and post-birth surgery.

Despite the desperate warnings, my husband and I chose to continue with the pregnancy, knowing God was ultimately in charge.

Not surprisingly, I prayed fervently during the rest of my pregnancy and faced my fears that God's answer to my pleas would be one I did not want to hear. I knew God could work miracles—I had experienced unexplainable answers to prayer many times. But I also knew His ways are not our ways (Isaiah 55:8–9), and that in His omniscience, sometimes His bigger plan includes our walking through dark valleys and not seeing the answers we want.

Thankfully, my husband and I were part of an extremely supportive church community, which committed to pray not only for our child's miraculous healing, but also that God would keep His hand on that precious life, bringing all of His plans for her to fruition.

When every weekly ultrasound showed the mass of intestine still outside the abdominal cavity, causing my hopes to plummet, my church family's continued faith and prayers provided the support that kept me believing for a miracle.

At week thirty-two of my pregnancy, my baby stopped moving, so an emergency C-section was performed. When the doctors lifted my daughter's flailing body, enraged cries emanated from her tiny lungs. I knew that even though God had not healed her before she was born, He had given her a fighting spirit—one she would need to survive the challenges ahead.

Although we had been cautioned that it could take months for all of the intestines to be placed back in our daughter's abdomen, the surgeon was able to place the entire mass—which spanned our daughter's shoulders down to her knees—back inside her underdeveloped body in one surgery. The surgeon said he didn't know how to explain what had happened; he could only say that it was a miracle.

The prayers did not stop for our daughter's continued well-being, health, and safety.

Even though her intestines had been placed inside her body during that one surgery, our daughter still needed to stay in the neonatal intensive-care unit (NICU) for an indefinite length of time to give her the best chance at healing and thriving. Every single visit included prayer for God's angels to continue to protect our daughter and for all of the potential physical and developmental concerns that the medical professionals still had to address.

Our daughter had been in the NICU for about a month, slowly and steadily healing and growing stronger, when I noticed that fewer babies were around my daughter each time I visited. At first, I thought they had improved and were simply being transferred to a level of less intensive care.

However, I knew something was wrong one day when I saw a man with a canister on his back with a hose leading to an instrument in his hand. As he scanned the NICU, he talked in low tones with a worried-looking nurse. When I asked the nurse later what was going on, she said it was part of the hospital's normal procedures.

I didn't buy it.

The next morning, a staff member met me outside the NICU doors to tell me my daughter had been moved to another floor. I was so excited that she could leave the NICU that all thoughts of the mysterious man fled from my mind.

Two weeks later, as I was getting my daughter ready to be discharged, I ran into a NICU nurse. After we chatted about my daughter's improvement, I mentioned the man I had seen in the NICU. The nurse nervously told me that she wasn't supposed to talk about it.

But then she told me something that floored me.

When I left the NICU the day that I had seen the man with the canister on his back, she had just started her shift. Right after I left, she noticed a nurse she had never seen before, so she assumed she was a new hire. That nurse cared solely for my daughter, hovering over her through the entire night, softly singing to my baby.

The next morning, as soon as my daughter was transported to the other nursery, the nurse disappeared. When the NICU nurse checked the security cameras to try to identify the disappearing nurse, there were no images of any nurse near my daughter all night.

Around a month later, I learned that a pathogenic bacteria had been introduced into the NICU and had been responsible for the severe illnesses and even death of some of the other babies. As a precautionary measure, the remaining babies were moved to another section of the hospital.

That fateful night, some friends from church had felt urged to go to the hallway outside the NICU and pray for God to send His angels to guard my daughter. These sweet people faithfully prayed all night long for my daughter's safety.

My daughter lived and thrived while those around her became ill and some died. I truly believe God honored the prayers of our friends by sending an angel—the nurse who was invisible to the NICU's cameras—to guard over my daughter, protecting her the last night she spent in the NICU.

That is not the end of the story, though. My daughter is now eighteen and is more vivacious than anyone I have ever known.

Despite the medical staff repeatedly cautioning that she would suffer developmental delays, my daughter met each milestone early. When she not only walked but also ran at the age of ten months, I knew God truly had miraculously healed her.

Despite warnings that she would suffer ill health and would probably have to return to the hospital many times, she did not even develop as much as a sniffle. She has retained that imperviousness to pathogens throughout her entire childhood, only requiring annual well-child checkups.

Despite predictions that she would not be able to perform activities requiring excellent gross motor skills, she won the Presidential Physical Fitness Award many times, has excelled in any physical activity she has attempted, and recently toured in Ireland with her Irish step dance group, performing intricate and challenging footwork.

Despite concerns that she would be cognitively challenged, she has excelled academically, completing an advanced high school course load and learning to speak and read Hebrew—for the fun and challenge of it.

Despite the warnings that she would not be able to exhibit high-level creativity, she has won awards for her art, plays the guitar, and oozes thespianism. Despite counsel that the dual factors of prematurity and being raised by very young parents would stunt her emotionally and make her unable to relate to others, my daughter tenaciously pursues justice and has a sacrificially compassionate heart.

Looking at this beautiful young woman, I know for a fact that God answers prayers and works ongoing miracles.

A Return to Sanity

Evelyn Rhodes Smith

I leaned against the wall outside the operating room door. Dr. Staats had said my father was unlikely to survive surgery, and even if he did, liver cancer would take him in a few days. I secretly praised God that years of agonizing care for my mentally ill father were about to end.

In two hours the door opened and the doctor emerged—I knew that ear-to-ear-smile would not be good news to me. It wasn't. He said my father did not have liver cancer. His problem was a ruptured gall bladder, and the infection had spread.

"I've removed it. He's going to be fine," he said.

A ton of bricks fell on me. I slid to the floor, sobbing. Did God not care for me at all?

Dr. Staats didn't know that during the Great Depression my father had deserted our family. Twenty years later, he showed up in my life again—but severely mentally ill. The courts had declared Dad incompetent. The doctor didn't know he had been in and out of our state mental hospitals a dozen times or that my father had tried to kill several people, and that I had prayed desperately for our loving God to remove him from my life.

How could I endure any more horrors of caring for an insane father?

The doctor misinterpreted my reaction. He thought I was relieved to hear that my father would live. He lifted me to my feet and led me to a chair. Sitting beside me, he put his arms around me and let me cry on his shoulder. He tried to encourage me. "There, there, now, everything will be all right. Your father is fortunate to have a daughter who cares for him so much."

The more he talked, the more I cried. I completely lost it when he added, "Your father will live a good, long life."

All that afternoon, memories of visits to mental hospitals played in my mind. There were no medications in those days to treat paranoid schizophrenia. Dad had welcomed the electric shock treatments because they temporarily stopped the voices in his head telling him to kill others. By the time he entered Staats's hospital, Dad had endured more than one hundred shock treatments. None stopped the voices for long.

Usually, my husband, Ted, went with me to the mental institutions to visit Dad. One time, however, I drove alone fifty miles to Huntington State Hospital. When I arrived, I learned Dad and four other men had attacked people at the mental hospital that morning. The men had been put in isolation.

Not understanding what I was getting into, I asked to see Dad. A guard took me to the top floor. The elevator doors opened, and I stepped into a bare room. No furniture, no draperies at the windows. Just bare floors.

Five men sat on the floor, each with one hand chained to the wall behind him. They wore little, if any clothes, and were wild-eyed and crazy. My father was in the middle.

"I'll return in five minutes," the guard said as I heard the elevator doors close behind me. Numb with fear, I stood frozen in place. Dad raised his free hand and waved for me to come closer. The other men glared at me.

"We've misbehaved," Dad said. "They won't keep us up here for long."

No words can explain the terror I endured until the guard returned. I could barely walk when I went out the front door to my car. I drove up old Route 60 toward Charleston and stopped midway at a roadside picnic table, where I collapsed, vomiting, with a severe migraine. I finally regained control enough to drive home. When Ted came home from work, he found me with an ice bag on my head. Years later, I still relive that experience through occasional nightmares.

Hospital visits during Dad's eighteen years of mental illness were just part of the problem. When he was out on probation, he was a constant danger to his neighbors. Pretending to be a calm, religious man, he would fool them into trusting him.

The odd thing was that when asked, my dad readily admitted his intentions. Since I was responsible for Dad, my call to the sheriff's department would send the deputies after him. Dad would relay the latest "message from God," and the deputies would return him to the mental hospital. That scene had been repeated a dozen times since he showed up on our doorstep.

At one time, a three-year-old girl lived with her mother in the house next to him. Dad told us that God had told him the little girl was the cause of all his mental problems, so he should kill her. I contacted the mother to warn her to keep her little girl away from him.

"Mr. Rhodes would never hurt anyone," she argued. "In fact, he babysits my little girl, and she loves him. I'm going to have my neighbors sign a petition to keep you from sending him to a mental institution!"

"Why don't you ask Dad if he intends harm to your child? You will hear it from him," I suggested.

When she asked, Dad admitted his plans. "God told me your little girl was coming in my house in the mornings and turning on my TV set! That's why I have to kill her."

As I sat outside the operating room door, all of the horrors filled my mind. I could not cope with it any longer.

When Ted came to the hospital that evening, I told him Dad was still with us. When we saw Dad, Ted and I noticed his eyes looked unusual. He was calm and smiling. On the way home, Ted said, "Something is different about your dad's eyes...."

As the days passed, his expression was still different from what I'd ever seen before. Calm, easygoing, he laughed and smiled a lot—which he had never done before—and he was pleasant. During previous years, his eyes had darted here and there, never settling down to look us straight in the eye. At our visits now, his attention focused on us. He was clearly looking at us through different eyes.

Dad was in the hospital for two more weeks, a total of forty-two days. His bill was over three thousand dollars. It took three years, but Dad paid it himself out of his Social Security disability check.

Paranoid schizophrenia is caused by an inherited gene and is incurable. Therefore, it took a while for me to realize that God had healed my father—totally and completely! Body and soul. Dad had been mentally ill since his early twenties. He had been declared legally insane by the Kanawha County Courts and spent eighteen years in and out of both Spencer State and Huntington State Hospitals. I could hardly believe it.

I finally accepted that God had performed a miracle in my father's life. Before surgery, he had gone to sleep insane. He woke sane. When Dr. Staats became aware of the circumstances, he called it a miracle and reported it to the mental health department.

I had never prayed for my dad's healing, because I thought it was impossible. Yet despite my lack of faith, God gave a very disturbed daughter her father back. His ways are above and beyond ours and sometimes hard to understand.

During the next two years, a dozen doctors who examined my father agreed it was a true miracle. None, including our family doctor, had ever seen anything like it.

The voices in Dad's head were gone. He realized the "god" he had listened to was not the true God. He found Christ as Savior and joined a church.

At age sixty-five, Dad applied for residency at Andrew Rowan Retirement Home in Monroe County, West Virginia. They accepted him, and he became a model resident. He was in charge of all the electrical equipment there and setting up and maintaining microphones and speakers in the main hall. Toward the end of his life, he was elected as a member on the governing board!

There's more to this story.

Several years later, Dad wondered if he could get his status as "incurably insane" removed by the courts. With that diagnosis, he was not allowed to vote, drive a car, or sign a legal paper. All legal documents had to have my signature.

I learned this kind of removal had never been done before, so I contacted a lawyer. When he heard my story, he became excited. "Let me check with my friends on the court, and I'll get back to you," he said.

The director at the Andrew Rowan Home sent a legal form documenting my dad's fifteen years of sanity. He submitted a request that I should "contact the Kanawha County Court and ask to have the incompetency decision reversed."

The Kanawha County Health Department reviewed the medical information and wrote a letter asking that my father's sanity status be restored.

The Kanawha county commissioner, whose office had declared my father incurably mentally ill with paranoid schizophrenia, agreed to change the status.

The judges heard the case and unanimously decided to reestablish my father's status as *sane*. My father could vote again. He could get a driver's license. He could sign his own legal papers—for the first time since he had been declared insane eighteen years earlier.

My wonderful Lord had answered my prayer. He did remove the mentally ill father from my life, but He replaced him with a new father who also became my brother in Christ!

Loving My Soldier

Ellen Farrington

On September 11, 2001, I watched my television in horror as the twin towers of the World Trade Center fell.

My telephone rang. My husband, Paul, was calling to tell me we would need to talk when he got home from work.

That night, I learned my husband had suddenly joined the army that day.

Although I disagreed with his decision, our house went on the market, and my husband took a leave of absence from his work. My four-year-old daughter, four-month-old son, and I moved into my parents' home in another state while my husband went to the other side of the country for boot camp and training.

Those months of separation were filled with loneliness. Besides losing my daily time with Paul, I had lost our home and community—our church family and friends.

After Paul finished his training, we cautiously moved forward with our lives, waiting in fearful expectation for his unit's call to action.

That dreaded call came on Valentine's Day.

Paul packed his gear, kissed the children and me good-bye, and joined his unit. For six months, we all lived in limbo as we waited for the final orders that would send his unit from the mobilization staging grounds over to join the war efforts.

We waited.

And waited.

Finally, Paul's unit was ordered to stand down.

I was ecstatic, thinking my husband would stay safely at home.

But as soon as Paul returned, he told me he was transferring to the infantry so he could actively fight overseas.

Despite my disagreement, Paul got his transfer papers signed, completed infantry school, and prepared to join his new unit, which was already overseas.

Those weeks of predeployment preparations were a blur for me. I felt numb and desperately wanted to remain that way to avoid the excruciating pain I knew would fill me when the numbness wore off.

The night before he left for combat, Paul packed and repacked his gear, telling me over and over that he loved me, that he loved our children, and that he would be all right. I tried not to cry, knowing that tears would make it harder for him.

I failed miserably.

The next morning, my husband left for war.

Saying good-bye was horrible enough, but having to go back home and be strong for my children was even harder. I don't remember the drive home—only walking through the door and seeing my children's faces. Thankfully, my son was too young to understand what was going on, but my seven-year-old daughter was very aware. Her tears broke my heart.

The next several months were awful. I did not regularly hear from Paul. Every communication blackout experienced by his unit caused me to live in terror that one day I would return home to find a notification that my husband had been killed in action. Every time I drove home from work, church, or errands with my children in the car, I would slow down before the last bend of the road in front of my house. I figured if a military vehicle bearing bad news was parked in front of my door, I could turn around and take my babies to someone who could shelter them while I returned to face my darkest fear.

I was living a nightmare.

I wasn't the only one living that bad dream. Despite my efforts to shield her, my daughter cried herself to sleep every night.

I couldn't blame her. I did, too.

There were some glimmers of light during those dark months. The night before he left, Paul had hidden little pieces of paper throughout the house, tucked in among the kitchen utensils, dresser drawers, and storage cabinets. Every time I read one of these love notes, I cried again.

Paul also wrote letters full of love for the children and me, including in these letters his requests for me to continue covering him and his squad in prayer. I did just that. I was not alone in my prayers, though. Friends, family, members of our church, and even total strangers prayed for the continued safety of Paul and the men in his unit.

As the months of war continued, my prayers morphed from requests for Paul's safety to continually begging God to let Paul come home quickly. I wanted my family together again.

Finally, I heard that Paul's unit was coming back to the United States. The families in his infantry unit were given a tentative return date and went through a debriefing of what to expect when the soldiers came back. In my excitement, I shoved this information to the back of my mind, telling myself it wouldn't apply to my family.

On New Year's Eve, at midnight, their unit finally returned. I jumped into Paul's arms, relieved that he was alive and whole and back with me. As he held me, I could only think that my husband was safe. Everything would be all right.

I noticed that Paul was terribly thin and that there was a new stillness to him. I told myself it was of no consequence.

After a week of debriefing with his unit, Paul came home. Our daughter had made a WELCOME HOME, DADDY sign that she struggled to hold aloft when he arrived back at our house. My brave little girl melted into a tiny sobbing puddle when her daddy finally held her again.

Over the next week, our family experienced the "honeymoon" phase of reuniting. Little signs here and there suggested to me that all might not be well, but I tucked those premonitions into a corner of my mind, emphatically telling myself that all was now well.

All was not well, however. The next period of our family's life was the most challenging as we walked through the aftermath of war.

Paul was angry all the time. I didn't know what to do to make him happy, and felt I had welcomed a stranger into our home. Home life was horrific, with a constant simmering fury that exploded without warning. Paul threw furniture across the rooms and punched holes into walls and through doors. He was constantly enraged and screamed at the slightest infraction. He regularly had nightmares and would abruptly wake, unconsciously thinking and acting as if I were the enemy. Sudden noises made him jump. If I forgot to do something as simple as latching a window shut at night, the potential threat to our safety would send him into a rage, veins popping in his temples and tendons straining at his neck.

Although Paul never physically harmed the children or me, the situation was so awful that I did not know if I could stay with him.

I prayed, begging God for direction. I had promised Paul "for better or for worse" and "until death do us part," but did that still hold in the face of constant fear of what would happen if I said or did the wrong thing?

I was not expecting God's response to my prayers: *"You must show him what real love is by loving him unconditionally."*

At that point, I wanted to do no such thing. I was worn, weary, and heartsick. Hadn't I already gone above and beyond what anyone—even God—would have expected me to do?

No matter how many times I prayed, I heard the same response: *"You must show him what real love is by loving him unconditionally."*

So I tried.

Paul's unabated rage continued for so long that I reached a point where I simply could not continue.

After Paul had erupted in an exceptionally horrific way, I told God that unless something radically changed in my husband that day, I was going to leave and take the children with me.

Then, expecting that nothing with Paul would change, I packed a bag of clothing and supplies for my children and me, shoved it in a closet corner, and waited for the end of the day and my escape from the nightmare that now was my life.

A few minutes later, Paul came back into the house and apologized for his explosion.

I was stunned.

He had *never* apologized for losing his temper. I grudgingly told God I would stay. Things gradually changed at our home as Paul's fury subsided.

Later, I found out that at the same time I had prayed my "this is it" prayer, my husband had heard a voice tell him that unless he changed right then, he would lose his family.

God's hand was on us the whole time.

Even though Paul was transforming before my eyes, growing into the person I had always known he truly was on the inside, I was not changing for the better. I was bitter and resentful over what I felt had been lost years, and I didn't trust that the change in my husband would last.

Instead of the happiness I expected would accompany the prayed-for difference in Paul, I was miserable. I became a version of the very person I had hated in my husband, spewing hurt and venom, erecting walls between my husband and me. Even though I could see the hypocrisy in the situation, I felt justified, convinced that nothing that changed in my marriage would ever address the deadness I felt inside.

Walking through his own pain, Paul continued to patiently love me, praying for God to heal me. My husband's kindness and compassion never faltered as God worked on my heart. Paul remained steadfast in prayer until God finally broke through my walls, uprooted my bitterness, and healed me.

Today, I love Paul more than when I first married him and thought that I knew what love was. Although we have faced some enormous hardships, through it all we have held on to each other and to God. Paul is a pastor today, openly telling how God has transformed his life to point others to the freedoms found in Christ.

Although we don't have a perfect marriage, I believe we have a good one because we have put God in the center of it and because we have allowed our trials to refine us, showing the beauty that prayer and forgiveness can bring.

Paul and I are still married today as the result of answered prayers.

We have used our story to show people the freedom that comes from giving our hurt, anger, and bitterness to God and choosing to forgive. Only God can do that. Only He can bring such miraculous answers to prayers.

He has done that for Paul and me. He can do that for you, too.

The Two-Percent Life Experience
Jan Apilado

"Oh, Father God," I prayed, "why won't Corky listen to me? Will You please speak to his heart just like You're speaking to mine?"

For two long years, the Lord had been pressing on my spirit: *"You're not where I want you to be. I want more of you."*

Each time I had tried to tell my husband, Corky, of this insistent, restless spirit prompting me, he simply did not take me seriously. I felt frustrated when he dismissed what God was telling me. He continued to go about business as usual, in the same life pattern we'd established while raising our family. Every time I told him of God's calling, he said, "Honey, we'll do more for God after we retire."

So during those years when God constantly leaned on me, my refuge was to lean right back on Him. After a while, I secretly referred to His call as my "God prod." My daily prayer to our Father was that He would change my husband's focus from the business of making money to the business of honoring God. If He would do this, once again we would be of one accord.

Over the course of more than twenty-five years of marriage, Corky and I had been partners in all facets of life. We were a team in work, in play, and in parenting our four children. During the early years of our marriage, we started a new business: a sales firm with income based on commissions only. Our finances were so tight that Corky taught me how to hunt and fish. All of us loved our family time—camping out while we filled our game tags and sometimes caught our limit of fish for our winter meat supply. We relied on the trout, venison, elk, and bear stored in our freezer. The kids loved eating the food we caught as much as they loved camping out.

As our kids grew, God also grew our business.

Before we married, I knew Corky believed in God and lived a life of godly ethics, but I had wrongly assumed that he knew Jesus as his Savior. After I learned that Corky had never actually experienced a specific conversion, I told him just how much Jesus loved him. After seven years of marriage, Jesus awakened Corky's spirit. He opened his eyes to just how much he needed a Savior. This was one of the Lord's answers to my prayers, along with the prayers of an entire congregation.

So there we were, in our fifties, with all our kids independent and building their own lives. Our business territory in the wholesale gift trade included five states of the Pacific Northwest. Corky was delighted that now, for the first time, I could travel with him in our motor home, which was custom-built as a showroom. Our business didn't feel like work because so many of our customers became our friends. They often shared with us both their blessings and their prayer concerns. Our days spent on the road together were such fun. The travel, good food, and fellowship with many Christians all gave us a very satisfying way of life.

But still the Lord continued to whisper, *"You're not where I want you to be. I want more of you."*

Summer business seasons were always exciting. We showed the new fall and Christmas merchandise at the gift shows the retailers attended. The travel schedule from the Salt Lake City show immediately to the Seattle show was always tight. To meet the deadlines, we had to drive straight through from Salt Lake City to Seattle. We were both exhausted after five days of twelve-hour shifts, standing on our feet. Seattle was our last show on the summer circuit, so after that we could head for home in Oregon. We could hardly wait to sleep in our own bed again.

Corky was at the wheel and had been unusually quiet, but I didn't think too much of it. We were both so tired. As we drove on Interstate 84, about fifty miles east of Portland, Corky suddenly asked, "What would you think if I tried to get into seminary?"

At first, I found it hard to believe he was actually speaking these words. Then my quiet response was "Praise God; it's what I've been praying for!"

Then nothing more—no words, not a sigh, not a sound, nothing—came from his mouth. I watched silently as his body sank down into his seat. He kept his eyes fixed on the road ahead. I felt as though an eternity had passed as I waited for what words might come next. But our silence went on for another ten miles. I dared not say anything, fearing he would recant his words.

Later he told me the thoughts that had been racing through his mind: *Oh, Lord, where did those words come from? I didn't really say that, did I? I couldn't have said that! That was not even a thought in my head. Oh, Lord, what can I do now? I can't disappoint You, God, and I don't want to disappoint Jan. And she said, "Praise God; it's what I've been praying for!" Lord, why, oh, why, Lord, did I ever say that?*

After the ten miles had passed, I saw a rest area sign and said, "How about stopping there? We need to talk."

In the parking area, we discussed what had just happened and wondered what we were supposed to do. We determined that it had not been Corky's choice to say what he did, but that God was speaking directly through his mouth. Since we'd drive right past the Multnomah Bible College and Seminary campus, we decided to stop and check the enrollment requirements.

When we entered the admissions office, a kind, young man was on duty. After we explained our experience to him, and he knew Corky was a few credits short of his bachelor's degree, he filed Corky's enrollment application to the seminary graduate-level program under a Life Experience category. After the paperwork was completed, our kind Multnomah representative delivered a caution: "Let me warn you," he said, "only two percent of the applicants who apply under the Life Experience Program are accepted."

Somehow we were not even fazed by the possibility of being denied admission, for it was God who had spoken. Our responsibility was to obey Him and let God take care of those two percent odds.

We drove on to Seattle, conducted our business for the week, and headed back home to Oregon. When we arrived home, we sorted our mail piece by piece.

Aha! Here it is—an envelope from Multnomah Seminary.

Corky handed it to me. "Here, honey! You open it."

Lo and behold, he had been accepted into their graduate program.

When God moves—look out! Just three days later, Corky found himself sitting in class, dazed, and still wondering what on earth had happened!

But God did not stop there. He worked out all the major and minor details. First, He opened a two percent–size door. Then He met our every emotional and physical need.

He answered every prayer all through this journey. We gave up our business, and God provided a good position for me. He gave Corky various jobs in nighttime security so he could study in between his duties.

Without our advertising it, God even sent us a buyer for our motor home showroom, so we no longer had the responsibility of the big payments. He also sent us friends to help fund the seminary tuition.

I so admire this man God gave me. He stayed the course in spite of the huge challenges of such a drastic life change. He had to relearn how to study. Thirty years had passed since his college days. During his three years in seminary, God clearly orchestrated all the events of our lives. We felt His love and His care so deeply that we said we were simply holding on to His shirttails. He was doing the rest.

Our God is a God of action! After Corky completed his seminary studies, we felt the call to serve as pastors to a few small, rural church bodies. Today, twenty years after God spoke, we continue to serve Him as volunteer chaplains to retired military groups. All our praise belongs to Him, for it is by His grace that we have His peace.

He Gives His Angels Charge over Us
Delores E. Topliff

"Delores, I'm terribly sorry, but while the children were playing hide-and-seek outside, there was an accident. Andrew's OK, but he hid behind shrubs by our concrete wall, and when his brother scrambled over the top, we guess, a loose block dropped down on Andrew's head."

As I listened to Lynda's voice on the phone, telling me about my son, I couldn't breathe.

"On his head? How bad is it?" I asked as I tried to calm the adrenaline suddenly shooting through my body.

"Surprisingly, it doesn't look that bad. He says to tell you he's fine. There's a one-inch cut that I think needs stitching. If it's OK with you, we'd like to get him thoroughly checked out. Our insurance will cover it.

"Meet us in the emergency room," she continued. "And it's the strangest thing. I had to call Wanda for your work number. She said she'd had a dream that you and your kids were in danger, so she was already praying."

I don't remember shutting down the office equipment or rushing outside to hop in my car. I dodged traffic, going over the speed limit, hoping a police officer would stop me so I could ask for help to get to the hospital faster—but none appeared.

We hadn't lived in Dallas long. After I finished graduate school at the University of Missouri, the three of us—my sons Andrew, eight, and Aaron, six, and I—moved south to live near families we knew who were part of a family-friendly church about to open a small Christian school.

One of those families, Wanda and Bill Rankin, lived on a thirty-acre ranch outside town with four nearly grown children. They assured me that they had lots of room and invited us to live with them until I found work and knew which part of town we should settle in. At that time, the whole Rankin family was packing for volunteer missionary service in the remote jungles of Colombia, South America.

Our family fit well with theirs. Bill was a gifted architect and lay pastor with a great sense of humor. He always put strangers at ease. Wanda was a tenderhearted Texan who tucked my guys into her arms and heart as if they'd always been there. She sang so beautifully in her church and at home that I'm convinced angels stopped to listen. When people had prayer requests, Wanda stepped into action. Sometimes she even sang her prayers and the Scriptures. Her favorite song came from Zechariah 4:6: "Not by might, nor by power, but by my Spirit, says the LORD of hosts" (ESV). Her singing made us believe it.

My kids and I loved those days with this warm, welcoming family. After we first arrived, I worked temporary jobs to find one that would be a good fit. I wasn't in a great hurry, since we were so happy in this home. Besides, I enjoyed helping Wanda prepare to move to South America.

As summer ended, the church's new school got off to a great start. My kids found friends and were invited to classmates' homes. The Nicholas family had two sons the same age as mine, so they invited my boys over for playdates. That's where they were after school that day while I was at work. All four boys had raced around the yard playing games. Andrew crouched behind a shrub in front of a six-foot retaining wall. His younger brother had climbed over that wall to hide behind it, but one concrete block in the top row was loose. Without warning, it dropped straight down.

While driving, I phoned Wanda to thank her for praying. "It was the strangest thing," she said. "I woke up from a nap, dreaming you and the boys were in danger. I'll tell you more when you get home, but I jumped up praying and shouting. I won't stop until we know everything's fine."

I cried as I swerved into the hospital parking lot and rushed inside. Lynda awaited me, looking pale, with my son Aaron and her kids at her side.

"Where is he?" I asked.

"Right there." She waved to the nearest curtained-off area. "I'll tell the doctor you're here. Our insurance is fine, but they need your paperwork, too."

"Sure." I fumbled for cards as we hurried to reach Andrew. Lynda parted the curtain, and there my son sat on the edge of an exam table, just as a doctor was putting neat stitches in the top of his forehead.

I couldn't hug Andrew while the doctor worked, so I gripped his hand. "Thank God, you're alive," I half sobbed.

He squeezed my hand back, looking like he was afraid he was in trouble. "I didn't mean to get hurt, Mommy. And it's not Aaron's fault."

"I know, sweetheart."

Aaron grabbed me. "I couldn't tell it was loose. I shouldn't have climbed up."

I hugged him close. "All that matters is that you're both OK." I turned to the doctor. "He will be OK, won't he?"

"Yes, I'm sure he will, and that's amazing."

The doctor tied the last knot. "You have quite a young man here. I hear a twenty-eight-pound concrete block fell on Andrew's head. It could have killed him." He gestured to the stitches. "Except for this cut near his hairline, X-rays don't show any problems. You should watch him for a concussion, but otherwise, he's great—one very lucky young man." He patted Andrew's shoulder. "And the bravest eight-year-old I've seen."

Andrew flushed with pleasure. After the doctor finished and we were released, our joyful drive home included stopping for ice cream cones. When we reached the Rankins' house, Wanda told us more of her vivid dream.

"I didn't know what was happening, just that something was very wrong. I saw you driving somewhere with your boys in the backseat of your car. You got out to take care of something, and the only place to park was on the edge of a hill. You were gone a minute when the emergency brake failed and the car started rolling toward the edge. There was nothing between your car and the cliff, so you started running but couldn't get there fast enough. That's when I jumped up, shouting prayers for God to keep you all safe. Next, I started singing, 'It's not by might, not by power, but by my spirit, saith the Lord.'"

"Do you remember what time it was?"

"Yes, I looked at my watch. I was on my feet praying at four fifteen." My knees became rubber. "Lynda says the accident happened at four twenty. How did you know? How can I thank you for praying? I'm sure your prayers saved his life."

"I just do what God impresses on me, dear." She wrapped us in the warm hugs we needed just then. "He's the one watching out for you to send help when you need it." And thankfully, God sends that help when others pray!

My Emmanuel Moment

Holly Blevins

I stood with my wet hands braced on the edge of the kitchen sink and looked up at the ceiling with tears in my eyes. I no longer felt God's presence. As much as I looked, I couldn't find Him.

We had stopped attending church, having watched every pastor and mentor we knew fall out of ministry. The disappointment had taken its toll on my faith and left me numb. I longed for the days when my faith was on fire, when I was passionately leading people to Christ and bringing the hope of the gospel to the lost. There was nothing that brought me more joy than witnessing people being reconciled to their Creator and being set free from sin.

Now that joy seemed like a vaguely recalled dream; I knew it had happened, but the details were a little fuzzy. Doubt had taken root and wound itself into my memories, causing me to wonder if my personal experiences were just a figment of my overzealous imagination.

I began to pray. I needed God to show me He was real. I knew I couldn't halfheartedly ask such a thing from God, that it needed to come from deep within. I looked toward heaven and simply prayed, "God, if You are real, and You are still here, please show me."

I did not believe God would answer me. I crawled into bed that night feeling hopeless. Then I began to dream.

I dreamed I was sitting down, surrounded by people crowding me and shuffling past—their dirty sandals kicking up dust and barely missing my fingers that rested on the ground. The large white columns of the inner courtyard made it difficult to see, so I stood and moved in a little closer to get a better view of the commotion. A Roman centurion was going through the crowd and questioning each person. I became frightened and turned to leave, but then I saw Him. When you see Him, you know Him.

It was Jesus. He was behind me, sitting casually against the wall and looking out at the crowd. The soldier raised his voice, demanding the people tell him who this man was. They started yelling, "Blasphemer!" and all kinds of names.

I knew Who He was. I knew He was innocent. I wanted to scream for Him to answer them, to put a stop to the false allegations! But Jesus didn't speak. He sat silently gazing out at His accusers.

When the Roman soldier had maneuvered his way over to me, he stopped. Looking directly into my eyes, he said, "Who do *you* say this Jesus is?"

I walked over to Jesus, let my hair fall to cover my face, and sat at His feet. As I did, the story of a woman who had followed Jesus just to be able to touch the hem of His garment flooded my mind, and I reached out and touched His leg. I was shocked to feel His hand rest on my head. I looked up into the gentlest eyes I have ever seen.

At once, my spirit was infused with supernatural peace, gratitude, and the joy of knowing and being known. His eyes pierced my soul so deeply that had I not known Him as my own, I would have been frightened.

I stood, shaking, but determined to speak to His accusers. In a loud, clear voice I answered them, "He is the King of Kings and the Lord of Lords. But His kingdom is not of this world, as you all fear. It is the kingdom of heaven. He alone can save you. He alone is our Savior and Deliverer from evil. He is Who He says He is, the Son of the Living God, and I believe Him." I looked into His gentle, sea-green eyes, and wished time would stop. His face began to fade as His Spirit spoke to my spirit. His soft smile was full of assurance.

As I woke, I knew this dream was a gift from God and a personal answer to my prayer—my very own Emmanuel moment.

Earlier that day, I had wondered if God would show me Who He was by performing an unmistakable miracle or speaking audibly, but that night in my dream He did the *unexpected*. He allowed me to have a glimpse of His glory, face-to-face. He gave me the opportunity to proclaim once and for all Who He is so that in every problem I face or trial I go through I can place my hope on the unchanging answer to the most important question: Who do I say He is?

Sometimes He sends His angels to protect and comfort His children or leads a dear friend to pray with and encourage us, but that day at the sink, Jesus heard my heart's cry and answered me Himself. To see His face is to see hope and to know truth. He is the Almighty God, Creator of the universe, and He will never leave us or forsake us. He is waiting to answer our prayers, but sometimes we are asking the wrong questions.

During faith-defining moments, the Holy Spirit is right there covering us with grace and mercy, leading us and guiding us toward Him. He knows our deepest needs, and He knew better than I did that what I needed was the strength to stand and declare Who He is in my life. I have never been the same.

An Unexpected Gift
David Michael Smith

*E*llen Knight decided she would do something about the one in six Americans who deal with hunger every day. She would fight back—at least for the needy residents on the lower Delmarva Peninsula near Berlin, Maryland. She campaigned to start a food pantry at her church, Holy Trinity Cathedral, and the parishioners warmly welcomed the idea.

Most of the donated food items were transported to the homes of hungry area residents, and occasionally visitors would come to the church for help. No one was denied. When pantry shelves started to empty, Ellen would stand up and make an announcement, and the faithful people of God would bring in more bags and boxes of nonperishable items to share with the less fortunate.

One anonymous parishioner wasn't sure what to bring in, so she purchased a gift card at a local grocery store and placed it in the box with a note that read, "Ellen, please use this to buy whatever is needed; God bless!"

Ellen held on to the card and forgot about it for several weeks.

Thanksgiving and Christmas were approaching with their normal emphasis on food distribution. Everyone tends to think about food when the holidays roll around.

Again the pantry was bare, supply and demand out of balance, and Ellen solicited donations. And although the people of Holy Trinity again responded, she remembered the gift card.

"Lord, what should I purchase with this card?" she prayed, only a week before Thanksgiving. She didn't perceive an answer, but she scheduled a trip to a chain store she seldom shopped at and trusted the Lord would lead her when she arrived. Ellen prayed daily and often, and she knew the Lord would respond sovereignly when the time was right.

After a busy day at work, Ellen headed home, exhausted and overwhelmed. Her mind was distracted. As she approached a busy intersection near the seashore tourist community of Ocean City, she sensed the Lord reminding her to turn at the light and visit the Food Lion storefront. She had forgotten completely, but with God's prompting, she made the turn, and a flood of energy returned.

"May Your will be done, Lord," she prayed as she pulled into the parking lot.

Inside the store, she pushed the cart around, oblivious as to what to purchase. The building was busy with shoppers grabbing things off the shelves for the upcoming holiday. Finally, she tossed in some boxes of Hamburger Helper, a few cans of vegetables and diced fruit, and some juice boxes for small children.

It wasn't much, and the randomly chosen items probably wouldn't expend the entire gift card.

Why am I even here? she asked herself, disappointed in her selections. Something didn't feel right. The church pantry had looked well stocked again when she last visited it after Sunday worship, and the purchases in her cart really weren't necessities. Still she pressed on, looking for the exit to this spiritual maze she found herself in.

As she approached the checkout lines, she noticed a solitary woman in the express lane. Ellen's cartload was small and qualified for the same lane, so she stepped in line behind the woman who apparently was shopping for her own Thanksgiving dinner.

The cashier scanned each item and slid it down for bagging—vegetables, frozen yeast rolls, a container of mashed potatoes, a box of stuffing, some macaroni and cheese, a frozen pumpkin pie, and a small turkey. The woman looked stressed, unhappy, and maybe even a little frightened. Ellen thought, *She must've had the same kind of day I've had.*

After the last item was rung up, the cashier announced the total: "Fifty dollars." The woman seemed to balk, and Ellen suddenly felt a presence.

Again the cashier repeated, "That'll be fifty dollars, please. Will you be paying with cash or with a credit or gift card?"

The woman made no movement to produce the cash or a credit card. In fact, she appeared forlorn, distraught, panicky. There was an uncomfortable silence for what seemed an eternity.

"I prayed this morning," the woman finally said, pulling at a scarf wrapped around her neck. "I know this will sound crazy to you, but God answered my prayer. I asked for a

Thanksgiving dinner for my family. We're broke, out of work, but God told me very clearly to come here to shop and that He would provide."

Ellen felt the presence of God nudging her; her mind and heart were racing.

"I'm sorry for your misfortune, ma'am, but I'll need payment or I can't let you exit with these groceries," the cashier replied firmly.

"You see," the woman started, "God said to come here and He'd provide a way. I came here in faith, but now I'm feeling a bit foolish…I am so sorry." She began to cry.

Ellen finally spoke. "Here, let me pay for your groceries." She handed the cashier the gift card, which was for the exact amount of the woman's purchase.

The woman praised God quietly and hugged Ellen for her kindness. Ellen wept. The cashier was shocked, but he accepted the card and completed the transaction.

"Thank you," the woman cried as she held Ellen in her arms. "You are my angel, the answer to my prayers."

"No," Ellen replied with a smile, "I am quite sure you are mine."

My Dream Husband
Laura L. Bradford

"*P*lease, God," I sobbed, "I know You can raise the dead. Could You please send my husband back to help me?"

It wasn't the first time I'd prayed that prayer in the six years since Jesus had called John home to heaven. I found it impossible to let go of my husband because he'd been my faithful hero, buffering me from the hardships of life.

It was wonderful to think that John had been set free from his sufferings caused by the increasing paralysis of multiple sclerosis. But whenever my life got complicated, I'd rattle heaven's gates again, begging God to send John back to help me.

"Lord, please?" I whined. "John would be able to handle this legal stuff so much better than I can."

The clock read 10:21 p.m. as I stared at the intimidating piles of paperwork. They were growing taller and more confusing with the arrival of each day's mail. John's mother had passed away only a few weeks earlier, and I'd inherited the job of handling her estate. Her attorney was an honest, experienced family friend. But I couldn't understand all of his instructions and legal jargon. I wanted to understand. I wanted to do all the right things for Mom—to carry out even the least significant aspects of her will. Yet I felt intimidated by the enormousness of the task.

I might have been less rattled if I hadn't been facing another huge battle. Only four days after Mom's funeral, a distracted driver in a large pickup truck had turned left immediately in front of my small car. The accident left me with another mountain of confusing paperwork, since my car was nearly totaled and I suffered numerous injuries.

"God," I begged, ignoring my body's need for sleep, "John was the one with a master's degree in business. This stuff would be easy for him. Could You please, ple-e-ease send him back to me?"

I heard only the ticking of my wall clock, reminding me of the late hour and of Jesus's earlier encouragement to get my rest. After a few more sobs, I fell into bed and drifted into a fitful sleep.

Morning's light was subdued by cloudy skies as I filled my teakettle at the kitchen sink. Out of the corner of my eye, I caught movement. Despite the early hour, someone was walking along the sidewalk in front of my house. Turning to see who it might be, I dropped the kettle in shock.

"John!" I gasped.

My husband was hobbling toward the front door on the crutches he'd used during the early stages of multiple sclerosis. He looked remarkably young, not at all like the emaciated man who died in his mid-fifties. The handsome man approaching my door was John at about thirty years old. He wore his favorite outfit—a pair of 501 Levi's jeans and a brown T-shirt that accentuated the ever-present twinkle in his deep green eyes.

In a mix of delight and panic, I tried to smooth my uncombed hair. Gazing down in horror at my raggedy bathrobe and slippers, I cried, "No-o-o! I can't let that handsome man see me like this. I'm more than twice his age and...what will he think?"

Nevertheless, I raced toward the front door and flung it open for my beloved husband.

He stood on the doorstep grinning at me.

The only words I could muster were "Oh, John, you're a sight for sore eyes!"

He cocked his head to one side, looked me up and down for a few seconds, then said, "Well, sweetie...so are you."

While I chuckled, John stepped into the house. At least, I think he stepped in. Astonishingly, I felt him pass right through me like the wind through a net.

Without warning, I was swept into a joyous whirlwind of heavenly love, freedom, and peace. With my arms lifted high, flailing in the breeze, I tossed my head back and laughed aloud while I twirled in that heavenly realm. No longer aware of John, I desired only the presence of my heavenly Father.

When one of my arms struck the bed's headboard, I bolted awake. The clock read 3:08 a.m.

"John?" I called. My husband had vanished with the dream. Yet my mind still lingered in the delight of my heavenly encounter.

With my heart pounding, I tried to distinguish the real from the imagined. Was it only a dream? Or had it really happened?

Regardless, God sent me a message through that experience. While I wondered why John had come to me on crutches, the Holy Spirit revealed what those crutches represented. If my husband were to return to earth, he'd have to face more suffering. Did I wish to see him endure more?

Absolutely not! John lives in that whirlwind of heavenly love, freedom, and peace. I would be selfish to insist that he return from a place of eternal bliss just to coddle me.

As my heart calmed, the path ahead became clear. I had to let go of John.

My compassionate husband didn't leave this earth without teaching me all he could about legal matters, finances, and the handling of estates, since he knew I'd face those things alone someday. He'd instructed me to lean on my "resource people," those who had the expertise to guide me through everything: lawyers for legal matters, bankers for money matters, and, of course, my Christian friends for matters of faith.

From professionals to friends, God had surrounded me with individuals who were poised to help. But best of all, God's Spirit is always with me, sovereignly guiding. All I have to do is follow.

In light of these revelations, I prayed, *Forgive me, Lord, for wanting John back rather than looking first to You. And thank You for setting my husband free.* With that, I lay back on my pillow and drifted into a peaceful sleep—something I hadn't experienced for a very long time.

A Heavenly Code Blue
Jeff Adams

*O*n July 5, 2001, I flatlined during my second heart attack. I heard the monitor and turned my head to see the horizontal green line.

Does that mean what I think it means?

I thought the nurse closest to me might faint.

I don't know if she did. I don't have any specific memories of when I woke. My wife, Rosemary, who stood at the end of the bed in the ER, told me what had happened next.

"They called, 'Code Blue! Code Blue!' and tilted your head down. But before the crash cart got there, you were back. They never used the paddles to shock you."

My first heart attack had followed what could have been my last supper. A delicious tender steak, baked potato, and salad would have been my demise—as is so often the case, especially for men.

That was in May 1998, when my daughter Meaghan was only three weeks old. I learned the digestive system uses enormous amounts of blood, which can overburden your heart.

The trigger of the second heart attack in 2001 remains a mystery.

It was past our bedtime when I was feeling the pain and learned Rosemary had forgotten to pay a couple of bills.

"I'll take them to the offices and put them in the drop box so they'll be there first thing in the morning," I said. It was a good excuse to get out of the house. *I'll stop by the hospital. They'll tell me I'm fine. She'll be asleep before I get home.*

As happened before, in the ER, God spared my life.

Somehow, Howard, our pastor, found out about my ER trip and pounded on our front door. "Rosemary! Wake up!" She opened the door. "Jeff's at the hospital."

When Rosemary got there, an ER doctor broke the news. "He's having a heart attack. The drug is working just the way it's supposed to." The cardiologist seemed surprised but glad. And since I needed surgical intervention they couldn't provide in that rural hospital, he told Rosemary, "As soon as he's stable, we'll Air Evac him to Phoenix."

I was afraid. I'd begged my friend Howard to pray for me. "You know what to say." Then he left.

Oh, God, not again. I can't take this. Dear God, please forgive me.

When you can't breathe, all you can think is what I thought. *I don't want to die!*

Some people think dying wouldn't be that bad. If you believe in Jesus, you expect to go to heaven. No more sorrow. No more pain. No more suffering. Perfect body. And much more. Reminds me of an infomercial. All yours for the low cost of leaving this world. But I'm in no hurry to do that.

I'll have all eternity to spend with God. I'm needed here. I have a wife, a daughter, a church that needs me. People who want me. I didn't want to leave. But it wasn't up to me.

What about Meaghan? Who will teach her what she needs to know? Who will hold her? Who will sing to her and dance with her?

I recalled our first night together. I sat in the hospital nursery rocking her. Our dear friend Gwen, one of the nurses on duty, handed me a bottle. "She won't eat. She hasn't."

I rubbed the nipple across Meaghan's lips. She greedily gulped, but milk poured out and ran down her chin to soak her nightgown. "Gwen, I think the nipple is too big."

"How did we miss that?" Gwen took the bottle, traded out nipples, and handed it back to me. Meaghan devoured the formula. I burped her, more by accident than expertise. We leaned back in the rocker. Soon, Meaghan drifted off to sleep to the lullaby of my voice singing the lyrics she would know so well—"Jesus loves me, this I know, for the Bible tells me so."

God, I want to sing again. I want to hold my daughter. I know it's a selfish prayer, but please, God. Don't let it end like this.

The pain increased. I couldn't exhale. A heart attack has that effect. It's the opposite of crucifixion, when you can't inhale. I imagined what Jesus must have endured.

I'm sorry. I'm sorry. God, please forgive me.

I felt calm, tranquil, peaceful, at rest, not a care in the world. Only later did I learn that Pam, Howard's wife, had begun to "storm the gates of heaven." That's how she described prayer. To Pam and others in our church that she enlisted that night, prayer was something akin to D-day—an all-out assault. I learned later that hundreds of people in other churches joined the fight for my life.

In the moment when I needed it most, God heard. He answered. He gave me His peace. *Does that mean what I think it means?*

"Code Blue! Code Blue!" No tunnel. No light. No welcoming committee. Nothing. Except serenity.

God answered my prayers. And the prayers of so many others. I know my wife prayed that July as she had done in May three years earlier. "God, no. I didn't sign on to be a single parent. I'm not doing this by myself. Bring him back. Now."

I'm grateful that family and friends and neighbors and strangers around the world prayed for me, with me. God can save by many or by few. But I am especially comforted knowing God heard my plea.

Semper fidelis not only describes the marines; it also describes God. Always faithful.

I'm not sure when I became aware of my surroundings again. Maybe it was later that night. Perhaps it was the next day or the day after or the day after that. It might have been morning. It could have been afternoon. *When* God answers a prayer isn't what we notice. I only knew I could breathe. My chest didn't hurt. I only knew that by the grace of God I wasn't dead.

After I was revived by someone besides the physicians, EMS personnel loaded me on a helicopter to the airport for another flight to Phoenix. Different hospital, different doctors. Same procedure. An angiogram became an angioplasty in order to place multiple stents. The tiny collapsed scaffolds, when deployed, would lock open and support my weakened arteries at critical junctures.

I became gradually aware at some point that I was in an ICU room. The recurring hum of a small pump measuring my blood pressure. The familiar blip of a monitor graphing my heartbeats. The ping of an alarm to alert the nurses that I'd finished yet another bottle of whatever they fed me through an IV. I dozed on and off as the TV faded in and out. I barely noticed the soft padded footsteps of various personnel who checked on me. My environment served one purpose: rest. So I did.

I still do. I rest in the goodness of God. And I pray. I'm thankful I don't have to be afraid. I pray others won't be.

The Prayer Stone
Ray Stenner, as told to Janice Richardson

*B*ill carefully placed the prayer stone with my name written on it under the altar of his church.

"This is for you, Ray," he whispered. "I pray that you will come to know Christ and give your life to Him."

The church was under construction, and the members decided to put prayer stones under the altar. Then they held a special service in which they prayed for the people whose names were on the stones.

Bill was my business associate and friend. We had often discussed politics, Christianity, and faith. I had been exposed to Christian teachings in my home as a child, but once I left home, I left Christ behind. Although I did not know it, Bill prayed for me every day. He had no idea how badly I would need those prayers.

Two years later, on June 2, 2005, I was doing what I enjoyed most, coaching my two daughters (ages seven and ten) in soccer and spending time with them. Early the next morning, I woke up with a severe ocular migraine in my right eye. I was headed downstairs to get some painkillers when I suddenly collapsed and tumbled the rest of the way down the stairs. My wife, Colleen, ran down to see what had happened.

"My eye! My eye!" I cried.

Colleen called 911, but I was unconscious before she got off the phone. By the time the ambulance arrived, I was no longer breathing. The paramedics resuscitated me twice because I had physically died for a few minutes.

I descended into blackness, and my human sensations started to disappear. I felt my spirit emerge. An unbelievable presence of love and peace overwhelmed me, like a mother's love as she snuggles her child, as well as a fatherly presence of strength and security giving me the will to live.

"You must go back," I was told. *"It is not your time to die yet."*

This was the first of several miracles and answers to Bill's prayers that changed the direction of my life.

My condition was an aneurysm on my right optic nerve. A massive vascular hemorrhage filled the right side of my brain with blood, causing a serious brain injury. While I was in a coma, the doctor said I would probably not live through the night. I was put on life support with no brain activity.

Colleen gathered my siblings for final farewells and decided to disconnect my life support and donate my organs. But a neurosurgeon on call arrived and convinced my family to let him perform a surgery.

The surgery worked! I remained in a coma for a week to let my brain heal. When I woke up from the coma, I could not speak but immediately wrote about my supernatural experience while in the coma.

The magnitude of my injuries from the aneurysm overwhelmed me. At the age of forty-four, I had partial paralysis on my left side, significant visual loss in my right eye, memory loss, and serious cognitive impairment. Having been a project manager and operations manager, I was devastated to know I would never be able to work or drive again. My former life had been ripped out from under me!

Learning to do basic skills again, such as taking care of my hygiene, walking, talking, and eating with utensils, was physically and mentally exhausting. A month and a half after my aneurysm, I was transferred to the rehabilitation ward and enrolled in speech and occupational therapy and physiotherapy. Feeling the tremendous impact these disabilities had on my life, I developed severe depression and anxiety.

One night, I woke up to see a small woman with dark skin at the foot of my bed. She exuded a loving motherly presence similar to what I'd experienced in my coma.

"Don't worry. You're going to be OK. You are loved," she reassured me. *"Be strong. Be brave. You will get better."*

I felt a deep sense of peace and fell back to sleep. The next morning, anxious to find out who that woman was, I stumbled to the nurses' station to ask. They told me no one of that description worked there. I eventually understood that she was an angel sent by God.

With renewed determination, hope, and confidence, I worked vigorously in all areas of therapy and could soon walk with only a cane. By the end of September, my dream of being home with my family again seemed closer when I was granted weekend visits. I could not hold back my tears as my youngest daughter ran into my arms, crying, "Daddy's home!"

The girls and I spent precious moments just hugging each other. I had missed them so much. I truly cherished my involvement in their lives—reading with them, cooking, swimming, taking them to dance lessons, and coaching their soccer teams.

Unfortunately, Colleen did not receive me the same way. She resented having to care for a disabled husband and did not think I could resume my role as father and husband. Her words and actions were hurtful and made me feel abandoned. To help me deal with this, my psychologist helped me find a church close to my home. The first day I attended, I was overjoyed to be warmly welcomed by friends whose daughter I'd coached in soccer.

Reading my Bible and being part of a loving, supportive congregation helped me to grow spiritually. Unfortunately, the situation with Colleen grew worse. I felt worthless after a difficult Christmas—my depression deepened, and I felt suicidal. I couldn't understand why God let me live after the aneurysm. I could not see a purpose for living.

On December 28, 2005, I prepared to end my life by jumping off a pedestrian overpass. Just before the fatal jump, my cell phone rang.

Through tears, I poured out my emotions to my friend. "No, Ray! No! Can you go somewhere safe? Is there a motel near you?"

He talked me into checking into the nearest motel, at his expense, and promised he would meet me there in the morning. Upon checking in, I was even more surprised to see that the front desk clerk was a former business associate of mine. He eventually helped me find a town house to live in near my girls. God's divine intervention saved my life for a second time.

When I moved into the town house, Colleen refused to let me have visitation rights, saying my daughters would be unsafe with me. I was very lonely without my girls. At an all-time low and unsure of my abilities and life as a disabled person, I cried out to God, "Lord, I give You my life! My former life is gone, even my family! You are my only hope! Please direct my life and please bring me the family that I need!"

My sister offered to visit every second weekend so my daughters could stay with me. Through the help of friends, I hired a lawyer. Eight months after I moved into the town house, the courts granted me visitation with my girls. The assessment stated that I was a better father than many fathers without brain injuries! This was a breakthrough for me, and wonderful times began again with my girls.

As the girls grew older, I got less time with them. My oldest daughter pulled away when she was fifteen. My youngest daughter still wanted to come but also pulled away when she started ninth grade.

Heartbroken and lonely, I prayed again for a family. I tried dating through Internet sites, but brain-injured applicants are not well received. After a nine-month relationship went sour, I believed I would never be able to have a relationship with a woman and decided that God was all I needed.

But God had other plans. I started attending a men's group at a different church and eventually started attending their Sunday evening services. Two months later, on October 21, 2012, I was taking Access taxi (a special transportation for disabled people) to the church and it stopped to pick up a woman, Rose, and her special-needs daughter, only a block from my house. We talked all the way to church and found ourselves looking at each other during the service. We talked more after church.

A few days later, I was reading the Bible in my living room. I glanced out my front window and saw Rose walking her dog in front of my house! I flew out the front door as best I could and surprised her with a hug. A few days later, Rose dropped a note in my mailbox, offering to help me rake my leaves. Unfortunately, her note slipped out and fell to the ground. Several days passed before I discovered it. I called her, and the romance bloomed from there.

Rose had been a single parent for many years. Raising a special-needs daughter, coupled with love for Christ, gave her a compassionate heart. Because she was coping with her daughter's seizures and a major concussion, Rose understood my brain injury and disabilities. God clearly orchestrated our meeting, because Rose had recently moved to my area to be closer to her job, and I had just started attending her church.

Rose and I had a very romantic engagement six months after we met and were married six months later. Rose's daughters openly embraced me, helping to ease the pain of losing my relationship with my own daughters.

God answered my prayer for a family. He provided me with a loving Christian wife, three fun-loving daughters, a son-in-law, and two adorable grandchildren—all who accept me as I am. I couldn't be happier! We continue to pray for my daughters and know that one day they will return to us because God has been so faithful to answer our prayers.

The angel from the hospital room told me I would get better. Although I have made significant improvements physically, my emotional and spiritual growth has been enormous. I not only came to know Christ, but have been able to experience the strength He provides.

One Sunday, Rose and I were sitting in the cafeteria at church. My friend and former colleague Bill walked up to us.

He stared. "Ray, is that you? How long have you been coming here?" After he heard my story, tears trickled down his face.

"I have been praying for you for ten years! I placed a prayer stone with your name on it under the altar of this church! Praise God! He's answered my prayers!"

Breaking Selfish Pride
Faith Turnet

$\mathcal{F}$acing the threat of lawsuits, job termination, and a ruined reputation was the best thing that ever happened to me.

I can utter those words with a peaceful heart now that I'm removed from the darkest journey of my personal and professional life, but it was a different story several years ago.

In April 2008, I was deeply engrossed in research and activities associated with a doctoral program to further enhance my profession as a public school educator. I had transitioned from classroom teacher to assistant principal and knew the next step in the journey was the coveted title of principal.

I had my professional career mapped out to the point that I could envision grandiose titles under the United States Department of Education in my twilight years. In my mind, I was an educational powerhouse who could do no wrong.

But those grandiose dreams came to a screeching halt in the spring of 2008, when the family of a student in my school became dissatisfied. The complaints moved beyond "We just don't like her" to "She struck our child, as evidenced by this bruise!" The bruise on the child's back actually came from a tumble on the playground, but the accusation of abuse was out there.

As a Bible-believing woman and a dedicated teacher and administrator, I would never even consider striking a child. I treated students fairly, loved them, listened when they were distraught, and disciplined respectfully when they disobeyed. But *abuse*? The mention of that word sent shock waves through my system.

A police investigator visited me at school with a long series of questions that drove my blood pressure through the roof. This interrogation was followed by phone calls with school district personnel and attorneys.

The family, besides requesting my dismissal from the school, also threatened to sue me. I was facing criminal charges, lawsuits, and termination at the ripe old age of thirty-five. With no history of legal concerns, I now faced the worst complaint possible.

During this painful season, I couldn't sleep, eat, think, or speak. I could only cry while friends or family members held me. My broken dreams, hopes, and reputation overwhelmed me to the point that I felt life really wasn't worth living. All I could do was cry and pray. Many days, my prayers were wordless. My agony was so intense that I could only ask God to hold me, love me, and somehow protect me through this horrible storm.

Like Jonah, I wanted to be thrown overboard. I wanted to disappear into the deep waters of confusion and despair and hope that everything was just a really bad nightmare. After all, how could a loving and faithful God allow a good, little Baptist girl like me to face such a frightening experience?

Some days, I felt like a persecuted Job who never asked for the hardship. Other days, I felt akin to a laughing, skeptical Sarah who doubted God's ability to do the impossible.

After weeks of investigative work, the good news came that the police saw no evidence of wrongdoing and would not charge me with a crime. Relief. Pure, joyful relief! But this was only the calm before the storm.

Within twenty-four hours, I was summoned to the school district headquarters, where I heard, "We don't think you can cut it anymore. You're not meeting our expectations. We're disappointed in you."

In the blink of an eye, I faced a decision I thought I would never have to face: walk away from the job that I loved deeply and leave public education or take a new job within the system as a writer until my contract expired. Option two was a professional demotion, but demotion seemed preferable to unemployment.

How would I explain to all of my colleagues and doctoral program friends why I was no longer in my dream job? How could someone working to obtain the highest degree possible explain that she was no longer "good enough" for this job? And how could I now report to a boss who looked me in the eye and told me I just wasn't cutting it? How could I endure this change?

The anger, frustration, and pain I felt when I had to kiss all of my professional dreams good-bye and with Christian kindness say, "Sure, I'll gladly make a professional change.

I'll take the demotion and subsequent pay reduction. I'll hold my head high and do a good job" is indescribable.

I made it out of the office and as far as the driver's seat of my car before I collapsed into a fit of fears and tears.

The days that followed the threats of lawsuits, termination, and a deeply bruised ego are a blur at this point, but they are days that I survived because of the power of a lot of prayer, and not just my own. I had been blessed with a devout mother, father, sister, extended family, and church members who believed that prayer held power. When I couldn't pray, they interceded for me. They went to their knees daily for me, asking God to make something beautiful out of this mess of my broken life.

In those dark days, it was powerful, on-your-knees kind of prayer that turned a charge of child abuse into a dismissal, a lawsuit into dropped litigation, and a termination into a testimony of God's provision for my life.

The new, demoted position to support district writing efforts actually offered me the opportunity to engage in rigorous research and writing for educational purposes. With less stress and better hours, I could concentrate on finishing my doctoral degree and finding balance in life, even though the paycheck and job title were less impressive. Furthermore, the new position allowed me to develop stronger writing, editing, and data-analysis skills, skills that serve me well today.

After four years as a writer, I was able to join an international education company. The demotion that I thought ended my professional success was God's first building block for future financial blessing and professional satisfaction.

But more importantly, the painful journey was God's plan at its finest—the first stepping-stone toward becoming a deeper, more devout, radically changed believer who finally grasped the power and purpose of prayer.

During this season, I came to a new understanding of Jesus during the final hours of His life. Mark 14:35 says Jesus "fell to the ground and prayed" (NIV).

Many of us gloss over this part of the crucifixion and resurrection story to get to the "really good part" about the angel and the stone. But the "good part" actually starts in that garden of Gethsemane, when Jesus fell to the ground in passionate, purposeful prayer. His season of prayer helped prepare Him for the most agonizing season of life. Prayer helped

Him face the ultimate betrayal with grace, dignity, strength, and compassion. Prayer prepared Jesus for the unthinkable.

My painful, life-altering season was nothing compared to what Jesus faced, but, like the Savior, I found that the best option, my only option, in the face of false charges and lies was to fall before my Daddy God, asking for strength to put one foot in front of the other.

Although the best part of my story may appear to be how God saved me from false charges of child abuse, permanent termination, and a frightening lawsuit, I learned in time that the best part of the story was the breaking of my selfish pride. Before this journey, I was so wrapped up in myself, my skills, and my experiences that I hadn't taken time to invite God into my life. God only factored in when I was the most desperate.

These circumstances forced me to look at the woman in the mirror and to question whether, like Jesus, I was praying, "Not my will, but thine be done," or attempting to be the author of my own story.

The greatest testimony of my journey is that God did the impossible, not only with my circumstances but also with me.

The Final Authority
Elfriede Volk

*I*n the spring of 1946, the war was over, but in our little city of Freiburg, now Świebodzice, a battle was still raging, causing more casualties than the war had. With immune systems compromised by malnutrition and starvation, people were falling victim to diseases brought on by parasites, polluted water, and a lack of hygiene. As no medical help was available, the result was a typhus epidemic that seemed to be unstoppable.

"If you get sick," people whispered to each other, "don't go to the hospital. The Russians will just inject you with some air, and when the bubble gets to the heart, it's over. One less German to worry about, as far as they're concerned."

We were not Germans. My father, the son of a Dutch fisherman, had come to Germany years earlier to find employment to help his family when pollution decimated the fish in the Frisian Lakes. True to his Frisian heritage, Dad stubbornly persisted where others would have given up long ago, and eventually he was successful. He was also devout and unfailing in his belief in God. He prayed before and after each meal and insisted that God's Word should be part of his daily bread.

In Germany, he met some Christians who worshipped on Saturday. Even as a boy, he had wondered why people went to church on the first day of the week when the Bible said that the seventh was the Sabbath, so he gladly worshipped with them. Falling in love, he married and settled in Germany, where we children were born.

When the Depression left many people unemployed, Dad embarked on a new venture, starting a business selling fish and fresh fruits and vegetables. After all, food is one of the most basic needs of life and always in demand. But the war ended this business because he was unable to obtain fuel to make his deliveries.

He was also unable to take his family back to his homeland. So to avoid being conscripted into the Organisation Todt, he volunteered with the Red Cross and worked in a hospital until the war ended. When armistice came, we were under Russian and Polish occupation and in the midst of a raging typhus epidemic.

Aware of the dangers of allowing infectious diseases to run rampant, Dad contacted the Russian occupation forces to offer his help. Since he had a horse and wagon, he was ordered to go from house to house each day to pick up the bodies of those who had succumbed to typhus overnight and take them out of town for mass burial.

Before he left, he gave us strict instructions: "Boil some water and use it to scrub your hair thoroughly with lye soap. Then comb your hair with a fine-tooth comb to dislodge any lice and their eggs. Don't drink water from the tap. Don't even use it to wash food or your hands. Boil it thoroughly first. Even boil the dishes you eat from. And pray. Don't forget to pray that God will keep you from getting sick, too."

Despite all precautions, my sister Ruth, thirteen years old, came down with typhus. Toward the end of the war, the school had been bombed, so there were no classes. Neither was there food. Some neighbors were eating rats and mice to keep alive, while one killed his entire family before taking his own life, as he could not bear to see them starve.

Since store shelves were empty, Ruth had gone into the country to forage for edibles. She had become thirsty. Though she had a bottle of boiled water with her, the cool, sparkling water in a roadside stream proved irresistible, and she drank. After all, she thought, it was not from the tap, and she didn't realize that the effluent from decaying bodies had leached into the groundwater.

Whether from the water or too close contact with friends, she developed a cough, a splitting headache, and a high fever a few days later. She lapsed into unconsciousness, and someone carried her home.

Mother immediately isolated Ruth in one of our two rooms, and she wore a mask and a long gown whenever she tended to Ruth, hanging these on a hook by the doorframe when she came out. She also set up a washstand at the door, where she washed her hands before going into Ruth's room and after coming out. Any linens or towels used for Ruth were boiled, as well as her dishes, which were boiled separately from ours.

The disease lingered for days. Each day, Mother spent more time with Ruth, and each day her eyes seemed to be more sunken in her worn face. At first, Mother had sung to Ruth, but after a few days her songs ceased. So did her smiles. They were replaced by a haggard, almost hopeless expression.

When they had not seen Ruth for several weeks, neighbors became suspicious, and then alarmed. They demanded that Dad take her to a hospital so that she would not infect others.

"She gets much better care here," Dad said. "But if you are worried that you might catch something, we'll keep the other children inside, too."

That was not good enough for one person, who lodged a complaint with the Russian authorities. Two officers came, did an inspection, and left again.

"We can't do more than what you are already doing here," they said. "Keep up the good work. And if anyone else complains, refer them to us."

After they had gone, we sent up a prayer of thanks. At home, Ruth had constant and undivided attention, whereas in the overcrowded hospital she would be but one patient among many.

As the disease continued and Ruth showed no signs of improvement, Dad's face also reflected his concern. His prayers became longer and more frequent, more earnest. He often relieved Mother at Ruth's bedside, passing long, sleepless hours in prayer.

Intestinal disturbances are part of the disease, and there was constantly a large kettle of linens boiling on the stove. Millie, two years older than Ruth, was responsible to do the laundry and hang clothes to dry. With widespread theft and pillaging, we could no longer hang clothes outside, so Millie carried the wet items up to the attic.

Crying, I followed her wherever she went. At four, I could not understand what was happening. I just knew that I was hungry, that I hurt, and that I missed Ruth and my mother. Since Mother had not been well even before I was born, Ruth had been the one who usually looked after me.

A few days later, I saw Mother crying too. She ran out of Ruth's room and didn't even stop to wash her hands or hang up her gown. "Ruth is dead. Ruth is dead," she wailed as she collapsed into Dad's arms.

Dad looked shocked. Then a determined expression settled on his face.

"I don't believe it," he said. "I *won't* believe it!"

Turning to us children, he said, "Come into Ruth's room. And, Mother, bring me some oil."

I could not recognize Ruth when I saw her. Her beautiful blond hair had fallen out and she was bald. Her once-rosy cheeks were white, the skin draped in folds over the bony structure underneath. Her eyes were closed and sunken into their sockets.

"She is not dead," Dad said, gently laying her bony hand back on the covers. "She is only in a coma. But the Bible gives us instructions on what to do when someone is sick. God can still help, even when the situation appears hopeless."

He opened his Bible to James 5:14–15 and read, "Is any sick among you? let him call for the elders of the church; and let them pray over him, anointing him with oil in the name of the Lord: And the prayer of faith shall save the sick, and the Lord shall raise him up; and if he have committed sins, they shall be forgiven him" (KJV).

"As our church members were scattered during the war, we have no elders to call on," Dad continued. "But we do have each other, and as a family we can pray for Ruth. As I was a church elder, I can anoint her. And while I am doing that and praying, I want each of you to pray, too. Remember what the Bible says: 'The prayer offered in faith will make the sick person well.' We need to take God at His Word and believe what He says."

I knelt down with Millie and my brothers at the foot of Ruth's bed while Dad and Mother were at the head. I had been taught to close my eyes for prayer, but I confess that this time I peeked. I wanted to see what God would do. I believed with all my heart. I knew I wouldn't be able to see Him, but I also knew He would do *something*.

God did not heal her immediately, but the fever left her. In the next few days, her rash faded and her intestinal disturbances settled down. She was able to open her eyes and speak. With help, she was even able to sit up. Before too long, she was feeling hungry and eating again. And Mother was singing and smiling again.

Slowly, Ruth regained the use of her muscles and limbs. When she held her arms up, the skin draped from them like limp rags.

"Look at what I can do," she said, smiling wanly. "I can push my finger between the bones of my arms. When I fatten up again, I won't be able to do that anymore."

The first time Ruth ventured onto the street, people ran away screaming. "What's wrong with them?" she asked. "They act as if they've seen a ghost!"

"Not a ghost," Millie laughed. "But you must admit that you look like a skeleton."

Through the Red Cross, we were taken to a refugee camp in Sweden not long afterward, and for the first time in years were able to fill our stomachs. With wholesome food, Ruth regained her health and strength and her hair grew in again. When we all were able to pass our medical exams, we were repatriated to the Netherlands, from where we immigrated to Canada. Here, Ruth met and fell in love with a young man who had also been displaced by the war.

"I'm sorry," the doctor told her when he did her prenuptial medical exam. "With what you have gone through, and with the seriousness of the typhus you suffered, you will never be able to have children."

Fortunately, God, and not doctors, is the final authority. And when God heals someone, He doesn't do it halfway. Ruth gave birth to five children and has numerous grandchildren. Now eighty-three, she never tires of telling people what God has done for her.

Home Is Where the Heart Is
James Stuart Bell

The idea of owning our own home seemed like a distant dream, and initially I didn't think there was any hurry. I had been a graduate student in Ireland, and my Irish wife, Margaret, got pregnant right away. We came back to the States and briefly lived with my parents as I looked for some type of writing or communications job. I found a low-paying job through a government grant with the American Heart Association as their public relations person.

After our adorable baby Rosheen was born, it was time to move out of my parents' beautiful home in a posh suburb and find a humble place of our own.

I had high expectations but very little money. Margaret was happy to find a place within our meager budget and begin the nesting process. We settled on a small one-bedroom apartment that was cozy enough for the three of us. But as time went by, we were expecting another baby and wondering how that would work with an apartment that had a postage-stamp-size kitchen, a bathroom that seemed about the size of a phone booth, and a bedroom that resembled an oversized walk-in closet.

Our apartment was on the second floor and had a stairway down to the entrance. We put up a gate to prevent our daughter from falling down the stairs. But it only took one moment of forgetfulness, and I watched in horror as she spilled down the stairs, feet entangled in her walker.

In addition, the neighborhood residents were having their own struggles a bit too close to home. The guy whose window we could look directly into from ours stuck his head in an oven after an altercation with his girlfriend. I could hear it unfold. It was time to consider moving.

Then it happened. My parents were casually looking for something larger to encompass our growing family. They landed on what seemed to be a bonanza—a brand-new housing development was going up with reasonable prices. I smiled as I thought about my own little plot of land and no cockroaches in the kitchen.

All of us took off on the weekend to see this smallish colonial. In my mind, nothing is quite like the excitement of new construction and watching homes going up with all new neighbors. I had experienced this three times in my own childhood when my parents built brand-new homes.

As we asked the realtor questions and toured the home, I felt like it was too good to be true. The finances just barely worked, but this was in a time when home values were escalating and, according to my parents, it would be a good investment. The only down-side appeared to be a dilapidated barn with a couple of old wrecked cars right behind what would be our backyard. Views and trees really appeal to me, but I thought I shouldn't expect too much and be content with this superb gift. Then, just as we were ready to leave, Rosheen fell down the stairs of the new home. We had been praying fervently for confirmation on our way to the house. Was this a negative sign?

When we came back to our little mole hole, we continued to pray. As a typical man, I was listing the facts, confident that my bride would see common sense and would also love a bigger home to take care of and decorate. But to my chagrin, she blurted out that she didn't have peace about it from the Lord. I was a bit shocked and asked her reasons. She said she had none but the intuitive check that we can sometimes get from the Holy Spirit. To my credit, I had to check my heart and seek out my own motivations before trying to pressure her with facts. What could possibly be wrong with a home that we could afford and that would be a good investment, especially with the prediction that mortgage interest rates would continue to go up?

Fortunately, I had learned a good bit from marriage conferences, books, and some other couples married longer than we were at the time. If you have a godly wife and after prayer on a certain issue you don't have peace or you are not in agreement, then don't move forward. She wouldn't budge because she didn't want to violate what she sensed the Lord was telling her. It was clear that we were being tested. It wasn't necessarily wrong to buy this house, but would we be willing to obey God for what He ultimately had planned for us? So we made the decision to pass it up, and we could find nothing else like it on the market.

Over the ensuing couple of years, interest rates did indeed climb, but so did my salary with a new high-profile job in New York City, and we were able to increase our savings. Our apartment began to feel like a sardine can when our son, Brendan, arrived, and then later a relative with her new baby for six months, to make a total of six sardines! But God was teaching us about sharing with others, learning to live on less, and putting Him above earthly desires. In fact, we put the goal of a new house completely out of our minds and asked God, when He was ready, to just give us a sign to pursue a change in our living situation.

One of our clients in a nearby tree-lined and more rural suburb had me come out for a visit. On my way back, I passed a sign saying New Houses For Sale. I cruised down the street, passing houses being constructed, to a dead end where there was an empty lot. As I surveyed the beautiful woods on three sides, I wondered why this lot was one of the last available and wished the fortunate person well. On my way out, I stopped at the builder's model home. He conveyed to me that the reason the lot was available was that the original owner's financing had fallen through at the last moment. What was really interesting was that this builder was the same one who built the home we had decided not to buy two years earlier because of our discernment in prayer.

I drove home at the speed of light and grabbed ahold of Margaret; we drove back to talk to the builder in greater detail. It turns out that he could put the exact same model that we had previously turned down on this prime lot. It would take him six months to build, and, because of my improved salary, we could save more for a down payment on what had become a slightly more expensive home. We had the additional perk, with new construction, of weekly watching our home ascend to the sky. And because of the location, we didn't have to forgo the joy of the trees or deal with the eyesore of rusted-out cars behind our backyard.

It was as if God introduced what was ideal for us at the time but was testing our hearts in terms of not getting ahead of His will. After we moved in, we realized that because of the cul-de-sac and no house across the street, our young children were able to play in the street in front of our yard without worry. Not so at the previous house two miles away. We were able to walk behind our backyard and follow a long path between the trees in solitude when we wanted to pray or think through a decision. Not so, again, with the first home two years previous.

Whenever we think back thirty-five years upon the joy of entering that house after waiting so long, and all the wonderful memories that ensued with our children, we ask ourselves: *Would we rather have lived in the first house with its downsides for eleven years? Or waited as we did for the additional blessings and the nine years we had at the second house?* The answer is always the same, and we praise God all over again for the house at 30 Pierson Drive.

Home is indeed where the heart is, and we'll find it by seeking the Lord's will and timetable and making sure He is first in our hearts.

No More Headaches

Marty Prudhomme

$\mathcal{A}$t seven years of age, I began suffering with headaches. My mom called them sick headaches because I would throw up. We had not heard the term *migraine*. Many holidays, picnics, and other family functions were ruined because I was ill.

My parents thought it was because I became overly excited, and the stress would bring on a headache. They often admonished, "Now, don't get too excited, but we are going on a picnic next week. You will be all right if you stay calm."

Their well-intended suggestions did not help.

We did not have money for doctors, except in extreme circumstances. Once, while I was playing with my brother, he fell and broke his arm. Now, that warranted a trip to the doctor, but headaches did not. My parents prayed that I would outgrow my inconvenient illness.

The headaches eventually tapered off, and by high school they were completely gone—although my parents began having headaches dealing with a typical teenager!

In college, I met Bill, who was to become my husband. He was a tall, very good-looking fellow. After we married, Bill's job required us to move to Virginia. I suddenly began to suffer with sinus headaches. Whenever the weather turned nice, the headaches would start. The beautiful fall days were the worst, but at least I was not throwing up anymore.

Eventually, Bill found a job in Louisiana. We thought I would be free from the sinus allergies, but the headaches continued. I would tease Bill that I was allergic to him, since the headaches started up again after we were married. He did not think that was funny.

We soon had two children, and the cares of life piled up around us. Our marriage felt the stress and started to break apart. All I ever wanted in life was to be a wife and mom. I would shout at Bill, "You never want to spend time with me; all you do is work!"

That did not go over very well, and Bill would yell back, "You are such a nag! No wonder I don't want to spend time with you."

Our marriage problems caused me to cry out to God. After seeking God for answers, I was invited to a prayer group by some wonderful Christian women. They often prayed with me and taught me what the Bible had to say about my circumstances. After accepting the Lord into my life, I asked Him to take charge. I knew God could do a better job of running things than I had. I surrendered my life, my children, and even Bill to the Lord. Slowly, things began to change; God took the anger in my heart and replaced it with His love.

Bill noticed the yelling diminished. He told me, "You should spend more time with those women; they are good for you."

Bill started going to a Christian men's group called the Full Gospel Business Men's Fellowship International. He gave his life to the Lord, and we began to hope that God could bring real change to our marriage.

I invited a friend to come and teach a Bible study in our home. God was at work in us, but my headaches persisted—they occurred every time we met for Bible study. The horrible nausea came back, but I would not cancel the study. The ladies prayed for me each week.

Doctors didn't have any answers. Pain pills gave me horrible side effects. I knew prayer was the only answer, even as the frequency of the headaches increased to several days a week.

Once I was to sing for a friend's wedding, but when the day arrived I woke in extreme pain. I was so nauseated I lay on the bathroom floor with my cheek on the cool tile. If I moved, the retching would begin. I was concerned that no one could take my place for the wedding. My friends would be terribly disappointed if there was no soloist for the ceremony.

Bill called Brenda to come and pray for me. Brenda was my teacher and mentor who had taught me the importance of prayer when I first came to the Lord. She prayed, "In the name of Jesus, headache, go and nausea, stop. We claim the healing that was paid for on Calvary."

Nothing special happened, but I soon realized the pain and nausea were gone. That afternoon, I was able to get dressed and made it to the wedding. I rejoiced in the Lord my Healer.

I thought I was totally healed, but when the Bible study came around that week, so did the headache.

As we joined hands, the Lord's presence was so sweet. The ladies' prayers warmed and comforted me. Jesus was my Healer, no matter my circumstances. I would often lie on the bathroom floor, praying, "Jesus, if You never heal me, I will praise You anyway, for You are worthy. As long as I have breath, I will praise You, O Lord."

I was very concerned for my children during this season. They were in school and still needed Mama to get them off to classes, to help with homework, and to cook their dinner. They needed me to tuck them into bed and say good-night prayers. Some days, it was impossible to give them the attention they needed, and I felt guilty. My friends' prayers sustained me as I continued to trust the Lord.

One day, Brenda phoned and invited Bill and me to go with her and her husband to hear evangelist T.L. Osborn speak. He had a powerful healing ministry in Africa and was traveling around the United States.

The evangelist shared many miraculous stories about what God was doing. He and his wife, Daisy, had seen thousands come to know Christ during their crusades. T.L. told us, "Jesus taught His disciples what normal Christianity was like. The gospel is to be preached everywhere, the sick healed, and the oppressed set free. God desires that His ministry be part of our everyday lives if we will only believe."

At the end of the service T. L. said, "This crowd is too large for everyone to come forward for prayer. I would like everyone who needs healing to place your hands where it hurts." He prayed, "Dear Lord, You see the needs and know every sickness in this room. In the name of Jesus, I ask for all sickness to leave—let all disease and all pain be gone."

His prayer was not lengthy, but I knew the Lord heard his prayer and all the prayers that had been offered over the past years on my behalf. I didn't have goose bumps or any warmth, as some say they feel when God has healed them. I didn't feel anything at all except a small pop in my ears.

As we left the church that night, I hesitated to say anything to my friends, because it was such a small sensation in my ears. When we got into the car, I thought, *By faith, I'm going to tell them I felt a pop in my ears, and I believe God has healed me.*

They did not seem very excited about my comment, but they talked about how the Osborns' testimonies had encouraged them. I silently thanked the Lord for His healing.

These events took place more than thirty years ago. Since that day, I have not had a single headache. No more sinus headaches when the weather changes, no headaches when I get hungry or when I'm under stress, and definitely no migraines. The Lord heard all those prayers over the years, and when the time was right, He answered. God miraculously healed me.

God exhorts us to pray, and then He answers our prayers. Even if the answers are delayed, God is faithful. Never, ever give up. Never stop praying. Praise the Lord, for He is a God who hears and answers prayer.

Father Knows Best

Dorothy J. Haire

A group of giggly twelve-year-old girls sat on the iron rail fence of the local elementary school, watching skinny boys play basketball. Suddenly, one boy broke away from the crowd and dribbled the ball to me. With his thirteen-and-a-half-year-old changing voice, he announced for all to hear, "I love you!" and dribbled back to the other boys.

The girls giggled, and the boys cheered! Refusing to admit I heard him, I continued to talk to the girl sitting next to me. I had no interest in boys in general, and not him in particular, since he had humiliated me in front of everyone. I never wanted to see him again.

I later found out that his name was Johnnie Lee Haire. For the next two years, he stalked me. He was everywhere: school dances, basketball games, walking home from school, always proclaiming his love.

By the time I was fourteen, my mother allowed him to come over and sit on the porch for a while. She loved his "Yes, ma'am," "No, ma'am," "Thank you," and "Can I pick that up for you, Ms. Bessie?"

Two weeks before my seventeenth birthday, I married that boy—my best friend and soul mate. Thirty-three years and four adult children later, we were making plans as new empty nesters to live our wildest dreams. We were so happy.

I could not imagine life without Johnnie. I was confident I would never have to live without him, because I had talked with God about it. Johnnie's possible death had become a concern for me when my friend Dee's husband suddenly passed away. They were such a loving couple. One night, they went to sleep; she woke up the next morning, but he did not. I was in shock. This was unbelievable. I went to their house to see for myself if this was true. The look on Dee's face said it all. I never wanted to experience that kind of pain.

I knew John 14:13–14: "Whatever you ask in My name, that I will do, so that the Father may be glorified in the Son. If you ask Me anything in My name, I will do it" (NASB).

I prayed all the way home, pleading with Jesus to take me home first. I explained to Him that I was an only child and all alone, except for Johnnie and our four children. Mama had passed years before. Johnnie had brothers and sisters who would help him finish raising our children. I told Jesus that I could not live without Johnnie—my friend, my lover, my soul mate, my everything.

When I got home, I sat Johnnie down at the kitchen table. I explained what had happened to Dee. I repeated to him my prayer to God. I made him promise he would not die before me. Confident that God and Johnnie understood the desires of my heart and agreed, I went on with my life.

A couple of years later, while we were laughing and talking, Johnnie began to cough. Then he began to hyperventilate.

"You caught a cold?" I asked as I passed him a brown paper bag to breathe into, which slowed his breathing.

"No, I don't have a cold."

"Lie down and rest. You'll feel better." I went to the family room to read so I would not disturb him.

"Hey, Mama, y'all got something to eat?" our son Tommie asked as he came in the front door headed to the kitchen. A few minutes later, we both heard labored breathing. Running into the bedroom, we realized Johnnie was in trouble.

"You are going to the hospital," I informed Johnnie while motioning for Tommie to help me get him dressed. We walked him through the house to the front door.

"What is this, Dorothy?" he struggled to ask.

"I don't know, but I know Jesus does," I answered. As I prayed, Tommie and I began walking his rapidly weakening body to the car to take him to the emergency room. He collapsed onto the backseat of the car. We arrived at the hospital in ten minutes, horn blasting all the way.

The police at the hospital entrance must have radioed ahead, because the ER staff burst out of the door with a gurney as we pulled up. They whisked him away, directing us to the waiting room. A few minutes later, the doctor came out to tell us that Johnnie had died of a massive heart attack.

There was no warning and no pain. He was not sick in any way. The love of my life, my soul mate, my best friend was gone!

Standing beside Johnnie's bed with my hand on his still-warm chest, I heard a loud voice say, *"Nothing left undone. Nothing left unsaid. No regrets."*

The authority and love in this voice prevented feelings of sorrow, anger, and betrayal from entering my heart. Peace filled me and encapsulated me.

As I stood beside the bed of my childhood sweetheart in the emergency room, the unthinkable happened. I was happy for him. After all, isn't that what all saints want—to finish their course in a way that pleases God? No pain. No time to fret. Just a call to come home, and it was over. Johnnie was with Jesus, and I was happy for him.

But what about me?

I prayed, "Jesus, help me through the next hour."

He did.

I repeated that prayer for a few days until it evolved to "Jesus, help me through this day."

He did.

Gradually, I started to pray, "Jesus, help me through this week."

He did.

I thought I could not live without Johnnie, and if I did I would be dysfunctional. It was not true. After the funeral was over and all my friends returned to their lives, God proved Himself to be more than enough for me. Daily, He stabilizes my heart with His love, which makes me strong. I feel God's presence every day, which gives me peace. I pray for guidance before going to sleep and wake with the answers to my problems.

Johnnie was a good provider. I also worked, and together we were able to afford vacations, a comfortable home, college educations, and nice clothes for our children.

God became an extravagant provider, not only taking care of my daily needs but also making my dreams come true. I had always wanted to travel abroad. So far I have been to London, Paris, Rome, Egypt, and Israel.

It was Johnnie's time to go home and be with the Lord. Now that it has happened, I am OK with it. My adult children have homes, children, and lives of their own, but I am not alone or lonely. Also, I have a new heart's desire. I want God to be able to say about me the words He spoke about Johnnie: *"Nothing left undone. Nothing left unsaid. No regrets."* My goal every day is to live in such a way that God would be pleased with me.

Often we think we are praying about one thing, when really we are praying about something else. My prayer was not motivated by love for Johnnie, but my unwillingness to live without him. God listens past the words of our mouths and hears the words of our hearts. In His infinite wisdom, He answers the prayers of our hearts in ways we could not fathom with our finite minds. I am so very grateful that our Father knows best.

Shortest, Biggest Prayer
Charles J. Huff

I heard an engine growl as the driver stomped on the gas pedal. I gave no thought to it until I heard the harrowing squall of brakes. I looked up and saw my five-year-old daughter, Nicole, in the middle of the street, staring wild-eyed at the approaching car careening toward her.

A friend of mine and I were working on a car across the street from our house. Nicole, wanting to be a part of what was happening, was watching everything we did.

The hood was up. I was sitting in the driver's seat as my friend worked on the engine. He said he needed another tool and headed for my garage. When he reached the edge of my yard, Nicole decided to chase after him.

Everything that happened and all that went through my mind in the next three seconds made time seem to stretch into minutes. I looked in the door mirror and caught the image of the bumper moving forward and then out of view. Turning to look out the window, I saw the fear in the eyes of the driver and his passenger.

Time stopped to allow me to recall a friend's story about a miracle involving his young grandson—a miracle that started as a horrible tragedy. He told how the preschooler had been struck by a car. Instead of being knocked to the side, clear of the car, he was knocked down and the car passed over him, stopping with the muffler resting on top of him. His grandson's flesh was seared and stuck to the muffler. Medics had to tear part of his skin off in order free him.

Through his tears, my friend gave glory to Jesus, saying that the boy not only lived but also had almost no scarring.

The thought of my beautiful little girl experiencing the same fate clawed at my soul. With the car passing beside me, I couldn't jump out and grab her or push her out of the way. This was one time all I could do was pray, but I didn't have time to tell Jesus all my fears. I didn't have time to tell Him how much I wanted Him to keep her from falling beneath the car.

Tires were still screeching, and the car continued to bear down on my little girl. The closer the car got to her, the more my heart collapsed.

I only had time to cry out, "Jesus!"

That one-word prayer contained everything I wanted to say to Him. He knows the thoughts of our hearts even before we speak them. I know this because she flew up into the air, not under the car, and the car continued skidding forward, moving underneath her. "Thank You, Jesus."

I saw her falling toward the car's windshield with the car still moving forward. A memory from my youth flashed in my mind—a young cousin of mine was struck by a car while he was riding his bicycle. He flew up and crashed down through the windshield, lost half of his face, and died of head trauma.

Again, I cried out, "Jesus!"

In that one-word prayer, I asked the Lord to prevent her from going through the windshield. With the car's forward movement, she hit the car just above the windshield. The impact caused her to fly forward, where she then grazed the front edge of the hood as the driver fought to stop the car. I again thanked the Lord for hearing and answering my prayer.

I had prayed against two immediate hazards, but now I realized other disastrous possibilities. What if she landed on her head? She could be killed, receive a concussion, or break her neck. She could already have broken bones and break more.

The car still had not stopped, so the fear of it moving on top of her speared me once more. For the third time, I cried out, "Jesus!"

I can still see her little body, arms, and legs flailing wildly like a rag doll tossed into the air. However, just as vivid in my mind is how her body turned after glancing off the hood so she rolled like a pencil in front of the now-stopped car. At last I was able to get out of the car and run to her.

I made her lie still in spite of her cries to get off the hot pavement. I prayed over her as we waited for an ambulance.

The driver kept apologizing, in his attempt to convince me he could have done nothing to prevent this. I told him I knew Jesus had already answered many prayers for her and that I believed she would be fine.

The ambulance came and took her to the hospital. The emergency room personnel confirmed God's protective power. She had only a couple of minor scrapes and bruises. I sent the driver the news from the hospital so he could know how great our God is.

We are so thankful to the Lord for all that He did for us in that accident. We thank Him and praise Him, too, for the lesson on prayer. Before the accident, our family had read and talked about King David's crying out to the Lord.

In Psalm 3, David wrote, "I cried to the LORD with my voice, and He heard me from His holy hill" (v. 4 NKJV). The heading to this psalm informs us David wrote it when he fled from his own son Absalom. David, God's own anointed. David, the King of Israel. David, the man after God's own heart. David, who slew Goliath, and the one of whom all of Israel sang, "Saul has slain his thousands, and David his ten thousands" (1 Samuel 18:7 NKJV).

This same David cried out to the Lord in desperation and taught us a valuable lesson on prayer. How long does a prayer have to be in order to be effective? How much detail do we need to express, or how many specifics do we need to give Him in our prayers?

According to David's example, not one of these questions or concerns really matters, since God knows what is in our hearts already. Like David, I cried out to the Lord with my voice, and He heard me, and He answered me.

A Race to the Bottom

Susan M. Watkins

*W*hen you're a tenured Christian, you've heard about multiple venues for answered prayers. God is indeed resourceful, and, like the flow of water, He effortlessly gets into the smallest cracks. He's never limited by calendars, geography, or hemispheres. Past, present, and future pose no boundaries. He doesn't need cars, airplanes, passports, or birth certificates. He truly is everywhere, and He truly does know all of our days before we reach them.

Some fifteen years before I uttered my prayer, God initiated His answer. He's like that. Isaiah wrote that God hears before we speak; answers before we ask (Isaiah 65:24).

Young and energetic and having recently moved to Arizona from a big city, I was always up for new challenges.

Quick to organize anything, I was often given the task of planning something fun and exciting. So one cool morning while doves cooed, perched atop abundant cacti, several of us loaded into cars to embark on a day of mountain climbing.

The day promised to be blistering hot, so we had to start early to get ahead of the heat. Despite our early start, the sun was fully awake and the car's air conditioner ran at maximum output.

Altitude popped our ears as we wound up the mountain's two-lane paved road. This peak's elevation reached ninety-two hundred feet. Boulders often littered the roadway and had shattered the pavement upon impact. Between the ponderosa pines we passed, we could see the city basin below with heat waves already dancing above it. Our engine's strain eased when we reached a cool enough altitude that we could turn off the air-conditioning and lower the windows. The mountain's fragrance filled the vehicle. I longed to stretch my legs as I thought about my childhood filled with riding trains, buses, taxis, and subways. The city idea of a "trail ride" was to let kids ride saddled horses on streets alongside rush-hour traffic. My new environment surprisingly suited me, and I was open to all possibilities.

This mountain range was becoming familiar to me. I'd already hiked it a few times, but this outing promised a higher trail. On the mountain's opposite side was a rugged cave for truly adventurous spelunking. It was not the destination for people who were unwilling to crawl in the mud on their bellies through extremely tight spaces. Within days of learning about it, I was facedown in the mud, scraping my back along jagged rock formations. I exited the cave twenty pounds heavier from caked-on mud and was recognizable only by my voice. This caused several waiting novices to change their plans. Personally, I felt my greatest accomplishment wasn't exploring the intimidating cave, but not losing my hiking boots to the viscous mud and its insatiable appetite for all it touched.

Hours later, we reached our target. It looked rather ordinary instead of the classroom it was to become. I tell people that the view is always worth the climb, whether spiritually or naturally. Only by our commitment to the resistance will we reach the top. The climb delivers the reward.

As the group chatted happily, I scanned the area. We'd never climbed this high before, nearly at the ridge.

Early into the excursion, the terrain became much steeper than we expected, and all but two less experienced climbers abandoned the journey. My friend and I pressed on well past the semblance of a trail until our passage narrowed sharply. Undeterred, we exited the tree line with unobstructed views of the glistening city. The altitude's beauty made me feel closer to God, not realizing how much I was about to need Him.

Our first dilemma was when we came to a ledge along the mountain's face that was only two feet wide, but it widened again twenty-five feet ahead. Evaluating the discovery, we continued. The mountain above and below this ledge was sheer; however, the lower portion sloped somewhat and was covered completely in loose rocks.

My friend took the lead and told me to follow her footsteps. I did, but suddenly the ledge gave way and I slid down the mountainside. A lovely day of escaping the heat was now a life-threatening situation.

Because the surface beneath me was loose shale of various sizes, it actually increased my speed as I slid downward. The land surrounding this barren swath grew abundant pine trees, but not a stem or root grew where I was plummeting. It was a race to the bottom, and I already knew I wasn't going to win.

I'm always amazed at how people describe such situations as going in slow motion. I believe God wires us this way to give opportunity for solutions. I, too, had this experience. Only I used the long seconds to unleash the greatest power handed to humankind: prayer.

All nineteen years of me asked the Almighty to be almighty. I had no chance of survival on my own. Even if I made it through whatever tragedy lay before me, I'd have a five-hour journey to a hospital. Being airlifted was unrealistic because I was literally on the side of a mountain. If the rocks didn't fillet me after shredding my thin clothes, at some point something yet unseen *would* stop me.

No longer able to hear my friend's screams, I implored God to solve this physics problem. It wasn't the temporary prayer for deliverance with empty promises of lifetime service, but the sincere cries of a redeemed child to her heavenly Father, Who'd granted another opportunity to prove Himself faithful on her behalf.

As suddenly as I'd lost my footing and begun to pray, God did what God does best and turned an earthly situation into a divine classroom.

Although I dug my heels into the shale, they failed to slow my ever-increasing speed. On my back, I continued scanning the surrounding landscape, hoping for something to grab. I prayed for any intervention to stop me.

I'd tried moving to the right and left, hoping it would create friction and reduce my speed. I crossed my arms and hands over my chest in an effort to protect them.

Desperately analyzing my situation, I finally visualized what was going to stop me. Jagged, sharp boulders formed a natural wall in all directions. They were impossible to avoid and a horrific collision lay just ahead. I couldn't even fathom the pain upon impact. Unless God performed the miraculous, death was imminent.

Preparing for the worst, I suddenly saw a green dot enlarging as I approached and realized it was a plant that could rescue me. Some spring day, years earlier, God had caused a little windblown seed to take root on a mountainside, and, despite rock slides and severe weather, it thrived until we met.

I began steering my speeding body toward the bush, hoping to crash into it instead of the boulders. With seconds left to maneuver into its path, I realized my "bush" was actually a wild prickly pear cactus covered with three-inch spike needles.

You've got to be kidding!

I rose, slamming my entire body against the unconventional rescuer, grabbing it with all my remaining strength.

Then I screamed.

This was not Moses's burning bush, but I was delivered just the same. Had it been any other type of vegetation, it could not have survived on that mountainside. It had to be a tenacious cactus to endure its commission.

I came to a halt and slowly peeled myself from that anchor. Crawling to the boulders just feet away, I discovered the road was on the other side, fifteen feet below. Had I survived the impact of smacking against the boulders, I'd have flipped over the steep embankment and potentially been run over by a car.

God answered numerous prayers that afternoon while He spared my life. Miraculously, my worst injuries were from cactus needles. The surface of the mountainside should have peeled me like a banana, broken several bones, and left me with severe internal injuries, but I sustained no injuries from sliding down the rocks, unprotected, at breakneck speed.

I learned our prayers are often answered in ways we're not expecting; however, He will *always* answer them.

Every single one of them—before we even ask.

Before the Snow Flies

LaRose Karr

Forging my car through deep, icy ruts was difficult and nerve-racking. It was unusual to have such a large amount of snow dumped on us this early in the season. Snow falls quickly in Colorado, and our city was not prepared to remove the heavy snow fast enough, so for three weeks, drivers barreled through unplowed snow, creating deep furrows of thick ice.

But sometimes you just have to brave the elements to do some shopping.

As I headed back home from my venture, suddenly I burst into laughter. The roads were just as bad as they'd been on my way into town, but instead of hunching over the steering wheel trying to deal with them, I unexpectedly exploded in glee.

I call this "holy laughter." It's when the joy of the Lord takes over and you laugh as you rejoice with Him. It's a simple pleasure, really, and just fun. Of course, it is perfectly fine to have a good time with the Lord, taking joy in the work of His hands.

And why were we rejoicing together?

The story began a year earlier in this same season of winter when I first heard the news: the structure of my longtime job was changing. Jobs do change at times, but I'd worked in this correctional setting for many years and had become burned out, as so many do from the stress and demands of a job.

With the new guidelines, I would still put in forty hours a week at my regular job, my *home*, as it was called. But now everyone at my level was being asked to fill in for others as needed. For example, vacations, sick time, and training would take me to other areas in my workplace while employees were away from their desks or while empty positions were waiting to be filled.

This new policy may work well in small facilities, but I worked in a megafacility, spanning eighty acres, and the walking distance from the entrance to some areas was often a quarter of a mile.

I followed this new work plan for six months, and I became even more tired than I already was. I was well equipped to handle one job, but adding in the distance between offices, differing work practices, policies, people, and extra duties made me begin to feel stretched. Factor in heat and blizzards while walking to the various areas, and I had approached my limit. Walking in the early morning in extremely cold winter conditions exacerbated my bronchial problems.

As a severe asthmatic, I knew I needed to cut back on work, so I began to ask God for a part-time job that would allow me to work less and spend some time with my grandchildren. I also asked others I trusted to pray.

Instead of my load at work lightening, it increased. I was asked to leave my desk again, not only to perform the extra duties but also to begin working two afternoons a week in another area.

That's when I knew it was time to make a decision. My workload, not counting the filling in for other areas, had now increased from forty hours per week to forty-six. But I was not allowed to count overtime or accumulate compensation. All the work was to be accomplished in a regular workweek. As I pondered this problem and prayed about my desire to lighten my workload, I kept hearing the Lord's voice: *"Before the snow flies."*

What did He mean? Would I have a job by then? Was I supposed to leave my position before the snow flies?

Lord, what are You saying to me?

I started interviewing for other jobs, but nothing seemed appropriate or worked with the schedule I wanted, so I hung on to the job I had.

However, one morning I woke up sick, and I knew without a doubt that this was the day I was to give notice and watch for the employment doors the Lord was going to open for me. I just felt in my spirit that this was the day to speak. So I did.

Later that day, while reclining on the couch, not feeling well and covered with a blanket, I saw a newscast on television. Speaking of an area high in the Colorado mountains, the newscaster said, "Snow is flying in Colorado."

I laughed, thinking of that phrase the Lord had given me: *"Before the snow flies."*

My, how the Lord had arranged this event! I knew then that my obedience was needed before the snow fell. I had made my requests known to the Lord. He asked me to step out in faith and let go of my fears, and I had cut it to the wire.

After interviewing for three months, I was able to cut back as I wanted to for my health with a couple of part-time jobs. One came about right away with some work from home for a friend. Then another person offered me a job with the opportunity to work around the times I watched my grandchildren. Surprisingly, this marketing and social media employment came because of my computer knowledge and my calm voice. The business owner had even planned to fix up an office for me. I certainly never considered that someone would create a job for me. There was no way my imagination could have dreamed of working with social media.

And six months earlier, when I had started petitioning the throne, how could I know that the job I would receive did not even exist yet? Perhaps the thought process of my future employer began at that time.

On this cold January day, I had driven the rutted, snowy streets of my town to shop. And as most small-town Americans know, local shopping is the social center for small towns. I came across two friends and told the story of how I acquired the jobs. One friend said, "I can see how this tickles you."

It did, indeed, tickle me. So as I drove home, I exploded with the joyous laughter of someone watching God's plans unfold precisely and completely, in God's way and in His timing.

Stepping out in faith for work provision is never easy, and because this was not the first time I had stepped out in faith, I already knew that the Lord knows the plans for us well in advance of our needs. He is not surprised when we become burned out or tired. He has doors in place for us to step through, and while we are constrained by time, He is not.

Ask.

Seek.

Knock.

He will answer. Laughter and rejoicing are just around the corner.

Dad, Let's Pray!

Bobbie Roper

One of the scariest experiences of my life happened on a snowy November night in the Catskill Mountains of New York. My husband, Jim, had gone hunting that afternoon. Though many local guys hunted for sport or for trophy mounts, Jim hunted for the meat. Raising four children on a missionary's salary was not easy. A deer in the freezer went a long way to providing for our family.

Jim had been out several times over the past two weeks to no avail. Today was different. Just before dark, he'd shot a young buck with his compound bow. Quietly, he eased out of the woods so the deer would lie down. After a couple of hours he would return, track it, bring it home, and prepare it for the freezer. Though he often did the tracking alone, on this night our twelve-year-old son, Jimmie, volunteered to help his dad. Not wanting to be left out, I decided to tag along.

We arrived at the spot where Jim had come out of the woods. We headed into the forest. I noticed right away that my nose hairs were freezing together as I breathed. Scattered patches of snow remained from a storm the week before, and the forecast called for heavy snow that night. The crunch of the frosty leaves reminded us how cold it was.

With thick cloud cover, our flashlights were our only source of light. I felt in the pocket of my heavy parka, making sure I had extra batteries. This cloudy night would not be a good time to run out of battery power.

Getting back to Jim's tree stand was fairly easy. He had glued squares of reflective tape to thumbtacks and placed a tack on every few trees at eye level. It amazed me how the tacks glowed when the light hit them. We found the tree where his stand was perched high above the ground. Now came the tough part—tracking the deer.

As we headed away from the tree stand, we could make out the trail of the buck through the heavy underbrush. A wounded deer always heads for the thickest cover, hoping to hide from whatever hurt it.

Eyes to the ground, ears alert for any sounds, Jim led the way. The deeper we went into the thick undergrowth, the harder it became. Blackberry vines ripped at our clothes, and in places we had to get on our hands and knees to make it through heavy underbrush.

As we pushed deeper, the temperature dropped. Snowflakes began drifting through the circle of light cast by Jimmie's flashlight. I asked Jim if we should turn around and head home.

"Just a little longer," he said. "That buck can't be too much farther."

After another ten minutes passed, we decided we would not find the deer. The snow was beginning to fall faster as the wind picked up. Even in this dense part of the woods the ground was becoming a white carpet. Pulling our hoods tighter, we headed back the way we thought we had come. We had been walking about fifteen minutes when Jim suddenly stopped.

"What's wrong?" I asked.

"We have walked in a circle," Jim said. "That's the same stump at the spot where we decided to turn back. But don't worry. I'll get us out of here."

Fifteen minutes later, we still could not find the trail we had come in on. Snow had already covered the ground, making it impossible to see any signs of where we had been. The way Jimmie was walking told me that his feet were cold. His cheeks looked like candied apples and his lips were chapped. Why hadn't I grabbed my lip balm and a scarf for him?

Jim stopped, pulling us into his arms. "Guys, I don't know how to get us out of here. It's hard to see with just our flashlights, and I left the compass in the truck. The temperature is dropping so fast, and between the wind and heavy snow I can't get my bearings. We will have to find a thicket to crawl into, and hopefully, if we stay close to each other we can keep warm enough to make it until morning. I am so sorry I let you come. I know you are scared. I just don't know what to do."

Sometimes as we raise our children we wonder if they are grasping anything we are trying to teach them. That night, we learned that our son had indeed been listening. We had always taught our children the importance of walking close to God. We also taught them that our God is gracious and loving and answers our prayers. They had seen many prayers answered during the years when we were in Bible college and in our time as missionaries. So on this cold November night, when his dad was at a loss as to what to do, our son said in a shaky voice, "Dad, let's pray!"

This was an earnest plea from a child who believed that we faced a dilemma and that the God we worshipped would hear and answer. To him it was simple: we were in a fix, and we needed to pray.

So there in the middle of the dark, ghostly woods, with the wind whistling through the trees and huge snowflakes falling around us, we knelt, joined hands, and lifted our faces heavenward.

"Lord," Jim prayed, "we need Your help, and we could sure use it now. Show us the way out. We praise You for what You are going to do. Amen."

It was a simple prayer, but as the snowflakes melted on our faces, we felt a sense of peace. Surely, the Lord was in this place. Jeremiah 33:3 came to mind: "Call to me and I will answer you and tell you great and unsearchable things you do not know" (NIV). We were certainly trusting in that verse.

Only a couple of minutes later, Jimmie shouted, "Dad, do you hear it?"

"Hear what, son?"

"I hear a car!"

We strained to hear something besides the wind whipping the bare tree branches, and, sure enough, we all heard the unmistakable hum of an engine. We only heard it for a few seconds, but that was enough. Jim led us toward where the sound had come from. Within half an hour, the woods thinned out, and we soon stepped onto the snow-covered road.

We made it out with only numb fingers, toes, and noses. To our amazement, we looked down the road and saw that we had emerged from the woods about fifty yards from our truck. What a wonderful sight!

After offering a prayer of thanksgiving for deliverance from what could have been a deadly situation, we headed to the truck and home. We were thankful for the faith of a child—faith not only in his earthly father but also in his heavenly Father. We also knew we would be more prepared the next time we ventured into the woods.

Some might say it was sure lucky we heard that vehicle. I don't think it was luck at all. We'd heard no sound from cars or trucks traveling that road before our time of prayer. I believe God answered our prayer by sending a vehicle down that snow-covered road just when we needed to hear a sound to lead us home. When God's children cry out to Him for help, He is quick to respond. We were all reminded that there is power in prayer.

And who knows? Maybe one of our guardian angels was driving that car.

An Earthquake Full of Blessings

AnnaLee Conti

The car door slammed behind me as Carol, Linda, and I dashed up the steps. As we entered the kitchen, Carol's mother asked, "Have you girls been watching TV?"

"No," Carol said. "Why?"

"I know AnnaLee grew up in Alaska." Her mother nodded toward me and gestured toward the television. "A few minutes ago, a news bulletin said the main street of Anchorage has been leveled by an earthquake."

"Oh, it must be an exaggeration." I laughed. "We have earthquakes all the time."

Just then the announcer again interrupted the programming: "And now for the latest on the earthquake that hit south central Alaska early this evening." We listened to a report by telephone from Fort Greeley.

I was eighteen years old and was visiting the home of a classmate during Easter vacation of my freshman year at Seattle Pacific College. Although I had grown up in a missionary family in Alaska and loved my home state, I was following my dream of attending a Christian college where I could enjoy fellowship with young people my own age and find a husband who shared my faith. To me, that had meant leaving Alaska.

Now, without warning, in a matter of minutes, my home was a disaster area.

I listened for news of Seward, where my family lived.

"The port city of Seward, a hundred and twenty miles south of Anchorage by car, has been wiped off the map by tsunamis, and the town is entirely engulfed by fire," the report continued.

As the full impact of those awful words hit me, I groaned. Did I still have a family? Had our home been destroyed? What would I do if my folks had been killed?

These questions and more played through my mind like a tape recording, but I was powerless to do anything but pray, "Oh, God, help them!"

I spent a sleepless night in front of the television and endless days listening anxiously to every news report and reading every newspaper. With each attempt to call home, I received the same robotic reply: "I'm sorry. Your call cannot be completed due to the Alaska earthquake."

When would I hear from my family?

Back at school, I checked the mail the instant it was distributed. At church, I heard that a minister friend of our family had died when the dock where he worked as a longshoreman in Valdez collapsed. Since my father supplemented his meager church income by working as a longshoreman, my fear increased to near panic.

The Good Friday Earthquake, centered in Prince William Sound, had registered 9.2 on the Richter scale—the strongest recorded earthquake to ever hit North America. It had wreaked havoc on every city, town, and village in south central Alaska and had shredded connecting roads.

Finally, a letter arrived. With trembling fingers, I tore open the envelope addressed in my father's handwriting and read quickly. Everyone was safe.

"Thank You, God!" I breathed.

Weak with relief, I sank into a chair to read my mother's postscript, which described their harrowing experiences.

To keep from being thrown to the floor when the violent shaking began, they had grabbed doorposts or anything else solid. The hard jolts seemed to go on and on. The earthquake lasted only five minutes, but that was a long time when they thought the house might collapse or that the undulating ground might crack open and swallow them.

When the quaking subsided, they ran outside. Smoke billowed hundreds of feet into the air from the huge oil storage tanks a few blocks away. The ruptured tanks belched burning oil that was being channeled through town along the railroad tracks. The quake generated an immediate tsunami that spread the raging inferno throughout the entire industrial area along the waterfront. To flee the flames, the eighteen hundred residents of Seward jumped into their cars and drove toward the lagoon, where cliffs on one side and the bay on the other straddled a two-lane road, the only route out of town. Traffic slowed to a crawl. Bumper to bumper, it inched along.

Midway across, my mother noticed that railroad cars and boats were being pushed up and over the breakwater as though by a giant hand. Puzzled, then horrified as everything raced toward them, she screamed, "Tsunami! Drive faster!"

My dad swerved into the empty inbound lane and passed the creeping line of cars. Waves swirled around the tires. Their car was the last to make it across before the tsunami crashed across the road, sweeping away cars and smashing houses, boats, and railroad cars against the cliffs like toys in a bathtub and snapping sturdy trees like toothpicks.

Still the nightmare continued. Burning debris from the exploding oil tanks rode the crest of the second tsunami, setting the forest at the head of the bay on fire. It spread quickly. About three miles out of town, the traffic stopped abruptly. Word passed from car to car: "The bridges are out!" People had been thrust eight to twelve feet above the broken roadway. They were trapped.

Just when it seemed they would all be incinerated, a third tsunami swept in and extinguished the fire. The stranded people spent the long, cold, sleepless night in the homes of friends in a development near the bridges.

When they returned home the next day, they found the church and attached parsonage still standing. They were fortunate. Everything south of their block was gone. The oil tanks burned for days. Homes would be without electricity, water, sewer, and heat for weeks until the ground thawed enough to allow repairs.

The Seward I returned home to that summer was nothing like the thriving port town I had left the previous fall. More than eighty homes had been destroyed and thirty lives lost. The docks, railroad yards, boat harbor, warehouses, and canneries had been swept into Resurrection Bay, stripping the waterfront of all industry.

Then I realized how much the earthquake had affected my life. I had worked several shifts in the shrimp cannery during high school and had planned to work there that summer to pay for my second year at Seattle Pacific College. But the cannery had vanished into the bay. With the docks gone, so was my father's supplemental income. My two younger siblings still lived at home and didn't have the financial resources to help.

Family men couldn't find employment, let alone a single girl with little training. With mothers unemployed, too, I couldn't even get a babysitting job. My one-year scholarship and savings had been used, and I had already taken a loan out for my first year.

Would I even be able to continue my college education? Nothing short of a miracle would enable me to go to *any* college in the fall. As the jobless summer progressed, I tried to believe God for a miracle, but my hopes dwindled.

My heavenly Father had met my needs before. Just a few years earlier, I had won an all-expenses-paid trip to the United Nations, including a monthlong, cross-country bus tour to New York City and back with thirty-five other teenagers. Summers in Alaska were cool, so I had no lightweight clothes for hot weather. My missionary family had no discretionary money, but we knew how to pray, and God had supplied the funds for every article of clothing I needed.

And there was the time four years earlier when our family had first moved to Seward— the airplane tickets and moving expenses had taken all of our money so we couldn't even stock the pantry. One day, my mother had no food to serve us for lunch. All morning she prayed.

Just before noon, a woman from the church called and asked my parents to babysit her children after school, since she had to make an unexpected trip to Anchorage. A few minutes later, she arrived with the children—and a large bag of groceries and some cash. In the bag, my mother found all the ingredients except bread for bacon-lettuce-tomato sandwiches, a favorite meal we could rarely afford. My father hurried to the store. Just in time, God had supplied not only our lunch but a treat, too.

Another time, my parents planned to take the church youth to a rally. We had already gathered at the parsonage when my dad told us there was no money for gas. We all held hands and prayed. The doorbell rang, and a man rushed in. "I don't know what's going on, but God prompted me to take my break now and come here to pay my tithe early."

I'd often experienced God's provision, but those needs seemed small compared to money for three years of college. I prayed and tried to have faith, but by late July I was in despair. Then our church held a series of special services. I shared my concern with the visiting evangelists.

"Nothing's too big for God," they said, and my faith grew.

The first week of August, our neighbor, the local librarian, asked me to help her catalog a shipment of new books for the library. "Two hours a day for two weeks, but I can only pay you fifty cents an hour," she said apologetically.

Fall was approaching rapidly. Time was running out. The job wouldn't pay my way to college, but I was happy to have something useful to do.

During the second week I worked at the library, a bulletin arrived from the Ford Foundation. The librarian showed it to me. "I think you'll be interested in this."

It announced that a scholarship had been set up for those who had lost family members, property, or employment in the Good Friday Earthquake. The scholarship would cover up to full expenses according to the student's need.

I was eligible.

There was only one catch. This scholarship was available only to those attending the two universities in Alaska.

Although I was disappointed that I could not go back to Seattle Pacific College, I knew this was God's answer to my prayers. I decided to apply to the University of Alaska in Fairbanks and immediately felt peace that I had chosen the right path. At least I would be able to continue my education.

Days before school started in September, I received my letter of acceptance, a scholarship covering full expenses for the year, and notification that all of my credits had transferred.

And that's not all. Seward, located in the coastal region of south central Alaska, has much milder winters than Fairbanks, where winter temperatures often dip to fifty and sixty degrees below zero for extended periods of time. I needed a fur parka but didn't have one. A well-made, moderately priced parka cost about five hundred dollars, and I had no money. The scholarship covered the purchase of the parka, as well as all of my books and even some spending money. Three years later, I graduated from the University of Alaska debt free.

Not only did God provide me with a college education but He also gave me the desire of my heart. The first week at the University of Alaska that fall of 1964, I attended an InterVarsity Christian Fellowship meeting on campus and met a tall, handsome young man named Bob Conti. Three weeks after we graduated in 1967, we married and have served the Lord together ever since.

I often say, "God had to send an earthquake to answer my prayers to meet the man who would become my husband."

The Message from Heaven
Betty Johnson Dalrymple

The funeral was over. The house was empty. I was alone—more alone than I'd ever been. Richard had always been there for me. We had been high school sweethearts, raised three children, and spent our time together whenever possible. He was my safe haven.

And God had always been there for me, too. He had been my companion during my early years, and His presence had seen me through difficult teenage months—during my father's death and my mother's depression.

God's presence also gave me courage when I responded to the surgeon's shocking announcement, "There is no hope. Your husband's cancer has metastasized. He has days, maybe weeks, hopefully a few months."

"What?" I stammered. "We are a family of faith. There is always hope."

This man in the green surgeon's scrubs does not understand, I thought. *Our prayers will be answered. We'll experience a miracle, and the cancer will go into remission. Maybe Richard won't live to be ninety as we'd planned. But he is not going to die. Not my big, healthy, I-can-do-anything husband.*

During the following weeks, I prayed. Our family prayed. Our fellow church members prayed. Our friends all over the country prayed. How could we not experience a miracle with all of these people praying?

There was no miracle and no remission. On a cold January morning, four months after the surgeon's shocking news, we were back in the hospital, and I was sleeping on a cot in the corner of Richard's room. I was wakened and led from the room while the doctor whispered, "Mrs. Johnson, your husband isn't breathing—his heart has stopped."

Stunned, I just sat on the stool and cried. *Where is my miracle, God? How did this happen? I was sleeping right here, and I didn't hear him. Did he call for me? I never told him good-bye. God, didn't you hear my prayers?*

Those questions haunted me during the first days, but I was too busy with friends and family staying with me, so I didn't spend any quiet time listening for God's answers.

Then came the night when I was finally totally alone. Tears poured from my eyes as I began to shout, *"Where are You, God? Do You hear me? Please, please help me. I'm begging You. If You've ever loved me, if You love me now, somehow, some way, show me."*

Desperate, I grabbed the booklet on my nightstand that my friend had brought to me the day Richard died.

"I was at Lisa's house when I received the call about Richard's passing," Bonnie had explained. "Lisa's husband died last year, and she said this booklet brought her great comfort. She sent it for you to read."

I'd read pages from it the previous night and found a bit of comfort in its message. It prodded me to trust in God.

Tonight I wanted more than comfort. I wanted answers.

"Do You have a message in here for me tonight, God?" I sputtered between sobs. When I opened the booklet, a small card fluttered to the floor.

"Where did this come from?" I mumbled. "I didn't see this in the book last night or the other day when Bonnie gave it to me."

I picked up the card, noticed the picture of Jesus on the one side, turned it over, and read the words written on the back. It began by telling me that Richard was safely home in heaven.

"It's a message from Richard," I whispered. I continued reading. "He's telling me that all the pain and grief is over, and he's at peace. God heard me. He heard my prayers."

Then the answers I'd so desperately sought began rolling out of the words as I read on. They reassured me that Richard was not alone as he passed through the valley of the shadow of death. Jesus's love brightened his pathway.

"Oh, thank you God. Thank you! Richard wasn't alone. I believe Jesus was with him," I cried. Now my tears had turned to tears of joy. I wanted to call someone, to share this wonderful news, but it was midnight.

A voice inside me broke into my time of joy. *I think you need to savor this moment, hold these reassurances close to your heart. You need to deepen your faith in your Father's will.*

A feeling of peace I have rarely experienced settled in my mind and soul. Finally, I read on and was told that my work is still unfinished, and when it is completed and God calls me home, Richard will receive me with joy.

Wow! When God answered my prayers that night, it was an awesome experience. I did not know then, and I do not know now, where that little three-by-five card was hiding during the previous night's reading. How did I not see it? And how did Bonnie just happen to be at her friend's house on the day of Richard's death? God knew what I needed, and He knew when I'd needed it most.

God heard my prayers and gave me answers. It wasn't the miracle I expected—the miracle of healing for Richard—but it was a healing miracle for me. It was a message for that night and for all of the days and years ahead.

The next time I cry out—and I'm sure there'll be a next time—"God, do You hear me?" I know He will be listening and I know He will answer.

The Nativity Baby
David Michael Smith

"*Let the little children come to me, and do not hinder them, for the kingdom of God belongs to such as these*" *(Luke 18:16 NIV).*

Right after Thanksgiving, it begins. Families and couples, people of all ages and backgrounds, begin their annual pilgrimage to the local Christmas tree farm to tag the perfect tree for the festive yuletide season. And at Turning Pointe Farm near Hartly, Delaware, tagging trees is commonplace.

But miracles?

Well, that's what makes the holiday season so magical.

Born and raised in New York City, and later residents of northern New Jersey, Tom and Roseann Conlon were familiar with traffic gridlock, high crime rates, high taxes, and a lifestyle that was far from tranquil. But in 1986, they purchased thirty-six acres of wooded farmland in the fertile epicenter of Delaware and became part-time weekend farmers.

After building a cozy log cabin on their own slice of earthly heaven, they planted three thousand evergreen seedlings by hand and named their picturesque property Turning Pointe Farm. For nearly two decades, they farmed the rich, flat acreage and planted additional firs, pines, and spruces until the fields were filled with beautiful boughs of greenery and trees that had matured to marketable heights.

After retiring in 2003, the Conlons moved to their Delaware farm and realized their longtime dream of operating their Christmas tree farm full-time. Because they now had more time to work the land, trim and sell trees, and assemble beautiful wreaths and holiday centerpieces, Turning Pointe Farm became a place that brought broad smiles to those who patronized it every chilly December.

But when they put up the annual crèche in 2004, things got *really* interesting. The Conlons and their son-in-law built a platform and a three-sided rustic shelter, covered with greenery grown on the farm, for the nearly life-size figures. Each piece was made of resin that resembled natural stone. There was a welcoming, watchful angel; the precious sleeping infant Jesus; and His earthly parents, a noble Joseph and a kneeling, prayerful Mary. A young shepherd came with his sheep to adore the holy child, while the three Magi patiently awaited their turn to present their gifts. The holy scenery was breathtaking.

Roseann was the inspiration behind the manger. She wanted to bring the reason for the season to tangible, meaningful life for her six grandchildren and to keep the holiday's focus on the virgin birth of the Son of God. So the day after Thanksgiving, the Conlon grandchildren carefully carried the still participants to the manger and set up the nativity. Then they added a large stone to the display with the word *Blessings* carved in it.

After the nativity scene was erected, Roseann and her husband told tree shoppers about it. People who wanted to could go to the manger and silently offer any prayer requests they had. And many did. At the same time, her grandchildren, ranging in age from three to eleven, prayed daily for all the people and their petitions. For the young prayer warriors, it was a faith-maturing ministry of goodwill.

The Conlon grandchildren didn't often know the exact requests, but occasionally someone would mention his or her need to Roseann. They prayed for people struggling with cancer, sickness, and disease. They prayed for broken relationships. They prayed for people suffering with depression, a common ailment during the holiday season.

But one desperate plea at the crèche stood out that first year.

Eric and Stephanie lived nearby and had frequented the farm. They were a fairly young couple, married for ten years, and in their mid-thirties with no children.

But they wanted children. Their hearts ached for children. For ten years, they'd tried every off-the-wall piece of advice from friends, neighbors, and family. They tried ovulation kits. They tried fertility drugs. They tried medical procedures like IVF and artificial insemination in an effort to have a baby and start a family.

And they prayed for a miracle, *their* miracle—one about seven or eight pounds, twenty inches long, and a grin to die for.

But absolutely nothing worked.

To deepen their sorrow, Stephanie's mother had cancer and a prognosis shrouded in darkness. Stephanie had always hoped her mother would live long enough to tenderly hold her grandchild and smile into the eyes of the little bundle that would carry on the family heritage, but it appeared this hope was wishful fantasy.

After the couple picked out a Christmas tree, a statuesque Douglas fir, they quietly walked to the manger. Roseann watched from afar and diverted foot traffic while the hurting woman and her husband clasped hands and bowed their heads. The Christ Child in the crib seemed to reach toward the husband and wife, as if to welcome their petitions. They were only there for a few minutes, and then they left. No one knew of their prayer appeal except God.

Christmas came and went, and another year passed. Soon, it was cold again and Christmas was gently energizing the winter.

Roseann was in her gift shop working on holiday wreaths when the door opened. It was Eric and Stephanie—another year older but with one noticeable difference. They appeared radiant and taller, as if they had grown like the hundreds of evergreens at Turning Pointe Farm. They bustled into the shop to blurt out their story, a miracle, but as Stephanie's heavy woolen coat parted, Roseann knew the story. Stephanie was quite pregnant!

"We prayed for a baby at your nativity last year!" Stephanie exclaimed with tears in her eyes. "We were distraught and sad, but standing there looking down at Jesus, we felt hope."

Roseann hugged the happy couple and then explained the motivation behind assembling the crèche, which was back up for the new Christmas season. And she told the soon-to-be parents about her grandchildren's faithful prayers, intercessory pleas made to the Creator on the behalf of total strangers.

"And guess when I'm due!" Stephanie added with a grin. Eric interjected, "Christmas! December twenty-fifth!"

When the faith of little children, or those who come as children, is on display, God cannot remain idle. Miracles, healings, blessings, and acts of wonder become the norm. Just ask Eric and Stephanie, and they'll gladly tell you all about their handsome little boy, the best Christmas gift they will ever know.

The Miraculous Ride
Jenni Davenport

"*H*ey, I enjoyed seeing Hunter at camp this summer," Cal exclaimed when I ran into him at the restaurant. Cal ran a Christian youth camp where we'd sent our kids every year. A frown lined Cal's forehead as he continued. "You know, he seemed a lot different this summer...."

Cal didn't have to go into more detail. I knew exactly what he meant. Over the past few years, I'd seen my son go from a boy who loved Jesus and asked Him into his heart at an early age, to a good, moral teenager who was totally disconnected from church and Christianity. In fact, it had been hard for me to get my almost-eighteen-year-old to go to camp that summer before his senior year.

"Please pray for him, Cal," I said. And I meant it. My heart had long been burdened for my son's spiritual walk. I had quietly asked family and close friends to pray for Hunter. I worked at a Christian organization, and every week as part of our staff meeting, we each placed a prayer request in the middle of the table. At the end of the meeting, we each took a request and prayed for it during the week.

Each week I'd put Hunter's name down as my prayer request. I might add other things, but I always asked my coworkers to pray for my son to walk in faith with God.

It wasn't that Hunter was a prodigal. He was a good, intelligent, moral kid who respected us and respected boundaries. His worst vice was the bad language that would sometimes float from his upstairs room where he was frequently gaming or hanging out with his friends.

Besides asking others to pray for Hunter, of course, I often prayed for my son during my long commutes to work and at other times when his soul was foremost in my mind.

I also talked to him. Hunter was always polite, but I would often see him zone out when I spoke about faith matters. Sometimes I saw his mouth tighten in disagreement. But I kept looking for opportunities to engage with my son spiritually. Sometimes I subtly brought up topics, and other times I was blunt so he'd know where I stood and how I felt. I asked the Lord to help me speak outside of the clichés to better help my son connect. It was one of those times that he let it all out. We were talking about his not wanting to go to church and avoiding anything with a spiritual focus when the flow started.

"I just don't know if I believe in God anymore," he announced, practically trembling with emotion. "It all just seems so unbelievable."

More than his words at the moment, I was struck by his countenance. He seemed so terrified to talk about it. *"He's afraid you're going to yell at him, that you're not going to love him as much if he can't believe,"* a voice seemed to tell me.

So I just listened with an open heart, and he gained confidence to tell me more. He went on with a few specifics, parroting some of the things I imagined he'd heard at school and from his older friends.

Finally, I spoke. "Hunter, it's OK to have a hard time believing. God can handle your questions. God can handle your doubts. God is big enough. It's OK to question Him. That's how we get to know Him."

While I spoke confidently, my heart wept. And I redoubled my prayer efforts on Hunter's behalf. My burden grew, and in the coming days I told the Lord, "I just can't handle it if Hunter doesn't know You. Oh, Lord, please draw my son to You."

It probably sounds crazy, but I was also burdened when I thought of the end times. I'm not a big end-of-the-world panicker. At my age, I've lived through times when Christians have gotten worked up and made predictions about the rapture and end times. I'm not dogmatic about when or how the church will be raptured or when and how Jesus is going to return. But I do believe the signs might be ripe in our world for the end times foretold in the Bible (I figure either the new earth or a revival is ahead). I was raised in the middle of the rapture focus in the '70s, so I lean toward that theology.

"Oh, Lord, what if the rapture happens before Hunter is ready to meet You face-to-face? He's driving now; what if he gets in a car wreck and dies?"

I didn't always focus on such things, but they did come to my mind at times, and I continued to pray...and to worry. The older two stepchildren my husband, Rick, and I had raised had fallen from their faith in their late teens (which made me fret about our parenting skills—or lack thereof!). They had walked more on the wild side than my son, but we had been blessed to see them come back to Christ with a passion—one was studying to be a missionary and one was winning her in-laws to Christ right and left.

It's not like I haven't been through this before, I thought.

But somehow it was different. We'd instilled more Scripture in the older ones. We'd been younger and more active in ministry. Some of that passion had decreased because of job situations and my husband's chronic health issues.

The world had changed a lot since the older two were teenagers. The battle against Christianity seemed so much stronger. And the older two didn't face the questions that Hunter was facing. Theirs was more of a temporary rebellion than an intellectual rejection of the gospel. I'd prayed and cared for them—probably even more than they realize today—but they didn't quite cause the angst in me that Hunter's spiritual coldness did. Hunter is our only boy, and everyone knows how mothers and sons are tied together. Could I really leave Hunter in the Holy Spirit's hands?

The days passed after Hunter's outburst, and outwardly I went on as normal—loving him, praying for him, and looking for opportunities to point him to God. Was the Holy Spirit getting through at all? I couldn't tell.

And then God answered my prayer in a way I never could have imagined! I was raised with Nazarene and Baptist influences. Whether good or bad, people in my faith culture don't often experience dramatic or unusual signs and wonders—I often envy my charismatic friends! So the last thing I expected God to do was to give me a dream.

I hadn't gone to bed that night with my mind on Hunter's spiritual state, so the dream wasn't arising from anything in my immediate subconscious mind. I hadn't eaten spicy food, hadn't done anything particularly spiritual before I went to bed. Just took my melatonin and was out quickly.

It was toward morning when the dream started. My husband was driving our family somewhere, as he often did. I was in the passenger's seat, and our two youngest kids were in the backseat.

Suddenly, something seemed to be happening. The top of the car disappeared, and it became the convertible my husband and I had always wanted. As Rick continued to drive, the car lifted off the ground. A light filled my heart and the sky as I realized Jesus had come for us and was drawing us to Him. We got to take the scenic route. The car flew over valleys and streams and mountains and oceans.

But there was something beyond the beauty and light—there was an indescribable joy. I've had a lot of happy times in my life, but this was something I've never experienced. It was like all of creation was bursting with joy and light and life.

And the best part was that my children were in the backseat. They were with us. We were being raptured, and our children were there.

The car continued to be drawn by an invisible force, like a *Star Wars* tractor beam. We were eventually pulled through clouds and into a world that was rising as we watched. As houses appeared, the car pulled into a driveway of a modest, pretty, little home—not the mansion by the mountains and ocean that I've hoped for, but I didn't care. My family was together, and we were in whatever world Jesus inhabited.

The dream ended. It was so wonderful and so peaceful that I tried to stay in a dozy state and call it back. But no luck. It had served its purpose. I woke up.

As I lay there, it was almost like my soul was coming out of anesthesia. My body was awake, but it was as if my spirit was still lingering in the land of confident peace, the land it was made for.

As I floated back to earth mentally, I surprised myself by bursting into tears. I'm not an overly emotional person—I tend to be too pragmatic for my own good. I only cry when I'm very upset about something. But this time, it wasn't tears of distress or disappointment. For the first time in my life, I was crying for joy.

I didn't tell my husband or anyone about the dream. One reason was that I'm a girl with a skeptical heart—only one other time in my life had God clearly spoken to me in a dream. The other reason was that whenever I even thought about the dream, I'd start crying—I couldn't have explained why and still can't explain why tears flow whenever I think about it.

I didn't have to ponder to know that the dream was given to me by God or what it meant. The dream meant God had heard my pleas and my tears for my son, that He understood my burden for Hunter. He was showing me that it's going to be OK. That He has His hand on Hunter and is drawing him to Himself. He showed me Hunter is indeed His child.

So I still talk to Hunter about his spiritual journey. But now I can do so in confidence, knowing God is working. I still pray for Hunter fervently, that God will become real to him and make him a godly man. I still pray that God will guard his steps and protect him from the wrong influences.

But now I don't pray with fear and panic. I pray with hope and reassurance, with the faith and confidence that my hopes will be realized. For a short time, I experienced the joy and light of heaven, and I know Hunter will experience it, too.

Nowhere to Call Home
Bobbie Roper

For most people, retirement is a bit scary, but senior folks usually have a house, with or without a mortgage. We live in the sunny state of Florida, where many residents have not one house but two. They have one up North for the warmer months and one here when the snow chases them south.

We were not so fortunate. My husband, Jim, was a pastor for over thirty years. His churches were small congregations in rural areas of New York, Pennsylvania, North Carolina, and Florida. Though the salary was low by most standards, all the churches provided a parsonage, so we always had a place to live.

When Jim reached age sixty-six and started drawing social security, we realized that retirement was right around the corner, as was the possibility of major health issues that could keep him from performing his duties as a pastor. If he suddenly needed to leave the ministry, what would we do? An even more serious thought was what would I do if he had a major heart attack that took his life?

We had sold our home in South Carolina thirty-one years earlier, enabling us to attend Bible college, so we had nowhere to call home. Our denomination had several retirement communities for pastors. There were also government-subsidized facilities for low-income people, and, of course, we had children who could take us in. None of those options felt right for us.

Our prayer was pretty simple: "Lord, retirement is close, and we have nowhere to call home. Please show us Your plan."

God had provided for our family in so many miraculous ways over the years, but what would He do now? James 1:5 says, "If any of you lacks wisdom, you should ask God, who gives generously to all without finding fault, and it will be given to you" (NIV).

So we asked for wisdom.

First, we had to decide where we wanted to live. We have four grown children. Two live in Florida, fairly close to where we were living, and two live up North. North was not an option, because Jim is a southern boy and had a difficult time dealing with the snow and cold. Being an avid saltwater fisherman, he wanted to be close to the water so he could spend his retirement years fishing. We finally decided on the west coast of Florida, a little further north of us in an area called the Nature Coast.

Jim began to search the Internet for homes in that area. As he searched for a place that wasn't too far from the water, I prayed for a place in the woods. His soul is refreshed breathing in the salt air, while mine is renewed listening to the wind whistling through the trees and soaking in the wonderful sights, sounds, and smells of God's fabulous creation.

Psalm 37:4 says, "Take delight in the LORD, and he will give you the desires of your heart" (NIV). I was wondering how God was going to do that when we had different desires.

Over the few months, Jim lined up places to look at. We knew our retirement income wouldn't amount to much, so we needed a place with a low mortgage payment. We needed a place with a shed. Jim dabbles in woodworking, so he wanted enough land to have a workshop. We also needed space for two vehicles and his flatboat. A porch would be nice, since we have his grandfather's wooden swing—an heirloom close to a hundred years old.

We looked at houses on our days off, but most of what we found didn't have usable acreage or the price wasn't workable.

Sometime in October, Jim lined up three properties. The first one was on two acres. It was a beautiful property, but the house was small with no storage building or garage. Since we were in the same area as the third property, we decided to go by and look at it before our appointment with the realtor at the second property. We drove down an asphalt road that turned into dirt right at the edge of the property. It was a manufactured home (not what we wanted but probably all we could afford) on two-and-a-half acres.

We parked the car and sat there for a moment taking it all in. There was a large storage building. Across half of the house front was a screened porch that wrapped around to a side door. Scrub oaks intermingled with pine trees filled most of the front and side yards, as well as the area behind the house.

As Jim walked the back area, I felt at home. When Jim came back to the car, he echoed the same words. Our dilemma was that the realtors had told us the property was under contract. A young couple was trying to buy it, but there had been many delays and problems with financing.

We drove to the second house on our list and arrived before the real estate agent got there. The house looked small and with the sloping backyard there was no place to put the workshop Jim needed. We called the realtor and told her we weren't interested.

Driving back to the "house in the woods," we wondered if this was the place for us. It seemed to fit what we both wanted. It was only about twenty minutes from the water, Jim's desire, and was sitting in the woods, fulfilling mine. If only someone else didn't already have dibs on it!

We drove to the back of the property, where the realtors met us. Jim told them we had looked around earlier and really liked what we saw on the outside. We would certainly be interested should the present contract fall through.

The Bible tells us in Philippians 4:19, "My God will meet all your needs according to the riches of his glory in Christ Jesus" (NIV).

God knew that we needed a house to call home even before we prayed, so we shouldn't have been surprised when the realtors told us that the contract had expired at noon—it was now 1:00 p.m. We wanted to shout our praise to the Lord! Did He hold the house under contract until we could find it?

Some would say, "Really? You really believe that?"

Yes, I really believe that.

This is not the end of the story. Though the house needed much work inside, we knew this was a gift from God and an answer to prayer. We put in an offer, the sellers countered, and we accepted.

Now we had to get financing. We sat for hours at our bank trying to get a mortgage. The computers were down, then slow—on and on it went until we finally had the loan papers in hand. After looking them over, we didn't see how we could possibly make the payments, and when we looked at the interest and what we would actually be paying for the house, we were flabbergasted.

We looked at each other, feeling deflated, not knowing what to do. We didn't believe God would have us get into debt like that, and we would probably both have to hold down full-time jobs till the mortgage was paid in thirty years. We would be in our nineties! We left the bank after telling the loan officer that we needed to think about it.

As we talked and prayed about it, God supplied the answer. Each denominational church Jim had served had put a small monthly amount into a retirement fund for him. Over twenty-plus years, that amount had grown, and without our even realizing it, God had been providing the money we needed to pay cash for our retirement home. We bought when the market was low and the property needed a lot of work, so the price was almost ridiculous for two and a half acres. But most importantly, God's hand was in it.

And that's not the end of the story, either. The Lord allowed us to work for the next nine months, which gave us the opportunity to put our social security into a building fund so we could make repairs. We closed on the house in November and traveled the two hours back and forth on our days off and vacation to work on it.

We retired in June and moved to our house in the woods on July 4. There was enough money left in the retirement fund for Jim to purchase the workshop he wanted with a few dollars left.

Every once in a while, Jim checks the Internet to see if there's anything comparable to our house-in-the-woods gift from God. Nothing even comes close. How awesome is our God!

Leaving the God of Money

Marleen McDowell

"Where, Lord? Where is that victorious life You promised?" I pleaded for an answer as I drove to work. Tears poured down my face, blurring my vision of the road. This had gone on so long the pain was too much to bear.

For years, our finances had been an endless roller-coaster ride. We both worked and made enough for a comfortable living, but we were always broke, always struggling, always worrying, and always fighting. Uphill, downhill. In debt, out of debt. We had just finished the long, slow, laborious climb out of debt, and here we were again, speeding over the suicide drop to the pit of easy credit.

So many times I had prayed for the Lord to change my husband, but now, ten years into the marriage, nothing was different. Repeatedly, promises were made and broken. Talking, pleading, reasoning gave way to blaming, shaming, and threats. The situation was hopeless. Why didn't God answer me? What was wrong? Did I need to pray more? Should I fast?

But we know God hears us. And God did hear it—all of it. He was just waiting for me to hear Him! That day as I cried my way to work, God answered my prayer. A voice spoke in my mind: *"If your happiness depends on the balance in your checkbook, you will continue to be miserable."*

I was shocked. This wasn't fair! I wasn't the one who spent all the money. My mouth opened. I tried to explain, but I could only repeat what I had just heard: *"If your happiness depends on the balance in your checkbook, you will continue to be miserable."*

Yes, I admitted, my moods did rise and fall with my bank balance. After all, it was stressful when the money wasn't there and the bills were coming in. My husband and I were so different! I wasn't the problem! I was a responsible person! I was a good steward!

I wanted to save our money. Wasn't that what we were supposed to do? Certainly, my way was better! Everything would be fine if my husband would only listen to me!

As I defended myself, I fought against the truth that was forming in my mind.

Something was wrong. Money was *too* important to me. It was my security. It was the answer to my problems. It meant more to me than my husband or my marriage or… The thought forced its way into my mind and I could not deny it: I trusted money more than I trusted the Lord. There it was. The ugly truth—money was my god.

Here I was, feeling self-righteous and putting all the blame on my husband. Yet I was the one with a serious problem. I was breaking the first commandment: "You shall have no other gods before me." Yet here I was, worshipping a money idol. My sin was directly against God!

With the truth in the open, a choice lay before me. I could continue to cling to my money idol and ultimately destroy our marriage, or I could turn to the Lord and trust Him to deliver me from my troubles.

I made my decision, and the helplessness dissolved. The tears started again, only this time they were tears of repentance.

That evening, I admitted my sin to my husband. I asked for his prayers and his help to tear down my idol with a money fast. For one month, I would not touch money in any form. He agreed to pick up my paycheck, take care of the bills, do the grocery shopping, put gas in my car, and handle all financial matters.

It was a long month. Coworkers invited me to lunch, friends asked me to go shopping, but each time a polite "Not today" excused me from the activity.

Frustration filled the first week as I automatically reached for my purse before I remembered it was empty. The second week, I was a bit resentful as I marked time waiting for the month to end. Yet by the third week, acceptance began to set in, and it wasn't such a big deal anymore.

A slow change was happening. I found that since I wasn't involved in the finances, the worries and responsibilities no longer consumed me. My mood stabilized. By the end of the month, the bondage to my idol was broken and joy was becoming my shy companion.

However, that was not the only blessing God had for me. For a time, the roller coaster continued to storm around the track. On the steep downhill rides, I learned to seek the

Lord first and to stay in the Word as He taught me to put my trust in Him so I could have peace whether the bank account was flush or had a zero balance. While we were in the pit of easy credit, He taught me to be thankful for the small things and to be content with what I already possessed rather than dwell on what I could not buy.

I learned that God can work all things for our good, just as He used my husband's financial weakness to change me. That taught me to look deeper into our problems in order to search out the hidden blessings. Most importantly, He taught me to take the log out of my own eye before I looked for the splinter in my husband's eye.

God is faithful. As I repented of my sin, He began to heal my husband's past hurts and deal with the mismanagement of our finances. Today, after more than forty years of marriage, we are retired and our income is half of what it was—yet we feel rich. Our wealth is not in our bank account but in the treasury of our strong marriage and our walk with the Lord.

So many times when the situation looked hopeless and the pain was too much, I wanted to take the easy way out and run away from that wild ride. Today, I am thankful that both of us chose to stay and work through the problems, because during that wild ride God gave us the tools to live a victorious life.

Paper Angels

Beth Duewel

I felt as if I'd met her before. Her gestures were calm and familiar. She was knitting when I burst into the room and interrupted her rhythm with a wail. Past the point of pain I could bear, I crossed the threshold into the small waiting room while suffering a moment of untamed grief.

Normally, I would have been self-conscious about such a dramatic show of tears. But on a normal day, I wouldn't be saying good-bye to my mama. On a normal day, I wouldn't have to leave the bedside of the one who had tucked me in, and know I would never see her again on this earth.

I was angry at myself. Frustrated that I was too weak to stay and hold her hand through those last moments, I ran to the family waiting room to cry alone. The room had been empty and had provided an echoing silence all weekend. It was a quiet respite with tiny chairs and outdated magazines.

But then I saw her.

She was an older woman, sitting across the room, knitting. She didn't seem upset that I was a maniac. She glanced over her glasses as if she had been expecting me.

At twenty years old, I couldn't help feeling robbed. My heart already missed my mom. My friends would have their mothers around to answer questions about how to make meat loaf and what to do with a colicky baby. As if those were major concerns. Either way, I wouldn't know how to do them—at least not the way my mom did.

I plopped down in a rust-colored chair, trying not to wail too loudly and disturb the tiny cubicle of peace. Jerry, my husband of a year, had stayed behind with my mom, dad, and uncle. He was the brave one. He was saying good-bye to a woman who'd become his second mother.

My mom had been unhappy until he called her by what she felt to be her deserved name. "Jerry, you need to call me Mom—I won't answer to anything else." She had been determined to nurture his heart.

Jerry had lost his mom at the age of eight; many memories of his mother had faded like a sunbathed watercolor. And my mom, raising three girls with hormones and bad-hair days, was eager to claim another son-in-law. Calm and collected, Jerry was as level as well-placed bricks. Jerry and Mom were a great fit.

And now I didn't know how I would replace the piece missing in both of our lives.

I'm not sure when it happened—maybe when I closed my eyes—but the knitting lady had put aside her needles. She was now sitting in the worn chair next to mine. Apparently, she was ready to console my fears.

I saw her curly silver hair through the puddles in my eyes. She pulled me close. And with her sweet hushes, I was a little girl again.

As my mind traveled back, I could hear my mom call my name while she stood on our porch. My favorite snack, celery sticks slathered with peanut butter, waited for me inside.

Earlier that morning, I hadn't wanted to go to school. At the bus stop, I held on to the stop sign, my normally compliant body refusing to let go, while I pushed the patience of the bus driver, who beat on the horn. Kindergarten can be tough for an insecure four-year-old, I suppose. My anxious body melted into the steel pole while Mom in her red robe and fuzzy slippers came to my rescue.

It could have ended badly. But it didn't. I could have been scolded in front of the last two streets of kids, their noses stuck tight to the windows. But I wasn't. Instead, my mom's words were calm and secure, "Let's go home, Beth-Anne."

Her fingers gently peeled me from the pole while she stroked my tear-soaked hair.

Now this woman in the waiting room pushed back the wet hair that stuck to my cheeks. "Oh, my dear child, your mom loves you very much." Her words floated like a hummed lullaby. "God loves you."

For the next however many minutes, she reassured me of God's love and plan for my life. It was as if she knew me. Or that she knew I had read Psalm 23 to my mom earlier that day and was reciting it back to me.

My mom and I had been alone together in her room, a room awake with alarms and respirator puffs, while her body slept in a coma. The doctors assured me that she could hear. Our one-way conversation was intimate as words bounced off the sterile sheets and sank into my heart—words that peeled my anxious heart off my stubborn will, promising calm pastures and a restored soul.

I wanted that. And in a hospital in the saddest of situations, I felt I could have it. I wish I'd been more observant that day. But my senses were numb, as if dulled by the selfishness of grief. There was no time for congenialities; my tears were interrupted by my husband's sobs trailing down the hall. He came in to tell me what I already knew: my mom was gone. A week before Christmas.

While I helped my father check out of a bed-and-breakfast that evening, the owner, hoping to console me for my loss, handed me a simple but appreciated gift—a paper angel.

That next day, I placed the gift on the top of our tree. It seemed the right spot for such a beautiful little item, as Christmas came quickly that year, leaving me with little motivation to decorate. After Christmas, Jerry, eager to lighten the load, offered to help wrap up the ornaments. That was usually not my favorite chore and was even more daunting with my heavy heart.

Reaching to the top of the tree, I lifted the paper angel.

"Honey, do you remember the woman who was in the waiting room with me the day Mom died? I've been thinking about her."

Jerry stared at me as if straining to fill in the blanks. "What?"

"You know—the woman sitting beside me when you came in—she had a bag with knitting needles and a blanket. I really don't know why I didn't introduce you, but I guess I didn't even ask her name…."

My voice trailed off as I remembered her words of comfort.

My husband seemed confused, with either the wrapping of ornaments or the conversation. Or both.

"Honey, no one was with you in the waiting room; you were all by yourself when I came in."

And as I thought it through, I really didn't remember seeing her after he came in.

Hmm. Now I was the confused one. Had my mental state been so altered?

No, I felt the touch of her hand—I heard her words. *But really, what color yarn was she knitting with? What was she wearing?*

Questions piled high in my mind. But thinking back, I was so wrapped up in the blanket of grief, I couldn't see through it. I guess everything seems a little blurry through a downpour of tears.

"No. She was there," I corrected. "She stroked my hair just like Mom used to do. She talked to me about God's love and told me it would be OK. I'd have gone crazy without her."

My husband's sideways glance was all the confirmation I needed. He felt I already *had* gone crazy.

Logically, I recognized his dilemma. And I had to agree—it didn't make sense. But then again, life hadn't made much sense in a while. And true, there were no streams of light, nothing shiny or attention-grabbing about the woman who so willingly kept me company.

"Well, she was a godsend." My tone sounded cliché even to me.

I stared at the paper angel resting in my hand and traced its subtle etching and delicately placed halo. Suddenly, it made perfect sense. I knew then that just one detail was missing from the paper angel—a tiny pair of knitting needles.

A Bright New World

Joyce Starr Macias

It was painful to see my father so weakened by disease. This man who had been so strong all his life now needed help to get out of his hospital bed.

But as much as I worried about the cancer spreading through his body, I was far more concerned about his spiritual state. I wanted to be sure he would be ready for heaven.

I knew both of my parents believed that God existed in a general sort of way, some kind of good God who lived too far away for ordinary people to reach. But I was sure they had no personal relationship with Jesus or even knew they could have one.

They were good parents—kind, moral people who taught my brother and me to be responsible citizens and to care about other people. I remember times as I was growing up when they showed their respect for God in ways that seemed odd to me—like when my mother made us eat fish on Good Friday because it was something her Catholic friends did.

I was married with three children before I heard the gospel for the first time and asked Jesus to forgive my sins and come into my life. The salvation I experienced that day changed me.

But I found it difficult to share my newfound faith with my mother and father. In the back of my mind, I'm sure I was thinking: *Who am I to be telling my parents what they need to do?*

But now that my father was so sick, I knew I had to share Jesus with him. At least I could try.

So before I left the hospital one evening, I got up my courage and asked, "Dad, may I pray for you before I leave?"

Instead of answering, he turned his head and stared at the wall of his hospital room.

I don't remember what I said after that, but I felt like a total failure. How could I share my faith with him before it was forever too late?

I lived about forty-five minutes away from my parents' home, and while Dad was sick I tried to get there almost every night to see them. With a demanding full-time job, that wasn't always easy. I'd rush home, make supper for my family, and hit the road.

Since Dad was in and out of the hospital a lot, I often didn't know until the last minute whether I'd see him there or back at home. And I still had no idea how to approach him about spiritual matters.

I'd already tried one method that hadn't seemed to work. I had given him tape recordings of myself playing the piano and singing. Dad was always proud that I could play. We weren't wealthy, and I knew it must have been a sacrifice for my parents to pay for my piano lessons year after year.

I had recorded a mixture of traditional songs and classical pieces, like "Clair de Lune," that I knew he liked. In between, I would play and sing hymns that I hoped would touch his heart. My mother told me he liked to listen to them, but they didn't seem to be having the effect I'd prayed for.

One day, when I telephoned my mother after work, she seemed more upset than usual. Dad wasn't doing well, and she was worried. His long illness was clearly taking its toll on her.

"Dad's back in the hospital. I don't know what's going to happen," she said, her voice quivering. She asked if I could stay overnight with her.

I hadn't planned on going that night, but what could I say? I told her I'd get there in time to take her out to eat before we went to see Dad.

As I rushed to gather my things, I prayed that God would strengthen my mother and give her peace. And I prayed that my father would open his heart to the Lord.

Mom had pulled herself together by the time I arrived, but her swollen eyes showed me she'd been crying. Dad was alert enough to enjoy our time together, but I still felt tongue-tied when it came to talking to him about the Lord.

Back at the house, I headed for my old room, which was next to my parents' bedroom. I had barely settled down when I heard Mom's voice: "Joyce, don't you usually read your Bible before you go to sleep?" she asked.

"Yes, I do, Mom."

"Would you mind coming in here and reading it to me?"

"I'll be right there," I answered, immediately changing my reading plan and choosing verses that would explain God's plan of salvation.

Mom listened intently as I read. She seemed so interested that I had no trouble asking if she had understood what the verses meant. When she said that she did, I asked her if she'd like to pray and give her life to Jesus.

With tears in her eyes, she nodded that she'd like to do that. For the first time, my mother and I prayed together. And when she lifted her head, I could see that something wonderful had happened. She had accepted Jesus as her Lord.

The whole world seemed brighter than ever as I drove to work early the next morning! My heart bubbled over with joy. I kept thanking God that Mom had given her heart to Jesus! I prayed that Dad would be next.

But weeks went by, and though Dad recovered enough to go back home for a while, the time never seemed right to talk to him about his spiritual condition.

One day, I drove to the town where my parents lived to attend a monthly meeting my denomination was holding. The meetings always began with a late-afternoon service, followed by a meal provided by the host church, a fellowship time, and an evening service. This time, they substituted a prayer meeting for the second service. That was fine with me. If ever I needed to pray, it was now.

The host pastor led the prayer time, and I immediately felt God's presence more strongly than I ever had before. People began to pray out loud for their needs, something I usually felt uncomfortable about doing. But this time I joined in, asking God to open my father's heart to the gospel and to give me boldness.

I felt such freedom as I pleaded for my father's salvation, and I could hear others agreeing with me in prayer. I'd never felt such awareness of the Holy Spirit's presence! Suddenly, God showed me that my father would turn his life over to Jesus before he died. That message was as clear as if God had spoken the words out loud.

All at once, I knew what to do. I would go and see my father right away, even though I hadn't planned on going there that night.

Mom and I hugged before I went into the living room to see Dad. He was sitting in his swivel rocker next to a little end table. As always, he was reading a book.

I told him I believed God had sent me. My statement surprised him enough that he set his book aside. He remained silent as I told him how much God loved him and that He'd sent Jesus to pay the penalty for our sins, including his, on the cross.

His eyes stayed glued to me the whole time I spoke.

At last, he's going to surrender his life to the Lord!

But he didn't. He wasn't angry or upset, but he didn't seem interested in what I'd said. I couldn't have been more disappointed.

I had envisioned him bowing his head and telling Jesus that he wanted to become His child. But he just thanked me for coming, hugged me, and went back to his book.

My heart ached as I drove home. But God let me know that I needed to leave the results to Him. I'd heard the expression "Let go and let God," but I had no idea that doing it could be so difficult.

"All right, Lord, I will believe You," I conceded as I turned into my driveway. "My father is in Your hands. Only You can convince him of his need. I certainly can't."

The next day, I phoned a pastor I knew who lived closer to my parents' home, and he agreed to visit my father the next time Dad was hospitalized.

We didn't have to wait long. Mom called me a day or two later to say that my father had taken a turn for the worse. When I called the pastor, he assured me he'd visit my father every day and would pray for him.

I didn't get back to the hospital for a couple of days because of icy road conditions, and by the time I next saw my father, he was so weak that he couldn't talk with me. But I could feel God's presence in the room, and I knew something supernatural was going on.

"Dad, is it all right if I pray with you?" I asked.

This time, he didn't turn away. Tears streamed down both our faces as I prayed, asking God to give my father faith to believe in Jesus as his Lord and Savior.

Somehow I knew that my prayer had been answered. My father couldn't utter the words to tell me, but I knew he had become a believer.

Here was the miracle I had sought for so long!

Within days, my father went home to be with the Lord. I was sure in my heart of the miracle that had taken place in his heart. But God in His mercy and kindness allowed me to hear more of the story.

During the funeral service, the pastor who had visited him spoke of my father's long involvement as a member of the Boy Scout council and his diligent work in developing a campground for the local Boy Scout troops.

I loved hearing the accolades about his Scout work, but the words that followed soothed my heart.

"The motto of the Boy Scouts is to 'be prepared,'" the pastor said. "This man taught many young Scouts that motto, but I want you to know that he had taken his own advice. He was prepared to meet God because of his personal faith in Jesus Christ. He wasn't able to say the words out loud, but I can tell you that I'm certain he gave his heart to the Lord before he left this earth."

God gave me the miracle I had prayed so hard for. Some people call it a "deathbed conversion," but I know it was a miracle. A last-minute miracle that God accomplished by His supernatural power.

Miracle Boy

Melinda Wright, as told to Anita Estes

"Do not be anxious about anything, but in every situation, by prayer and petition, with thanksgiving, present your requests to God. And the peace of God, which transcends all understanding, will guard your hearts and your minds in Christ Jesus."

The pastor had barely finished reading Philippians 4:6–7 (NIV), when my phone rang. I answered and heard the words in every parent's worst nightmare.

"Your son has been in a terrible accident. A car hit him head on and catapulted him off his bike into the air. He has multiple lacerations and fractures and is in severe condition. He's being airlifted to Rhode Island Hospital."

When I told my husband, Richie, he turned pale and felt numb, but my reaction was different.

What normally would strike fear in a parent's heart had the opposite effect on me. I felt a strong sense of God's presence. An incredible peace washed over me.

During the service, I'd been praying for another crisis, regarding my nephew, and afterward we received a text message that he was safe. I felt elated that God had answered our prayers so quickly. When the bad news came about our son, I felt God would do the same for him. I believed it was the perfect opportunity for us to put into practice Philippians 4:9 (another verse we had just heard): "Whatever you have learned or received or heard from me, or seen in me—put it into practice. And the God of peace will be with you" (NIV).

As we drove the three and a half hours to Rhode Island, anxious thoughts tried to assault us. My son's landlord filled in the details, telling my husband that David had severe head trauma and had lost a lot of blood. His collarbone was sticking out from a huge wound in his neck. "They don't think he is going to make it," she said.

A flood of anxiety could have overtaken us, but I still felt an incredible peace. When my husband called the doctor, he was informed, "David is in critical condition. Get here as soon as possible."

God did something miraculous for us that night. He gave us a gift of faith-filled prayer and all-encompassing peace, which helped us to believe Him over the reports we were hearing. We were thankful that our pastor had prayed for us before we left, and we knew many others were praying for our son. Then we prayed in faith, knowing that God loved David more than we did and that He knew what was best for him.

"You're a healing God!" my husband declared. We believed for a miracle.

When we arrived at the hospital at 2:00 a.m., we couldn't find the right building. Finally, a nurse escorted us to the trauma center. Another nurse greeted us and searched for a place where we could sit and discuss the facts and prognosis with the doctor. As we passed one room, we noticed a circle of doctors standing around a patient in a bed with light radiating from it. I peeked in, not knowing it was David. A nurse pulled the curtains shut.

Finally, we were escorted to the consultation room. The doctor started with the positives. David was moving his fingers, he didn't appear to have brain damage, and there was no internal bleeding.

I felt God had already answered our prayers. Everything would be OK. I asked, "So what's the problem?"

"He received a major blow to the heart, and we're concerned it will give out," the doctor explained. "We've given him three different heart medications, but he's not responding. His blood pressure is dangerously low, hovering around 59/24. He's not stable enough for exploratory procedures, so the next twenty-four hours will be critical."

When we walked into the ICU room, the consultants still circled my son's bed. As we moved to his bedside, the doctors' eyes fixed on us. Richie asked if we could pray.

"Lord, we trust You. You're a healing God. You've raised people from the dead, and now we're asking You to heal David. Our confidence is in You! We're asking for a miracle."

Since God's Word tells us to come boldly to the throne of grace, we did just that. We wanted God to shine through this situation. We decided that we wouldn't let the facts hinder our faith. And one by one we witnessed a series of miracles.

The next morning, David's blood pressure had stabilized enough so they could put in a balloon pump. I felt encouraged, though later I found out this procedure was considered a last resort. They told us the pump could stay in for up to seventy-two hours to enable David's heart to work on its own, but he only needed it for twenty-four hours!

Another small miracle. That night, the resident doctor gave us a positive report. My husband told him that many people were praying for David and for us. God's peace surrounded us like a warm blanket, though there were still more hurdles ahead.

Our once energetic and athletic boy now lay surrounded by tubes and monitors, pale and immobile. He had been in a drug-induced coma for three days and had only briefly opened his eyes to say hi. By Wednesday, he began to talk, though he didn't remember anything about the accident. It was the first time after the trauma that he ate any food— mashed potatoes. The following day he underwent extensive surgery on his neck and arm.

On the night of the accident, the gash near his collarbone was five inches wide and eight inches long! If paramedics who lived near the scene had not responded quickly, David would have bled to death. We were so thankful God had provided exactly what David needed, and we rejoiced. The surgery was successful.

A week after the accident, David was moved to a regular hospital room. I soon realized the staff there didn't know much about him. Though strict orders had been given for David to stay in a neck brace, the doctor on that floor ordered it off because David pulled at it. Then they wanted to insert a feeding tube, even after he had begun to eat on his own. My heart took a nose dive when I saw how they mishandled situations and called him "unresponsive." I felt that all the gains David made would be lost if we didn't do something. Once again, we turned to God and the power of prayer.

After these events, we went back to the trauma ICU and explained that we weren't happy with his current care. The following day, they moved David into a step-down unit. I felt that God had, once again, answered our prayers. Many people had been alerted in our church and around the country and were still praying for him. By then, even the doctors had started calling him the miracle boy. They originally hadn't expected him to make it through the first night.

Though the facts appeared depressing from the start, God kept giving me hope and comfort. He surrounded me with His awesome peace even when the nurse gave us a disheartening report: David would need three months of rehabilitation and up to a year of around-the-clock in-house care. She read a litany of things David would no longer be able to do, such as feed or clothe himself. At first, I felt confused, but I continued to pray God's Word.

The resident doctor gave us a very different account. He said David should be back to normal within three to four weeks instead of months. My heart soared.

I remember when David was given permission to get out of his hospital bed and sit in a chair. I remember how excited he was. Instead of just sitting up, he hopped over the rail with his heart monitor and catheter trailing behind. He nearly knocked over all the machinery. It was an exasperating, yet exhilarating, sight.

Soon, he was receiving a ton of visitors. David loved it and couldn't stop talking. He discussed in detail how to put together a complicated bicycle. Every day after that, he gained more and more intellectual and physical ability. God was miraculously answering our prayers, minute by minute.

On the day of David's release, all the doctors were happy to see their miracle boy walk out the door without a wheelchair. The same nurse who had given us the hopeless news early on discharged him with tears in her eyes, saying, "I've never seen someone who needed an aortic balloon pump walk out of the hospital."

I didn't really understand the full extent of that miracle until we visited David's home, Block Island, a week after his release. People recounted the serious accident, all the blood he lost, and the thirty-second response of the neighbors who just happened to be paramedics. I knew it wasn't just coincidence. It was God's provision for David. Throughout this whole ordeal, God spoke to me over and over again about the power of faith, of believing His Word over the facts.

Eight years have passed since his accident, and David is doing well—no rehab for him for the rest of his life! He now has a son, a good job, and a winning smile. He's heard over and over again that he's a miracle boy, and I'm praying he'll realize just how much his life is a living, breathing testimony to God's healing power.

A Sparkling Miracle
Gail R. Helgeson

May this be a trip that will awaken my desire to trust God more…to trust that He will keep us safe and teach me to thrive. Maybe it will open my eyes to see Him; I want more of Him.

Those words from my journal haunted me as we stood at the airport in Rome after a delayed flight from Paris. Hungry and worn, my husband and I had shuffled off the plane and followed the other passengers, herded together like a flock of sheep, to the baggage claim area. As the baggage carousel circled, black bags descended the chute and into the arms of the waiting travelers. So many bags looked alike; I wondered how they didn't get lost.

Then I looked around and realized everyone had grabbed his or her bags and left. That is, everyone but us. Only after the carousel stopped did we realize our bags had taken an alternate vacation.

In the days leading to this vacation, I had spent much time in prayer and journaling. That's when I'd penned my paragraph about trusting God and wanting more of Him.

But now, on the first leg of our journey, I didn't expect the trust to have to start so soon.

There we stood, marooned in a foreign-to-us airport. We couldn't speak the language, and had no idea when, or if, we would see our bags again. The harsh glare of fluorescent lights stalked us as we hunted down the customer service counter.

The man behind the desk seemed to care more about the score on the TV screen than about our missing luggage. We couldn't do anything except fill out forms and let the airport officials know where we would be should our bags appear.

Frustrated, we left empty-handed through the airport doors. Soon, we discovered luggage wasn't the only thing we would lose.

Travel can be exhausting. You have to be even more aware of your surroundings than normal. We read that taxi drivers may try to rip you off. We were determined not to let that happen as we flagged down a taxi and slid into the backseat.

With a cigarette drooping between his lips, the driver pushed the fare button. We rolled the windows down and gasped for air that wasn't smoke-laden as we took off. Horns blew, cars whizzed through red lights, and scooters buzzed around like mosquitoes.

We arrived safely at our hotel, passed the fee to the driver, and exited the vehicle. The irritated man waved the money at us and shouted, "No, no. No enough. You short me."

We apologized and handed over more euros. He smiled, gave us a thumbs-up, and helped us cross the busy street to our hotel. Only after we checked in did we calculate and realize we'd been had.

With no luggage, and fifty euros poorer, we were crabby. We got to our room, and although we were tempted to sulk and stay in for the night, we realized Rome was out there. The Vatican walls stood directly across from our hotel window. Grateful that I had my journal tucked in my backpack, I opened it to the verses penned inside the front cover. One in particular jumped from the page—Psalm 31:14: "But I trust in you, LORD; I say, 'You are my God'" (NIV).

My husband and I prayed and asked for protection and for God to give us glimpses of His presence. I wiped some tears, washed up as best I could, and off we went. We enjoyed our first bites of fresh Italian pizza and scrumptious gelato. Airplane food had sustained us, but this feast replenished our souls.

We wandered back to the hotel, and before I collapsed into bed, I removed my earrings and laid them on the desk. *I probably should not set them here,* I thought, but I did anyway.

My husband uses a CPAP machine to sleep, and, of course, it was in his AWOL suitcase. Between his snores and the adjustment of an unfamiliar place, we spent a restless night.

Thankful we packed some clothes in our carry-on bags, we prepared for the day ahead. Our first full day in Rome involved a tour of the Vatican. I reached for the earrings I had placed on the desk, baffled to find only one. Distressed, I looked all over. The earring was gone! I was devastated, and since my husband had fumbled around at the desk the night before, it was easy to play the blame game.

What made it worse was that these were my favorite pair of earrings—diamond teardrops I'd bought in England a few years earlier and wore everywhere.

Their sentimental value meant more than their monetary value. I'd dreamed of taking a trip to England since I was in the eighth grade and had never imagined that day would come. My parents had known about my dream but died before it came to fruition. I finally did get to go years later, and those earrings were my keepsake; I often thought of my parents when I wore them. When I was packing for this trip, I'd thought about leaving the earrings at home, since they meant so much to me. But I'd squelched the idea, thinking, *What could go wrong?*

I could taste the salt from the tears that rolled down my cheeks. Heat rose up my neck, and anger clouded my judgment. Venom spewed from my mouth straight at my husband. "Why didn't you see my earrings on the desk? You lost my earring. The pair I adore most. It's all your fault."

"Me? You're the one who put them there. Why is it my fault?" he retorted.

In the twelve hours we had been in Rome, we had managed to lose our luggage, euros, sleep, patience, tempers, and now my favorite earring.

Dejected, my husband picked up his backpack and pulled out a flashlight. I'd kidded him about the flashlight when we were packing. I'd laughed and said, "What are you bringing that for? You don't need that."

"You never know when you will need one," he'd responded.

I recalled those words and hugged him. I said I was sorry and thanked him for his wisdom. We dropped to our knees and shone the light in the dark corners of our hotel room. We shook the curtains and inspected every piece of paper on the desk. We checked windowsills and overturned garbage. We made the bed three times and rubbed our bare feet across the tile floor. We found plenty of dust bunnies but no earring. It had simply disappeared.

We needed to go; the Vatican awaited. But first, I wanted to get alone and pray. Outside our room, a deck beckoned. Small tables with fresh flowers filled the area, and none were occupied. I settled into a cushioned seat and pondered the fact that losing the earring was my fault, too. I should not have loosely placed them on the desk. Perhaps those earrings were a possession I held too tightly to, or maybe they were tied too closely to the memory of my parents, who supported my dream. Either way, I had to learn that I could trust only in God. I prayed and asked God to somehow help us find that earring, and if not, to help me to let it go. I couldn't ignore the irony of being in a part of the world to where the faithful journey on pilgrimages while I was undergoing my own trust journey.

We visited the Vatican and learned how Michelangelo painted the most famous ceiling in the world, and then we toured other famous sites. But at the end of the day, we still didn't have our luggage, and the earring was still lost.

We woke the third day to find my husband's luggage outside our door. Opening his suitcase was a bit like opening a gift on Christmas morning. There were toiletries, his sleep machine, and some of my clothes, since friends had advised us to load clothes in each other's bags "just in case your luggage gets lost."

Time was running out. The next day we would leave Rome—possibly without my luggage and, even more likely, without my earring. Once again I whispered a prayer, asking God to specifically supply my earring.

That afternoon, I sat in a pew in a cathedral, staring at a statue of Jesus bearing His cross. In the quietness, God had my full attention. Did I have enough faith to trust Him with my whole life, even a lost earring? Finally, I had to let go. *OK, God. You win. You get control. Help my unbelief.*

We woke our last day in Rome without my luggage. We peacefully walked downstairs and enjoyed a fresh breakfast. When we were about to enter the elevator to return to our room, the gal at the front desk stopped us. She spoke with such excitement I had to ask her to repeat herself. "Your luggage here!"

"Really? Are you serious? It's here?"

She wheeled the familiar black bag with the pink bandanna from behind the desk. I was in awe, but God wasn't done yet.

After I enjoyed a shower using my own items, I changed and zipped up the suitcase. We closed the hotel door and rolled our bags to the elevator. I decided to leave my address with the front desk just in case my earring was found. I gave it to the same woman who had delivered my luggage.

"We do find thing sometimes and put in this drawer," the woman said in her broken English. She opened a cabinet under the desk. "I remember housekeeping telling me something like you say was found while empty vacuum. She say she almost dump, but she notice sparkle. Not sure it yours, but let us look."

She dangled my diamond earring between her fingertips. I trembled as I scurried behind the desk to hug her.

"You have no idea what this means to me!" I exclaimed.

"I think I do," she replied.

I wept. I looked toward my husband, who, through his own tears, replied, "We are blessed. This is a miracle."

I had never seen a housekeeper at the hotel. Only once could we tell someone had come in and cleaned. The fact that she had noticed a flicker through the dust and dirt in that vacuum bag speaks of God's hand. She could have thrown the contents into the garbage. Perhaps she could have kept the earring for herself. Who would know? Instead, she gave it to the front desk.

Angels come in many forms. In my case, the angel was a housekeeper. That earring was nowhere to be found. We looked everywhere. There is no other explanation as to why I wear it today. Ephesians 3:20–21 (NIV) states, "Now to him who is able to do immeasurably more than all we ask or imagine, according to his power that is at work within us, to him be the glory…for ever and ever!" And Luke 15:8–9 tells the story of a woman who loses a coin and rejoices when she finds it.

I, too, have rejoiced since my earring was recovered. True, it is a small miracle. But it is a constant reminder, whenever I wear my earrings, of His longing to give me the desires of my heart. My job is to simply trust Him.

A Precise Prayer for Healing

Susan L. Tuttle

"*Y*our mother has cancer."

I gripped the phone as I listened to Dad's choked-up voice. In my thirty-four years, I'd heard that word more times in relation to my mother than a daughter ever should.

I didn't want to go on this ride again, but cancer offers no choice. It tosses you to the front of the line and thrusts you onto its crazy roller coaster without asking permission.

Silence hung between us. Dad always had positive words to say. Encouragement to give. But not this time. It was so unlike the other times he'd delivered this news.

I sucked in a fortifying breath, resolving to once again believe and speak the words Dad couldn't. Those words he'd used with each previous diagnosis that now seemed stuck in his throat. "We'll beat this."

And we would. I didn't want to consider any other option.

"It doesn't look good." Tears filled his voice. It was the first time I'd heard my father cry over my mother's health.

My stomach tightened. With my free hand I massaged my temples as I lowered myself onto my bed.

"What did the doctor say, Dad?" I wasn't sure I wanted to know.

He cleared his throat and took a moment. "We've been to several, and they're all saying the same thing." Again he faltered. "They're telling her to go home and enjoy the time she has left. Six months, a year tops. There's nothing they can do."

A lump lodged in my throat. Six months? She'd never been given a time allotment before. The calendar flipped through my mind, time slipping away. How do you plan your last Thanksgiving, your last Christmas—your last anything with someone you love?

"How's Mom?"

With a shaky voice he answered, "She says this might be the one she doesn't beat."

Cancer hadn't come only to do battle this time. It had come to wage war and win.

We regrouped as a family. Reading over her diagnosis in black and white made things look dark. A tumor was growing in close proximity to her pancreas. They'd tested the cells. Pancreatic cancer. The five-year survival rate fell under 5 percent, but they reiterated that because of the intricacies of her case, they couldn't even guarantee a year.

With the tumor encased around a major vein, no one wanted to touch what promised to be an impossible surgery. At best, it would extend her life by a few months. Worst-case scenario: she could bleed out on the table.

All doctors in our area refused her case—which spoke volumes. We lived in the suburbs of Grand Rapids, Michigan, known as the Medical Mile, aptly named for the millions of research dollars that had been poured into our city. Schools had added campuses simply to be close to the medical advances in the heart of our downtown.

If no one there was willing to help her, who would be?

We prayed desperately for wisdom, and God led my parents to a doctor nearly three hours away on the east side of the state. My parents met with a surgeon who agreed to evaluate her case. We gathered as a family shortly afterward.

"So?" My older brother voiced the question we all wondered.

Mom, perched on the dark wooden chair at the worn kitchen table where we'd grown up eating, folded her hands over her stomach. "The surgeon took my case before the tumor board. They agreed I at least deserve a chance." For the first time since this started, she smiled. "They're going to do the surgery."

We clung to that hope, and it bolstered our spirits, even if we knew the tumor board was humoring us. They didn't truly believe the surgery would be successful. With the tumor measuring eight centimeters and its precarious location, this surgery was more about allowing us to let her go, knowing we'd tried everything we could before uttering our good-byes. It was their way of offering hope.

But the hope we felt wasn't from the doctors.

Our hope came from the Lord.

With a new plan facing us, we bathed the day of surgery in prayer, our church congregation, extended family, and friends joining us. Hope continued to rise even in the midst of an impossible situation.

The night before the procedure, as I packed at my own home, my parents received a call from our pastor.

"I've been praying for you, and God has placed on my heart something specific to share. I wonder if I can come over."

"Definitely," Dad answered. Prayer was the most important action we knew we could take, and we'd absorb all the prayers we could.

Pastor Sam arrived at their house, and the three of them huddled in the family room. Mom settled into the red recliner she'd purchased for my father, but which had quickly become her favorite chair. In the comfort and quiet of their own home, our pastor anointed her with oil and prayed for her healing. In that prayer, he declared five specific things:

The tumor would be completely encapsulated.

The tumor would separate from the main vein without the need to cut.

The tumor would fall out into the surgeon's hands.

There would be clear margins on the tumor.

And regardless of what the pathology report currently said, when they tested the tumor after removing it, there would be no evidence of pancreatic cancer at all.

After praying these things, Pastor Sam left.

The next day, my entire family caravanned across the state to the Karmanos Cancer Institute. On March 11, 2008, we hugged Mom good-bye as they wheeled her into the operating room. We then settled in the large waiting room with so many others who longed to see their loved ones healed.

The chair crinkled as I sat, hard beneath my weight. How unreal. Had I just said good-bye to my mother? Yes, my hope came from the Lord, but it was feeling battered. With every cancer diagnosis, I wondered if it was the last one she'd receive—and this time the foe was so formidable. Could I trust Him again? I struggled to hold tight to the truth I knew: God is the greatest physician of all.

And He was the one who operated on her right now.

Throughout the morning, friends and other family members showed up to comfort us, sharing stories that made us laugh or simply waiting with us in silence. Unsure as we were how long we would wait for the surgeon and his report, this outpouring of love helped us pass the time.

Several long hours ticked by before a nurse came into the waiting room. She approached Dad. "We'd like to have you all come back to a room so the surgeon can speak with you."

Wide-eyed, my sister and I gaped at the woman. There was only one reason I'd ever heard of them delivering news in seclusion.

"What if we don't want to go back to that room?" I asked.

She smiled. "You do. It's good. I promise."

The bands of anxiety squeezing my chest released.

She led all of us to a tiny gray room with a small wooden table and chairs. Some of us sat while others leaned against the wall. As awkward silence descended, we began to recount more funny stories about Mom. In the midst of our nervous laughter, the surgeon entered the room, his blue scrubs showing a few faint lines of sweat while his hair remained hidden under his cap and a white surgical mask hung around his neck.

He crossed his arms, slightly shaking his head. His eyes focused downward before scanning each of us.

"I don't know what you're doing, but whatever it is, keep doing it." Then he stared Dad in the eye. "That tumor was completely contained. It wasn't involved with the vein. I didn't even have to cut"—again he shook his head—"I don't know why, but it just fell out into my hand. All margins were clean." He paused. "We'll have to wait a few weeks for pathology reports, but it appeared to be nothing more than a cyst. Not at all what we saw on the reports."

This surgeon unknowingly had just repeated nearly verbatim the words our pastor had prayed over Mom.

Dad smiled. "We know why."

It was the second time I'd ever seen him cry over my mother's health, and this time they were tears of joy.

Six weeks later, Mom and Dad sat in the oncologist's office as she repeated the final item our pastor had been led to pray. "Your pathology report is clean. There's not one pancreatic cancer cell in that tumor." She lifted her shoulders, in awe of what she saw on the medical report. "Other than healing from the surgery, there's nothing else to do."

The medical community was amazed at Mom's case and left without explanation, but my parents offered it to them anyway. God instructed our pastor to pray over her. He was obedient and delivered the words he'd been given, praying specifically how the Holy Spirit led him. Yet our pastor's words didn't heal her; he was simply a messenger. The surgeon didn't heal her, either; he was simply an instrument.

The Great Physician alone deserved all the credit. Not only did He sew together my battered hope and remind me that in all situations I could trust Him, He ultimately did what no one else would or could do. He healed my mom. Once again. Miraculously.

3

A Guide for Prayer

Learn, Grow, Practice Prayer

*O*nce upon a time, you didn't know how to talk. Or walk. Or feed yourself.

Those skills are among the simplest in the human experience, but you still had to learn how to form sounds into words, to put one foot in front of the other, and even to get a spoonful of peas into your mouth. But you did it. You learned. Now each of those tasks is second nature to you. Elementary. You do them without realizing you're using a skill you learned long ago.

It can be intimidating to watch or hear someone pray who seems to be so good at it. The words just seem to roll off the tongue. The door of heaven seems to open. The presence of God seems to fill the room when some people pray. But learning to pray is much like learning to talk, walk, or feed yourself. It involves certain steps, a few skills, and some practice. But it does not take long, even for someone who has never tried to pray before, to learn and grow in the practice until it becomes second nature. Elementary. Like something you've always known how to do.

Andrew Murray, South African pastor and author, wrote in the book, *Lord, Teach Us to Pray*, "Prayer is so simple that the feeble child can pray, yet it is at the same time the highest and holiest work to which [we] can rise. It is fellowship with the Unseen and Most Holy One. The powers of the eternal world have been placed at its disposal. It is the very essence of true religion, the channel of all blessings, the secret of power and life."

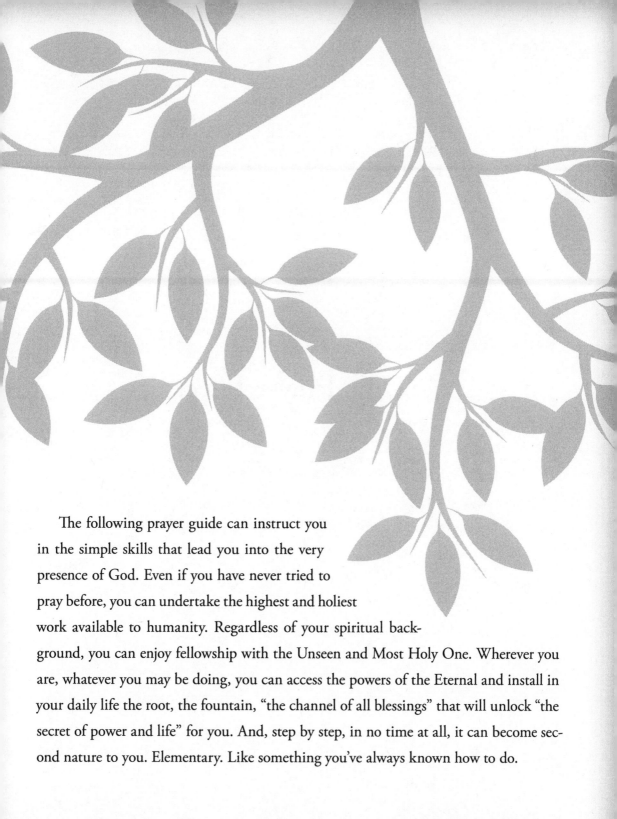

The following prayer guide can instruct you
in the simple skills that lead you into the very
presence of God. Even if you have never tried to
pray before, you can undertake the highest and holiest
work available to humanity. Regardless of your spiritual background, you can enjoy fellowship with the Unseen and Most Holy One. Wherever you
are, whatever you may be doing, you can access the powers of the Eternal and install in
your daily life the root, the fountain, "the channel of all blessings" that will unlock "the
secret of power and life" for you. And, step by step, in no time at all, it can become second nature to you. Elementary. Like something you've always known how to do.

The Prayer Effect

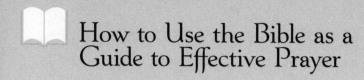

How to Use the Bible as a Guide to Effective Prayer

Some of the most profound prayers in history are recorded in the Bible. Two of Jesus's prayers are among the most quoted words worldwide in every language. God's people are a praying people. Since God is the leader, His people follow Him and communicate with Him. And yet prayer is stronger than a fiber-optic telephone line and faster than a walkie-talkie. The Bible becomes a powerful guide and model for your prayers as you follow God and communicate with Him.

The Tone, Attitude, and Content of Biblical Prayers

Imagine having video footage of all the prayers in the Bible edited together in a tight sequence. Watching the prayers back-to-back, you would see a pattern emerge. God's people pray in a personal tone, with a reverent attitude, and they speak blunt words.

- Adam and Eve walked and talked with God in the cool of the day. They talked with Him as if He were their neighbor.
- God called Abraham His friend, and yet Abraham prayed with a reverent heart. Many times, Abraham prayed bold prayers without any "spin."
- In Moses's landmark interaction with God, he removed his sandals because he was on holy ground. Reverence marked his prayers, but Moses was not afraid to ask hard things of God.
- David and the other psalmists provided some of the greatest language for your prayers. They demonstrated great agony and joy, sincere devotion, and acute doubt.
- Jesus taught us in the model prayer—known worldwide as the Lord's Prayer—to go to God as a child to her father, a radical concept in Jesus's culture. In His prayer for all believers—the High Priestly Prayer—Jesus prayed with reverence, with familiarity, and wasn't afraid to ask God to be generous to His people.
- The apostle Paul is a great mentor for your personal prayers. In each of his letters, he let you see the content and intent of his own personal prayers.

Even with these great prayers at your disposal, using the Bible as a guide is a daunting task. The Bible is full of history. What one person prays is not necessarily what you should pray. Others' lives and circumstances are different from yours. Look more to their hearts and the big pictures of what they prayed than to the specific words or requests.

The Bible is God's story of interacting with His people. Adam and Eve were kicked out of the garden of Eden because of their sin. Noah and his family were the only ones to survive the worldwide flood. As you fast-forward through history, Jesus, the Ultimate Redeemer, came to earth, died for the sins of God's people, and gave us new promises and a new commandment. When you use New Testament prayers as your model, remind yourself to pray in the light of where God is in His story—after the cross and before heaven.

Dear brothers and sisters, I urge you in the name of our Lord Jesus Christ to join in my struggle by praying to God for me.

ROMANS 15:30 NLT

Listen, GOD! Please, pay attention! Can you make sense of these ramblings, my groans and cries? King-God, I need your help. Every morning you'll hear me at it again. Every morning I lay out the pieces of my life on your altar and watch for fire to descend.

PSALM 5:1–3 MSG

Getting Started

Use the following suggestions as training wheels for your prayers. The Psalms and the prayers of Paul provide rich content and the fewest mousetraps for your words.

1. Read a phrase or a verse of Scripture.
2. Pray the intent of the phrase or verse in your own words. When praying for someone else, follow the same pattern.
3. Repeat the process for several verses in a row or until the natural end of the passage.

An example of praying for yourself:

- Scripture—"The LORD is my shepherd; there is nothing I lack" (Psalm 23:1 HCSB).
- Prayer—Thank You, Lord, for being my shepherd. Thank You for protecting me and providing for me. Thank You for always being beside me. Even though You're beside me, I'm fearful. I can't say like David, "I shall not want." Help me to trust You like that.

An example of praying for someone else:

- Scripture—"Since the day we heard this, we haven't stopped praying for you. We are asking that you may be filled with the knowledge of His will" (Colossians 1:9 HCSB).
- Prayer—Dear God, please help Jim find a job. He's struggling to keep going. God, please fill him with knowledge of what You want him to do. What should he do today? Help him to make the phone calls, set up meetings, and carry out the follow-up necessary to get a new job.

> *Moses said,*
> *"I pray You, show*
> *me Your glory!"*
>
> EXODUS 33:18 NASB

Final Thought

Spiritual disciplines have been taught through the ages from the early church fathers to modern-day megachurch pastors. Praying the Bible for yourself and for others integrates many of the spiritual disciplines: prayer, Bible reading, Bible study, and Bible meditation. Praying through the Bible is a practice that will encourage your heart and enrich your soul.

How to Be Moved to Pray

Jonah had a problem. Jonah was an Old Testament prophet sent by God to the city of Nineveh. God commanded him, "Go to the great city of Nineveh and preach against it, because their wickedness has confronted Me" (Jonah 1:2 HCSB). God was going to wipe out one of the enemies of God's people. Jonah worried that if God heard their prayers, He wouldn't destroy the city. He worried that God might be moved to change His mind.

What Happened in Nineveh

Instead of going to Nineveh, Jonah fled to the sea. The crew threw Jonah overboard to save themselves from a wrathful storm. Jonah was swallowed by a big fish, and he repented of his disobedience. The fish ejected Jonah onto dry land, and Jonah traveled immediately to Nineveh.

Jonah preached that in forty days God would destroy Nineveh. Word of Jonah's warning reached the king, who ripped his clothes and decreed that all the citizens should repent and pray to the God of Israel for mercy.

Jonah's worst fears came true. "God saw their works, that they turned from their evil way; and God relented from the disaster that He had said He would bring upon them, and He did not do it" (Jonah 3:10 NKJV). Because of their prayers, God did not punish this group of people.

Seminary professor and theologian Wayne Grudem explained it this way: "These instances should be all understood as true expressions of God's present attitude or intention with respect to the situation as it exists at that moment. If the situation changes, then of course God's attitude or expression of intention will also change. This is just saying that God responds differently to different situations."

Conversely, think about Egypt during the days of Moses. Moses and Aaron stood before Pharaoh eleven times. Even when Pharaoh relented and released the Israelites, he didn't show sorrow or repentance. His heart was hard. God brought about His original plan—the delivery of His people. Pharaoh's kingdom received no relief. Eleven times destruction followed Pharaoh's refusal to let God's people go. God brought about ten plagues and then the destruction of the military in the Red Sea. The circumstances did not change, so God brought about the plan as He communicated to Moses.

How This Truth Affects Your Prayers

Jonah warned the people of Nineveh, who in turn begged God to relent and not destroy their civilization. Another prophet, Isaiah, confronted King Hezekiah. Isaiah told him to get his house in order because he would die soon. Hezekiah responded in prayer, repenting and pleading for God's mercy. God extended Hezekiah's life by fifteen years.

God probably will not send a prophet to your doorstep with a specific message of doom. Instead, look to your circumstances. If you continue to make similar decisions and act in similar ways, what is the most likely outcome? If your answer to that question makes your knees knock, cry out to God and ask for mercy.

Remind God of His Promises

The Israelites had front-row tickets to the hardhearted behavior of Pharaoh and the consequences that rained down on Egypt. However, many years later in the wilderness, their hearts started to calcify. God told Moses to duck because He had grown tired of their behavior and disbelief.

Instead of covering his head with his arms, Moses asked God for mercy. He reminded God of His covenant with His people. Had God forgotten the promises He had made to Abraham, Isaac, Jacob, and all their descendants? Of course not. By reminding God of His words, Moses heard the promise and reminded himself that God keeps His promises. You can do the same in your prayers. Remind God of the truths you've learned from reading the Bible.

 Check Your Understanding

- **What criteria does God use to decide between carrying out His original plan and changing according to different circumstances?**
  God always remains consistent within His character. God is eternal, holy, unchanging, infinite, all-powerful, all-knowing, self-existent, self-sufficient, merciful, just, gracious, and sovereign.

- **How does God remain consistent in His character yet seemingly change His behavior?**

  Here's an example: God cannot tolerate sin. If you break God's rules, He will not let you into heaven. He sent Jesus to earth to pay for your sins. When Jesus died on the cross, the circumstances changed, and thus God's attitude toward you changed.

- **What can I do when I struggle to believe this truth?**

  Proverbs 3:5–6 offers great advice: "Trust in the L<small>ORD</small> with all your heart and lean not on your own understanding; in all your ways submit to him, and he will make your paths straight" (NIV).

Does God Move You, or Do You Move God in Prayer?

You are moved because you move toward God in relationship. God is moved because His ultimate desire is a deeper relationship with you. Through prayer, your outlook on your circumstances changes as you see through God's eyes. Through prayer, your circumstances change and God then acts based on the new circumstances.

There are dozens of promises within the pages of the Bible. The following chart is merely a partial list for reference.

When God Closes a Door, How Do You Know if He Opened a Window?

Imagine a little boy asking his father, "Daddy, may I please have some popcorn?" The father extends a plain brown paper bag. The bag is too high for the boy to see into, so he must reach his hand over the rim of the bag. He feels inside and pulls out the contents. What does he remove? The potential answers to this question illustrate how God answers our prayers. God always hears your prayers and always responds. His responses can be divided into four categories: (1) yes, (2) no, (3) later, and (4) something better.

If the father said yes to his son's request, the boy would have reached in to find warm kernels of popped corn. If the father had said no, the son would have felt only air. If the father had planned to delay his yes, the son would have found a handful of unpopped kernels. And if the father had wanted to exceed his son's expectations, the child would have discovered caramel popcorn, cheese popcorn, or kettle popcorn.

"Yes!"

God revels in answering His children's prayers. The people of God rejoiced when He answered their prayers. They often gave God a new name to celebrate His intervention. These terms of endearment became spoken reminders of the faithfulness of God.

One of the most poignant yes answers came when Abraham trudged up Mount Moriah to sacrifice his son Isaac (Genesis 22). Abraham surely questioned why, but moved forward anyway. He told Isaac, "God will provide for Himself the lamb for a burnt offering" (v. 8 NKJV). Abraham must have prayed with every step. When Isaac was bound, he must have prayed for a substitute with every huffing breath. The Lord waited until Abraham lifted the knife before telling an angel to shout, "Abraham!" Abraham loosed Isaac, and together they sacrificed the ram stuck in the thorns. They called the place Jehovah-Jireh— The LORD Will Provide (v. 14 NIV).

"No!"

God also says no to prayer requests. The negative response often produces doubt, disappointment, or anger. When God says no, remember that He is acting in your best interest. When you ask why and receive no answers, remember that He loves you and is protecting you.

He might have said no to you in the same way He refused Jim's request. Jim's car died on the way to a job interview. As he watched the news that evening, he marveled at the report of a fatal accident a few blocks and a few minutes from where his car broke down. He wondered if he might have been the victim instead.

On the night before His crucifixion, Jesus agonized in prayer at the garden of Gethsemane. The Bible tells us that He sweat blood, a condition that occurs only under the heaviest stress. He asked, "O My Father, if it is possible, let this cup pass from Me" (Matthew 26:39 NKJV). The cup equaled His execution on the cross. God said no and Jesus was crucified. God acted in the best interest of all creation. Jesus had to die so that God could carry out His plan to rescue humankind.

"Later!"

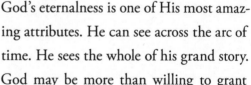

God's eternalness is one of His most amazing attributes. He can see across the arc of time. He sees the whole of his grand story. God may be more than willing to grant your request, but He may see a better time for your prayer to come to fruition.

The prophets foretold the Messiah's birth for hundreds of years before Jesus arrived. The apostle Paul told us, "When the fullness of the time came, God sent forth His Son, born of a woman, born under the Law" (Galatians 4:4 NASB). A modern-day proverb quips, "God is seldom early, but never late."

"Something Better!"

God longs to bless His children. The apostle Paul discussed the amazing riches of God's kingdom. You can almost hear him growing louder and more excited with each sentence until he proclaimed, "To him who is able to do immeasurably more than all we ask or imagine, according to his power that is at work within us, to him be glory in the church and in Christ Jesus throughout all generations, for ever and ever! Amen" (Ephesians 3:20–21 NIV).

God longs to pour out the riches of His kingdom into your life. He surprises His children. When God closes a door (says no), sometimes He opens a window. And sometimes He takes the whole roof off.

🌿 Final Thought

When Jesus prayed in the garden of Gethsemane, He closed with the words "Nevertheless, not as I will, but as You will" (Matthew 26:39 NKJV). God's will supersedes your will. All of His answers—yes, no, later, and something better—come from His master plan. The key to accepting any of the four answers is trust. No matter what answer you receive to your request, trust that God knows what He's doing.

When You Can't Find the Words

One of the most encouraging verses in the Bible is found in Romans 8:26–27: "In the same way, the Spirit helps us in our weakness. We do not know what we ought to pray for, but the Spirit himself intercedes for us through wordless groans. And he who searches our hearts knows the mind of the Spirit, because the Spirit intercedes for God's people in accordance with the will of God" (NIV). What happens when you don't feel like praying but pray anyway?

When Life Overcomes You

A cynical man once said, "You are either in a crisis, coming out of a crisis, or about to go into a crisis." Jesus put it another way: "In this world you will have trouble. But take heart! I have overcome the world" (John 16:33 NIV). When life overwhelms you, you may not have the words—or the desire—to pray.

Classic commentator Matthew Henry pointed out that the word Paul used for help, *synantilambanetai*, means "The Spirit heaves with you," like a friend helping you dump a heavy load over a wall.

> GOD *is in his holy Temple! Quiet everyone—*
> *a holy silence. Listen!*
>
> HABAKKUK 2:20 MSG

> *Rest in the* LORD *and wait patiently for Him; do not fret*
> *because of him who prospers in his way, because of the man*
> *who carries out wicked schemes.*
>
> PSALM 37:7 NASB

The Holy Spirit Makes Intercession

Henry said, "Why, the Spirit itself makes intercession for us, dictates our requests, invites our petitions, draws up our plea for us. Christ intercedes for us in heaven, the Spirit intercedes for us in our hearts; so graciously has God provided for the encouragement of the praying remnant. The Spirit, as an enlightening Spirit, teaches us what to pray for, as a sanctifying Spirit works and excites praying graces, as a comforting Spirit silences our fears, and helps us over all our discouragements. The Holy Spirit is the spring of all our desires and breathings toward God."

God is not uncomfortable when you fumble your prayers. He does not grow impatient as He waits on you to say what you want to say. To the contrary, God looks upon your heart and feels your prayers in the same way you do. While you struggle to put them into words, God comprehends and responds.

Points to Remember

When you feel overwhelmed, try one of these four practical activities:

- *Sing.* Find a recording of your favorite hymns or worship songs and sing along with them. Singing can focus you on the One to Whom you can't pray.
- *Borrow Words.* Praying written prayers can break the dam holding back your thoughts and emotions.
- *Pray the Scriptures.* Even reading the Bible aloud can bring comfort and peace.
- *Enjoy the Silence.* Sitting quietly will let you hear God's voice more easily.

 Final Thought

Despair and stress are not the only reasons you may find yourself without words to pray. Singer-songwriter Steven Curtis Chapman lost his voice in 2001. His career was over. Chapman said, "I didn't lose my speaking voice, which was the weird part. I thought maybe God was saying, 'I'm done with you.'" After three months, his voice miraculously returned. He was overwhelmed by God's grace.

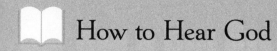

How to Hear God

Busy signals. "Please leave a message after the tone." "The number you have called has been changed." Jeremiah 33:3 is often called God's phone number: "Call to Me, and I will answer you, and show you great and mighty things, which you do not know" (NKJV). God spoke these words to His people through the prophet Jeremiah.

These words are also a promise. When you call out to God, you will never hear silence or be placed on hold. God longs to hear your prayers and respond. God is part of the dialogue of prayer through His still, small voice and the Bible.

Listen for God's Voice

God's voice is hard to hear. God worked through Elijah to demonstrate His power to King Ahab, Queen Jezebel, and their entire kingdom. Jezebel became enraged and threatened Elijah's life. Despite God's amazing pyrotechnics show the day before, the prophet fled in fear. He cowered in a cave, awaiting more marching orders. As you read 1 Kings 19, you can almost see Elijah turning his head and pointing one ear toward God. The winds blew, an earthquake erupted, and fire swept over the mountain, but Elijah didn't hear God amid the fireworks. Suddenly, the Bible tells us, Elijah heard a still, small voice. A whisper.

The culture fills every second with fireworks of its own. Three hundred television channels compete with Internet videos. Satellite radio wars with the iPod. Your senses can easily be overwhelmed and stressed. Just as suddenly, just as quietly, God can speak to you. Are you turning your head and bending your ear toward His voice?

Here are a few ways to listen for the voice of God in a noisy world:
- Set aside a special chair and lamp in your home. Spend the first fifteen minutes of each day in prayer. Allow the chair to become a special meeting place for listening to God.
- Use your car as a sanctuary. Drive for a while with the radio and cell phone turned off. Or, after driving to a destination, sit quietly in your car for a few minutes before going inside.

- Make your hectic morning routine meaningful. Write prayer requests on the shower wall with children's bathroom markers. Pray and listen during bath time.
- Don't fall asleep with the television on. Instead, spend a few minutes praying and listening before fluffing your pillow.

Search the Bible

As hard as God's voice is to hear, it's even harder to make sure you heard it right. Compare what you've heard in your conscience to what God says in the Bible. This is not a display of doubt; it's a noble pursuit.

The apostle Paul and his friend Silas visited the city of Berea in Greece. They were impressed. The Bereans listened like anxious students hanging on every word of their professor, but when the teaching was over, they "searched the Scriptures daily *to find out* whether these things were so" (Acts 17:11 NKJV).

Don't take what you hear at face value. Take a cue from the Bereans and search out the Scriptures for confirmation. How large is your decision? How deep is your crisis? How wonderful is your possibility? Depend on the Scriptures in direct proportion.

Hearing God's Voice

In addition to listening for God's voice when you pray, you should also look for God's message to you when you read the Bible. Throughout history, Christians have tried a number of creative—but dangerous—ways to find God's message. Some have approached the Bible with eyes closed, opening the book to a random page, pointing a finger at a passage, then opening their eyes to see what God would say. Equally dangerous, some have chosen a series of numbers like a telephone number. For 123-555-1212, they've opened the Bible to page 123, counted the lines to find number 555, then read the next 1,212 characters.

Instead of hunt-and-peck spirituality, seek the whole counsel of the Bible. Any less is like assuming you've seen a movie just by watching the trailer.

A topical Bible puts all the verses addressing a subject at your fingertips. Editors arrange verses by issue or thought. Look up the subjects in the same way you would use an encyclopedia. Under each division, you'll find the addresses to the Scriptures that meet your needs.

For example, if you're praying about a new job, look up words such as *work*, *talent*, *labor*, and *prosperity*. Write down the references in your journal, and then look up each one, listening for direction.

Points to Remember

A game called "Word Scramble" appears in hundreds of newspapers worldwide. Readers work hard to figure out anagrams—rearranging the letters in one word to form another. One of the anagrams that can be spelled from the word *listen* is *silent*. Will you rearrange your life in small ways to hear God's voice more clearly?

Myth Buster

Some say that God used burning bushes, talking donkeys, and angels to deliver His messages in the Bible but that He doesn't do anything like that anymore. Every year, Christians worldwide report hundreds of fascinating encounters with God. Your job is to have your eyes, ears, and heart wide open. Don't be like Jim Carrey's character in the movie *Bruce Almighty*. He prayed for a sign, and God sent him a truckful he didn't see.

Final Thought

"God, please rescue me!" a man prayed as he watched the lake flood over its banks. He waited on God's answer. The mayor ordered evacuation over television, but the man waited on God's answer. Two men came by in a canoe offering a ride, but he waited on God's answer. He crawled up on the roof. A helicopter lowered a ladder, but he waited for God's answer. God talks to you. Are you listening? Hearing God requires an understanding of the many ways He responds to people. The answer to your prayer may come in unexpected ways. By remaining spiritually alert, you'll be better able to recognize the answer when it comes.

What God Says when He Talks to You

A politician gives a speech that lasts thirty minutes. The pundits spend hours—sometimes days—telling you what the politician meant. A speaker from a foreign country teaches a class. Phrase by phrase, the interpreter standing next to her translates the concepts and words into your language. The God of the universe whispers to your heart. The Bible's text is ancient, and you must work, at times, to understand its meaning. How do you know what God is saying? How do you differentiate between His voice and the voice of the devil, the enemy of our souls?

You Know His Voice

A baby knows the voice of his mother. Just a word can soothe a cry. A toddler can tell the difference among all the vehicles that come down his street. When his father is nearing home, the toddler moves to the door. In the same way, you know the voice of your God.

Jesus was teaching a crowd with many religious leaders looking on. He compared himself to a shepherd and said, "The sheep follow [the shepherd] because they recognize his voice. They will never follow a stranger; instead they will run away from him, because they don't recognize the voice of strangers" (John 10:4–5 HCSB).

Take comfort in this knowledge, but be sure to take the time to distinguish between all the voices you hear in a given day. God's voice has many distinct qualities.

The Qualities of God's Voice

You know the voice of Don LaFontaine (1940–2008). He became known as "the Voice of God." The voice-over actor recorded thousands of movie trailers. He is famous for the phrase "In a world where…" His "thunder throat" had many distinctive qualities. God's voice has many as well. His voice has richness and tones that set His voice apart.

James reminded us that when God speaks, He will do so with kindness and gentleness. God's wisdom comes to help and to build up. The tone of voice God uses with His children points toward peace.

The apostle Paul, in his last letter to his apprentice Timothy, summarized the roles of the Bible in your life. When God speaks in prayer, His voice will carry the same roles.

God desires to teach you like a parent teaching a child to walk. He will reprove or reprimand you like a parent pulling a child back from touching a hot stove. He will correct you like a coach working on the fundamentals of a sport. He will also train you in small increments like a dance instructor.

The tone of God's voice will sound more like that of Mr. Miyagi, the long-suffering sensei from *The Karate Kid*, than Foley, the rigid drill sergeant from *An Officer and a Gentleman*.

Recognizing the Voice of Your Enemy

Many voice-over artists have tried to imitate LaFontaine. In the same way, the devil tries to imitate God's voice to fulfill his ultimate directive—to deceive you. He hissed his way into Eve's heart and pulled her from God's instructions in the garden of Eden. He tried to outwit Jesus after He fasted for forty days before launching His earthly ministry. Later, Jesus would tell a large group of followers that the devil "was a murderer from the beginning, not holding to the truth, for there is no truth in him. When he lies, he speaks his native language, for he is a liar and the father of lies" (John 8:44 NIV). The devil is also called the accuser (Revelation 12:10).

When you hear a voice, listen for half-truths, twisted words, and accusation. The enemy wants "to steal, and to kill, and to destroy" (John 10:10 NKJV). God seeks to heal the brokenhearted and bind up their wounds (Psalm 147:3).

The Content of God's Communication

Two famous songs summarize what God will say to you. The children's song "Jesus Loves Me, This I Know" is profound in its simplicity. God loves you. The Bible is often called God's Love Letter. The most famous verse in the Bible, John 3:16, is one of dozens outlining how much God loves you. God loves you with an everlasting love.

The world's most famous hymn, "Amazing Grace," reminds us that God's messages will be full of grace. Grace is not escaping punishment; it is receiving a reward when you should be receiving punishment. Jesus sacrificed His life on your behalf to cover your sin so that you might go to heaven.

When you hear a voice, listen for messages filled with love and grace and discard the others. Know the differences between God's voice and that of the devil.

 Final Thought

When listening for God's voice, remember these truths:

Jesus was crushed. He will not crush you.

Jesus was bruised. He will not bruise you.

Jesus was mocked. He will not mock you.

Jesus was spat upon. He will not spit on you.

Jesus was abandoned. He will not walk away from you.

God's voice will never speak destructive, hurtful, derisive, degrading, or forsaking words to you.

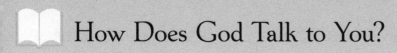

How Does God Talk to You?

Same room. Same people. Different emotions. When they arrested Jesus, the disciples retreated to the room where they had shared the Passover meal. They locked the door and wondered when guards would kick down the door and drag them away. The resurrection changed their outlook. Jesus gave some instructions and reminded them of His promise. Then Jesus ascended to heaven. They returned to the same room without fear, and they waited for the promise like eight-year-olds in late December. How does God talk to you? Through the fulfillment of that promise to the disciples—and you. The fulfillment of that promise enables and empowers your prayers.

During the Passover meal with His disciples—the Last Supper—Jesus saw twelve distressed faces. He comforted them with many truths, including His promise to send the Helper. This Holy Spirit was a new concept. Jesus described the Spirit as full of truth, living in you, and staying with you no matter what.

The Holy Spirit Helps You in Your Weakness

The Holy Spirit isn't Alfred to your Batman. He is more like a battlefield medic always nearby with words of comfort and plenty of bandages.

Derek Redmond was expected to medal in the four hundred meters during the 1992 Olympics, but a torn hamstring crashed him to the track with seventy meters to go. He stood and limped forward, determined to finish.

His father, Jim, burst past heavy security to wrap his arm around his son. He supported his weak side all the way across the finish line.

When you pray, the Holy Spirit is like Jim Redmond—He supports you where you're weak and comforts you where you hurt.

The Holy Spirit Helps You Understand the Mind of God

When you bring your questions to God, you hope for answers. The Helper is with you and in you to help you hear and understand God. The apostle Paul described the Spirit's mission statement. He is "the spirit of wisdom and revelation in the knowledge of Him" (Ephesians 1:17 NKJV).

God talks to you in prayer through the Holy Spirit. The Spirit helps the lightbulb of comprehension glow brightly above your head.

 ## Check Your Understanding

- ### Is the Holy Spirit equal to God?
  The Holy Spirit is God. Orthodox Christian belief holds that God is one God in three Persons—Father, Son, and Holy Spirit. The Holy Spirit is the third part of the Trinity. He is described through the Bible with the same attributes as God. The Spirit is eternal, omnipotent, omniscient, omnipresent, and was part of creating the universe.

Final Thought

Bill Bright (1921-2003), the founder of Campus Crusade for Christ, always spoke of the Holy Spirit as a friend: "He makes me glad. He fills my heart with joy. He inspires me with marvelous ideas. He energizes me. He surprises and blesses me daily. He listens when I need help. He has incredible wisdom and insight. When He speaks, it is as if a light goes on in my head and heart."

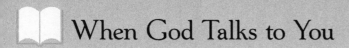

When the night started, Samuel must have wanted a cup of warm milk and an extra blanket. His eyes had barely drooped when he heard his name. Like a good apprentice, he reported for duty to his mentor, Eli. But the aging priest hadn't called him. Samuel returned to bed only to hear two more summons. Eli figured it out and sent Samuel back to bed with instructions: if you hear your name again, it's God calling. God did call his name. Samuel responded, "Speak, for Your servant hears" (1 Samuel 3:10 NKJV). When God calls your name, how do you respond?

Are You Listening?

When Eli sent Samuel back to bed to listen for the Lord, he must have heard every creak and every puff of wind. His ears were alive with anticipation. Are yours?

Eugene Peterson, pastor and creator of *The Message* Bible paraphrase, said, "We're in a hurry and not used to listening. We're trained to use our minds to get information and complete assignments; but the God revealed to us in Jesus and our Scriptures is infinitely personal and relational. Unless we take the time to be quiet, in a listening way, in the presence of God, we never get to know Him."

Train your ears to pick out the voice of God from the surface clutter of daily life.

Are You Responding?

When God called Samuel, he must have popped out of bed like a husband nudged by his expecting wife to take her to the hospital.

Do you respond like Samuel? Do you spring into action with anticipation and eagerness like a young groom pursuing his bride? Do you respond like Pharaoh? Moses approached him seven times and said, "Thus says the LORD God of Israel..." (Exodus 5:1 NKJV). Each time, Pharaoh turned a deaf ear. Do you respond like a cautious business owner with words like "We need to study several alternatives to determine the best course of action"?

Decide today to grow in how you respond. As you quiet your heart and surroundings to hear His voice more, choose to answer God with increasing devotion.

Something to Ponder

The English language distinguishes between the words *listen* and *hear*. In a restaurant, you hear the music on the speakers, chairs scraping, waiters taking orders, and cell phones ringing. Your ears process these sound waves and relegate them to background noise. In the same restaurant, you listen to the voices of those at your table. When God talks to you, will His voice be in the background noise with clattering plates or at the table in intimate conversation?

 Final Thought

Samuel wasn't the only man or woman chronicled in the Bible who had nocturnal visits from on high. Spend a few minutes reading about the encounters these men had:

Jacob (Genesis 32:24–30)
Solomon (1 Kings 3:5–15)
Joseph (Matthew 1:19–25)
Peter (Acts 12:3–11)

Common Barriers to Prayer

Prayer is sometimes like a journey through a construction zone. Potholes jar your body as your car bounces through. A flag-waving construction worker cuts you off. Orange barrels narrow the road, and large wooden signs announce a detour. You wish you could turn your car into a helicopter to fly over it all or just go back to bed and forget the entire trip. What detours—or derails—your prayers? Most barriers fall into two categories: "I" barriers and "God" barriers. This chapter addresses the "I" barriers, and the next chapter will cover the "God" barriers.

"I Am Busy"

No matter how busy you are, you always have time for one thing—a crisis. Crises come when you least expect them. They storm into your life, laying waste to your schedule. Crises bring crystal-clear clarity to the essentials and priorities of life. You have no choice but to fit a crisis into your life. What if you treated prayer with the same respect as a crisis?

Pastor and renowned church growth specialist Bill Hybels observed that we are trained to believe that time is money, but that the training leads to some dangerous behaviors. Hybels wrote, "The archenemy of spiritual authenticity is busyness, which is closely tied to something the Bible calls *worldliness*—getting caught up with the society's agenda, objectives, and activities to the neglect of walking with God. Anyway you cut it, a key ingredient in authentic Christianity is time. Not leftover time, not throwaway time, but quality time. Time for contemplation, meditation, and reflection. Unhurried, uninterrupted time."

So how do you cut a swath across your schedule to accommodate prayer? The high school and college campus organization Fellowship of Christian Athletes uses a sports metaphor. Leaders encourage the student-athletes to go "first and ten" with God. Spend ten minutes in prayer each morning as the first part of your routine. This technique isn't for "the entire game" but just to get you started. You will seek to increase the minutes once you feel the benefits of committed time to pray.

"I Am Distracted"

Those who have many distractions have many things to pray for. There are two major types of distractions: internal and external.

Internal distractions are thoughts and feelings that captivate your mind. When you quiet yourself for prayer, these gremlins turn up the volume to get your attention. To combat these internal distractions, create a list of all your concerns. Use that list as your guide until you experience a time of prayer not marred by random thoughts.

External distractions include ringing telephones and interrupting children. Electronic devices are easy to disable or unplug. Moms in particular struggle when their children disrupt their times of prayer. They've overcome the barrier of being too busy, but as soon as they take a deep breath, a child needs help. Children require care and attention. Many moms report that they need to wake up before their children do or put the to-do list on hold during nap time in order to pray for just a few minutes without distraction.

"I Am Sleepy"

If bowing your head is a better cure for insomnia than counting sheep, perhaps your environment is more conducive to sleep than it is to prayer. Classic paintings and the monastic life have been combined with the solemnity of prayer to create an expectation that prayer is best when on your knees in silence.

That might work for some Christians at times. Silence and solitude are positive elements to your spiritual life. However, prayer can be just as meaningful while out for a morning run or an afternoon walk. If you have a long commute, spend part of your time in prayer. Keep a three-by-five-inch card full of prayer requests behind your visor. One young businessman likes to pray aloud, so he wears his earphones so that it appears he's on a telephone call. In essence, he is talking over the communication line that's never busy.

"I Am Inadequate"

Even those who have prayed for years feel inadequate from time to time. This barrier rears its head when the basics become dusty. If you feel this way, remind yourself that prayer is simply having a conversation with God.

Something to Ponder

French theologian François Fénelon once tutored an unruly seven-year-old boy. Their relationship thrived, and the boy became a responsible young man. Years later, Fénelon wrote to his former protégé, "An active personality, accustomed to lots of activity, will faint in solitude. For a long time you have been distracted by much outward activity. By being fruitful you will gradually come to experience a deeper inward life with fewer distractions." Persist in prayer.

Points to Remember

- People have no choice but to make time for a crisis, and yet many crises could be averted or better handled if people made time for prayer.
- Until you find a way to handle distractions, you can use them as a springboard to prayer.
- If you find that prayer lulls you to sleep, pray when you're most alert or when you can't fall asleep, such as when you're walking or driving.

 Final Thought

The most troublesome "I" barrier to prayer is "I Don't Want to Pray." Many are afraid to admit this core thought and choose to voice other barriers that seem more "religiously correct." When you feel this way, ask yourself how God has disappointed you or frustrated you, and then take your feelings to Him. King David, the apostle Paul, and many others complained to God. When they did, God drew them closer to Himself.

Praying in the Middle of Life
for You and Others

How to Pray with Longing while Trying to Discover God's Will

Should you accept that job offer? What's the best way to help your daughter decide which college to attend? Does God really want you to serve on the worship team when you're already overextended? These and similar questions send Christians on a relentless pursuit to discover God's will for their lives. Sometimes the questions apply to everyday matters, sometimes to life-changing decisions, and sometimes to big-picture scenarios like God's purpose for putting you on earth. And sometimes the best way to find out what you don't know is to figure out what you do know.

What do you already know about God's will? You know that

- God has plans for a hopeful future for you (Jeremiah 29:11).
- God wants you to understand His will (Ephesians 5:17).
- Your plans need to take second place to God's (James 4:13–17).
- His will is good, acceptable, and perfect (Romans 12:2).
- His will is for everyone to come to salvation and knowledge of the truth (1 Timothy 2:3–4).
- If you ask for anything according to His will, God will hear you (1 John 5:14).
- If you do what you already know of God's will, His love is in you (1 John 2:4–5).

Teach me to do your will, for you are my God. May your gracious Spirit lead me forward on a firm footing.

PSALM 143:10 NLT

Trust GOD from the bottom of your heart; don't try to figure out everything on your own. Listen for GOD'S voice in everything you do, everywhere you go; he's the one who will keep you on track.

PROVERBS 3:5–6 MSG

God Wants to Reveal His Will

You probably know even more than that about God's will, but this is a good start. Looking over that list should give you the confidence of knowing that God wants to reveal His will to you. Pay special attention to the last item, because if you're not already doing what you know to be God's will—His revealed will in the pages of Scripture—it would be a good idea to start there. Christians who want to know God's specific will but aren't following God's will as revealed in the Bible have it all backward; they need to start following what they know—love God, love your neighbor, and other equally clear commandments—before they ask Him to fill them in on what they don't know.

Praying the Scriptures

Praying the Bible back to God is a great way to talk to God about anything in your life that you're uncertain about. Whenever you're seeking God's will for a specific situation, try this method of praying. Here are some examples:

"God, I need Your wisdom for this situation. James 1:5 says that You will be generous with Your wisdom if I ask for it. I believe the Bible, and I'm asking for wisdom now."

"God, I'm trusting You with all my heart. I'm not relying on my own understanding. You said in John 16:13 that if I acknowledge You in everything that I do, You will show me the way to go. I need to hear Your voice. I need You to guide me toward the truth in this situation."

"God, You say in Proverbs 12:15 that a person who is wise will seek the counsel of others and listen to their advice. I need to know Your will for my life, and I'm trusting You to speak to me through the people I trust to give me direction."

There's no lack of passages in Scripture that you can pray back to God. If you search the Bible, you will no doubt find many verses that express the longing of your heart to know God's will. Praying in this way assures you that you are praying in God's will as you pray for God's will.

Relax and Wait

During this time of seeking, it's important that you relax and wait on God. It's tempting to want to rush things and try to determine God's will right away. But as you've probably already learned, God is seldom in as much of a hurry as you are. Relaxing is tough when you have a deadline—you have until next week, say, to let a prospective employer know whether you'll take the job—but it's in those situations that you discover the depth of your trust in God.

God's guidance for your problem may not always be as spelled out as you might want. Be alert to your intuition, however. That is often God's will making itself known to you. Have you ever had the experience of sitting down to write a check or make an offer and had a number pop into your head? Have you ever "known" something without thinking about it? Oftentimes that is God talking to you. Does God say yes or no to the new job? You may already know.

Don't forget to thank God for revealing His will to you. Thanking God in advance, before you have the slightest inkling of what His will is, shows that you are praying with anticipation and the expectation that He will answer you.

The Bible offers lots of advice on how to determine God's specific will for your life.

> *"I know the plans I have for you," says the LORD. "They are plans for good and not for disaster, to give you a future and a hope."*
>
> JEREMIAH 29:11 NLT

 ## Final Thought

God wants what's best for you. Prayer is a way to reassure yourself of that fact. Remember, you know God's will. Your knowledge of the Scriptures is an important foundation for understanding Him. Rest in that knowledge and continue to trust that God will provide what He already knows you need when the time is right.

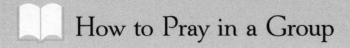

How to Pray in a Group

The practice of praying together originated in the first gathering of believers after the ascension of Jesus Christ to heaven. The book of Acts records exciting and transformative events. While the apostles waited for Pentecost, they gathered in a room with other close followers. The activities of these early gatherings included listening to the apostles' teaching, spending time and sharing meals with one another, and praying for one another's needs. When you pray with a group, you are continuing an unbroken chain from the days of the New Testament.

Praying in a group should be as natural as conversation. Throughout the centuries, habits and unofficial rules have shaped the way groups pray. These practical guidelines help make group prayer more meaningful and natural, but they shouldn't become legalistic requirements.

How to Take Prayer Requests

Many groups begin their prayer time by soliciting prayer requests. This custom communicates the details and the story behind a request. Requests should be offered in an attitude of reverence. Some requests can become announcements or gossip. Check your motives before you add your request to the list.

Appoint a scribe to write down and distribute prayer requests. A list allows members to pray for one another throughout the time between meetings. It also becomes a living document. Brief notes about how God answered the prayers broaden your group's journal. You can see the hand of God moving in your midst. Log the dates of the requests and the answers.

Taking prayer requests can burn precious time intended for actual prayer. Fern Nichols, founder of Moms in Prayer International, encourages her chapters to spend the majority of their time together in prayer. If a group desires to keep a journal, they have the freedom to take notes during prayer.

Unspoken Requests

Since God knows everything, He knows the hearts and needs of the members of your group. Everyone should feel open and free to share concerns, but human nature can get in the way. Allow a group member to say, "I have a private request." Others can then reach out to God in prayer on his or her behalf. This routine also opens up prayer opportunities about confidential matters.

The Health Rut

Asking for prayer can sometimes feel like inviting a camera crew from a reality TV show into your life. Groups often gravitate toward safe requests such as physical health. Everyone experiences health problems from time to time.

Do not forsake praying for health needs. There are serious health concerns that should be a part of the fabric of your group's prayer life such as cancer, a problem pregnancy, and trauma. Chronic conditions such as Alzheimer's, autism, and arthritis should not be overlooked. The admonition is to pray for "health and more," not health alone.

If you are facilitating the prayer time for your group, consider asking questions to help your group pray for a wider variety of needs: Is anyone praying for the salvation of someone? Is anyone struggling with a relationship issue? Are there any workplace or unemployment issues? Is anyone struggling to trust God with a need?

Giving Everyone Time to Pray

Group dynamics should not distract your group from the focus of your time: talking to and hearing from God. However, prayer time can feel dicey. Questions abound. Is he finished praying yet or is that a pause? Has anyone's request been left out? How long should I wait after she's finished before I begin?

Discuss these issues with your group. The conversation will be insightful and downright funny. Here are a couple of suggestions to ease the tension:

If your group is small enough, hold hands and pray in order. Person #1 opens in prayer and will close when all are finished. When he is finished, he squeezes the hand of #2. If #2 doesn't want to pray aloud, she then squeezes the hand of #3. This continues around the circle until #1 closes.

If your group is larger, two members might begin praying at the same time. Just laugh it off. A shrewd leader could say, "Anita, why don't you pray first? Then Eric can pray."

🍃 Final Thought

The larger the group, the more difficult closing can be. The group leader should designate someone to close in prayer. If your group struggles to end on time, the group leader should feel the freedom to say, "We have time for two more prayers before we close."

Technology has enabled churches and other organizations to distribute prayer requests faster and invite a larger sphere to join in prayer more often. These tech tools are often praised for bringing a church closer together, but have raised some security and privacy concerns.

How to Pray with Determination during Suffering or Persecution

Even those who know little about the Bible are often familiar with the story of Job, the man whose faith was tested after he lost his entire family and all his possessions. Not surprisingly, Job's name has become synonymous with suffering. Far fewer people are familiar with the story of David and Nancy Guthrie, although their story was compelling enough to warrant coverage by several major news outlets. To many who know what happened to the Guthries, their name has become synonymous with modern-day suffering.

The chances that the Guthries would suffer as they did are actually measurable. Zellweger syndrome is a disorder for which there is no treatment or cure. David and Nancy both carry a recessive gene for Zellweger syndrome, and the odds of that are one in a hundred thousand. They learned that they both had it a few days after the birth of their second child, Hope. Just over six months later, Hope died. David got a vasectomy; Nancy conceived anyway, a one-in-two-thousand probability. This baby was also born with Zellweger's. Gabriel lived just under six months.

> *Blessed are those who are persecuted because of righteousness, for theirs is the kingdom of heaven. Blessed are you when people insult you, persecute you and falsely say all kinds of evil against you because of me. Rejoice and be glad, because great is your reward in heaven, for in the same way they persecuted the prophets who were before you.*
>
> MATTHEW 5:10–12 NIV

Suffering Serves a Purpose

At one time, people might have believed the Guthries were being punished for their sins. Most Christians today agree that suffering serves a purpose. That purpose may not be known this side of heaven, however, and bearing up under the weight of agonizing pain—physical, emotional, mental, spiritual—requires more than the promise of an unknown purpose.

Suffering Christians through the centuries have found comfort by viewing their pain in light of the cross—a symbol of suffering that led to a resurrected life. By sharing in the suffering of Christ, their pain became a pathway to a new life.

Contrary to conventional wisdom, the Bible frequently points out the benefits and rewards for those who endure suffering and persecution, particularly those who suffer for their faith.

🍃 Final Thought

There is another example of suffering for a purpose: Jesus. He suffered and died on the cross for the ultimate purpose to restore life everlasting. Jesus bore our sins and endured great suffering out of love for each of us. He continues to walk with us in our darkest hour. He is the light to see us through.

How to Pray with Power while Wrestling with Temptation

Throughout history, groups of Christians have separated themselves from the mainstream—even from other followers of Christ—in an attempt to avoid temptation. But their efforts have always proven to be misguided, because their objective was misguided. Can anyone avoid temptation altogether? No. That's where separatist groups get it wrong. Everyone, however, can avoid situations that are likely to prove tempting. And everyone can resist giving in to temptation by drawing on God's power. The Bible is so frank about the prevalence of temptation that the message comes through loud and clear: expect to be tempted.

People may try to flee worldly enticements, but they always have with them a primary source of temptation: themselves. James 1:14–15 minces no words about that, especially in this paraphrase: "The temptation to give in to evil comes from us and only us. We have no one to blame but the leering, seducing flare-up of our own lust. Lust gets pregnant, and has a baby: sin! Sin grows up to adulthood, and becomes a real killer" (MSG).

You are tempted in the same way that everyone else is tempted. But God can be trusted not to let you be tempted too much, and he will show you how to escape from your temptations.

1 CORINTHIANS 10:13 CEV

Since we have a great high priest who has passed through the heavens—Jesus the Son of God—let us hold fast to the confession. For we do not have a high priest who is unable to sympathize with our weaknesses, but One who has been tested in every way as we are, yet without sin.

HEBREWS 4:14–15 HCSB

More Than One Kind of Temptation

That's how author Eugene Peterson interpreted the words of James. But don't let that lust-related imagery fool you into thinking sexual temptation is the only kind there is.

Think of the temptations you could face in a single day: gossiping about that new couple at church or spending money you don't have on a suit you don't need or getting back at your spouse by shutting him or her out. Those and other seemingly innocuous situations start with the urge to do something you know you shouldn't.

God Always Provides an Escape

Can you see how prevalent temptation is? Try shutting yourself off from all outside influences for just a few hours—and notice how many temptations surface during that time. But there's good news. God always provides an escape (1 Corinthians 10:13). Friends can steer you away from the temptation, or a Bible verse can give you the strength to resist. As you wrestle with temptation, show God that you are willing to take His way out—and trust Him to reveal that escape route to you.

 Final Thought

Here are five steps to help you resist temptation:
- *Acknowledge the temptation to God, yourself, and a confidant.*
- *Run from the situation. If you're tempted to overeat, leave the kitchen.*
- *Call to mind appropriate Bible passages (such as the "armor of God" verses in Ephesians 6:10–18).*
- *Praise God. Turning toward God diverts your attention from harmful things that entice you.*
- *Thank God immediately for helping you overcome the temptation.*

Mental health professionals consider the loss of a job to be a major life crisis on a par with the death of a loved one. Why? Because the stages of grief that accompany a job loss are identical to those that accompany the death of a close relative or friend: denial, anger, bargaining, depression, and, eventually, acceptance. Job loss carries with it several additional complications, such as feelings of shame, embarrassment, loss of identity, and loss of self-worth. Despite such a grim diagnosis of the problem, sudden unemployment is not a hopeless situation.

This Can Happen

Whether you've been downsized, laid off, or fired, the sudden loss of a job leaves you reeling. Even if you heard rumblings that you might lose your job, when you actually get the word, it feels like a sucker punch. *This isn't happening,* you immediately think. *No. This isn't possible. This can't happen to me.*

When it does happen, your world is turned upside down. It will take time to get it turned right side up, but the sooner you turn to God in prayer, the sooner the journey through job loss will begin to go more smoothly. That's partly because prayer is proof positive that you are still in a relationship with God—even if you don't understand how he could let this happen to you.

> *God is our refuge and strength, an ever-present help in trouble. Therefore we will not fear, though the earth give way and the mountains fall into the heart of the sea, though its waters roar and foam and the mountains quake with their surging.*
>
> PSALM 46:1–3 NIV
>
> *The LORD gives perfect peace to those whose faith is firm. So always trust the LORD because he is forever our mighty rock.*
>
> ISAIAH 26:3–4 CEV

Brand-New Opportunities

Maintaining that relationship offers the best chance you have of finding needed direction and peace to think clearly about what to do next. Losing your job may open up brand-new opportunities; trusting God enables you to calmly sort out your options and make decisions based on the wisdom He gives you.

No matter what, surviving unemployment requires tenacity, perseverance, and energy, all of which are easy to lose when your job pursuit fails to yield any real opportunities. Discouragement can quickly set in. But David, who knew a thing or two about discouragement, was able to attest to the fact that the Lord "gives His people strength; the LORD blesses His people with peace" (Psalm 29:11 HCSB).

Something to Ponder

Westerners in particular often link their identities with the work they do. When they lose that work, they run the risk of losing their identities as well. Think about how closely your sense of identity is tied to the work you do, whether you have a traditional job, own a business, or work in the home. Who are you without your work?

 Final Thought

Here are some suggestions for surviving job loss in a healthy way:
- *Find a prayer and accountability partner who will come alongside and help you through this.*
- *Volunteer, which may or may not lead to a job, but either way, volunteering will keep you active and focused on others.*
- *Realize that seeking work is harder than working. Have fun in the process.*

How to Pray with Insight about Time Management

Sometimes it's downright baffling. The people who seem to have the fullest lives also seem to have the most time for activities like volunteering, socializing, and even taking a course or two for personal enrichment. How can that be? You imagine all sorts of things about their lives behind the scenes: they must have full-time assistants, housekeeping services, personal chefs, and live-in nannies, at the very least. Then you discover they don't have a staff attending to their everyday needs. So what gives? What's their secret? It turns out that what they have is no secret at all.

Mention time-management techniques to some people, and their eyes glaze over. They feel they've heard it all before, and they don't believe any technique will work for them. You've probably heard it all as well: Write everything down. Prioritize. Limit commitments. Reduce large projects to manageable chunks. Avoid time-wasters like TV and long phone calls. Set deadlines. Just say no.

> *Come now, you who say, "Today or tomorrow we will travel to such and such a city and spend a year there and do business and make a profit." You don't even know what tomorrow will bring—what your life will be!*
>
> JAMES 4:13–14 HCSB

> *There is an occasion for everything, and a time for every activity under heaven: a time to give birth and a time to die; a time to plant and a time to uproot.*
>
> ECCLESIASTES 3:1–2 HCSB

Gaining Control of Time

Those and other practical time-management suggestions are important. But gaining control of your time is as much a spiritual activity as it is a practical one. It's a matter of the heart as well as the mind. "We have time and prayer backward," wrote Christian author and philosophy professor Peter Kreeft. "We think our lack of time is the cause of our lack of prayer, but our lack of prayer is the cause of our lack of time."

Giving God Your Time

When he gives God his time, Kreeft said, he miraculously seems to have more of it: "I have no idea *how* he does it; I know *that* he does it, time after time." He compared this phenomenon to the miracle of the loaves and fishes, when Jesus took a meager offering of food, blessed it, and fed more than five thousand people with it (Matthew 14:15–21). Kreeft believes Jesus multiplies his time in much the same way.

You don't need a staff of assistants to manage your time; you need the assistance of the one who created time. Give God your time in prayer, and watch how He increases it.

Digging Deeper

Delegating responsibility as a time-management technique is found in the Bible. When Jethro saw how much time Moses was spending settling disputes, he advised his son-in-law to appoint judges to assist him (Exodus 18). Jesus gave the twelve disciples the authority to minister in His place (Mark 6). In Acts 6, the apostles appointed others to serve the needs of the Christians in Jerusalem so they could spend more time in prayer and preaching.

🌿 Final Thought

Is your life all work and no pray? Consider Martin Luther's daily routine. While Luther was busy reforming the church, translating the Greek Bible into German, and dodging assaults by church leaders, he also spent time in prayer: "I generally pray two hours every day, except on very busy days. On those days, I pray three," he wrote. The more he prayed, the more productive those busy days were.

How to Pray with Endurance
while Raising Children

Imagine being notified that you will be required to run a marathon, a feat for which you have had no training. Actually, you would be required to run more than a marathon, much more—and its length would be measured in decades, not mere miles. There is one primary rule: no fair dropping out. That's what parenting is like, isn't it? Sure, you can try to train—caring for other people's children, reading everything in sight about parenting, absorbing the wise counsel of experienced parents. But all that pales in comparison to having your own children. For this leg of life's journey, you need endurance.

Parenting—The Hardest Work

If you ask people from all walks of life what is the hardest work they have ever done, the men and women in the group who have reared children will answer without hesitation: parenting. That's partly because it's a 24/7 job. Your children are never far from your thoughts, even when you're not physically with them, and there is tremendous responsibility involved.

There's much work to do in caring for children, many needs to anticipate, many dangers to be concerned about. And all of this is on many levels—physical, mental, emotional, and spiritual. And then there's your spouse, your friends, your coworkers or your staff, and your extended family, all of whom need you to some degree. Whew! Parenting is much more challenging than a simple marathon.

Since we are surrounded by such a huge crowd of witnesses to the life of faith, let us strip off every weight that slows us down, especially the sin that so easily trips us up. And let us run with endurance the race God has set before us.

HEBREWS 12:1 NLT

Patient endurance is what you need now, so that you will continue to do God's will. Then you will receive all that he has promised.

HEBREWS 10:36 NLT

Learn to Pace Yourself

How will you ever make it? You need to do what every long-distance runner learns early on: you need to pace yourself.

Even for experienced runners, that's tough to do in the beginning. Runners see their competition getting way out in front; as a brand-new parent, you see a helpless infant with a seemingly endless string of needs. Slow down? No way! Cut yourself some slack. This phase will feel more like a sprint, and that's to be expected. You're doing everything for the first time.

But as your firstborn outgrows the need for your constant attention, and as more children come along, the long haul begins. This is when you need to start pacing yourself so you can run the parenting race with endurance.

Take a Break and Breathe

First, take a break and breathe—prayerfully. Praise God for the joy your children have brought into your life. Thank Him for the work He is doing in the lives of your children and for bringing you through this initial stage of parenting.

Then remind yourself that this is not a competitive race. There's no point in competing to come in first. There's no point in competing against other parents. And there's no point in anticipating the finish line, because there isn't one. You will always be a parent.

Even though the culture may tell you—sometimes jokingly, sometimes not—your parenting duties are over when your child turns eighteen, you will continue to be on call as a parent for the rest of your life. Your active parenting days will subside, unless you have a special-needs child, but as a loving parent, you will always be available to your adult children.

Pray with Endurance

That means you not only have to pray for endurance; you also have to pray with endurance; you have to pray for the stamina to continue praying! It means praying during the good times as well as the bad, during the so-so times as well as the exciting times, and on the days when you don't feel like praying, when you don't feel as if God is listening, when you're not sure that your prayers are doing any good at all.

Keep this in mind: even when you're praying for your own endurance—the strength to continue, the energy to keep going—in a sense you're also praying for your children. A parent who feels like giving up is a testy, edgy, cranky parent who is likely to take his or her fatigue out on his children.

Pray that you will be the best parent you can possibly be—but only in God's power. If you try to do this on your own, everyone will suffer. Focus on the joy and on the specialness of every day. Give your children whatever you can, whenever you can, and however you can, but pace yourself in the process. They will need you all along the journey; make sure you'll be there for them.

> *Parents, don't be hard on your children. Raise them properly. Teach them and instruct them about the Lord.*
>
> EPHESIANS 6:4 CEV

Points to Remember

- You're in this for the long haul; pace yourself.
- This is not a competition, nor is there a finish line.
- Focus on the joy your children have brought to your life.
- Don't try to be a good parent in your own power; rely on God to give you strength.
- Pray with endurance as well as for endurance.
- Give your fatigue to God so you don't take it out on your children.

Check Your Understanding

- **Why is parenting so difficult and so overwhelming—even when you tried to prepare for it?**

  Parenting is a job that never stops; you're either meeting your children's immediate needs or anticipating the next round. There are some situations involved in parenting that you can't prepare for.

- **Does it ever get easier?**

  Yes—as long as you pace yourself. You may feel as if you're running a fifty-yard dash when your first child is born, but then you settle down into an endurance race.

- **Won't it get even easier when they're adults?**

  The everydayness of parenting will be over, but they will still need you. Your love and concern for them won't diminish. And you never know—they may end up moving back home, bringing with them an entirely different set of challenges!

 Final Thought

Every family dynamic is different. Parenting techniques that work for one family may not work for yours. But there is one sure thing when it comes to being a parent—the wisdom you can glean from the Bible. Keep it close by and read it daily. In addition to its direct advice to parents, it has a great deal to say about relationships in general.

Only those who are also infertile can fully understand the pain and heartbreak of a couple unable to conceive. The desire for a child is unlike any other. You want a child that your love has produced, a girl or boy who carries not just your DNA but so much more—the essence of who you are as a couple, two people united as one. Although nearly 20 percent of all couples experience infertility at least temporarily, some infertile couples suffer from an acute, indescribable loneliness. Their yearning for a child consumes their lives.

If the desire for children is consuming your life, you've probably had well-meaning friends, relatives, and acquaintances offer advice on how to improve your chances of conceiving. But none of that advice helps you endure the emotional roller coaster you experience month after month.

> *The LORD is close to the brokenhearted; he rescues those whose spirits are crushed.*
>
> PSALM 34:18 NLT

> *The LORD'S kindness never fails! If he had not been merciful, we would have been destroyed. The LORD can always be trusted to show mercy each morning. Deep in my heart I say, "The LORD is all I need; I can depend on him!" The LORD is kind to everyone who trusts and obeys him. It is good to wait patiently for the LORD to save us.*
>
> LAMENTATIONS 3:22–26 CEV

Pray to Strengthen Faith

Infertile Christian couples across the country have a different kind of advice for you— suggestions about how to pray to strengthen your faith in God and your relationship as a couple, as well as how to maintain your sanity. Here are some ways of praying that have helped other childless couples:

- Be honest with God about your anger, disappointment, and doubts.
- Ask for contentment with your family of two.
- Thank God for His blessings on your life.
- Ask for compassion for struggling parents and joy for new parents.
- Seek God's purpose for your life and ways to serve Him and others.

Will praying in this way erase the pain? Perhaps not, but it will likely ease the pain. And one day, despite the pain, you'll be able to utter these words with complete conviction: "Though the fig tree should not blossom and there be no fruit on the vines, *though the yield of the olive* should fail and the fields produce no food, though the flock should be cut off from the fold and there be no cattle in the stalls, yet I will exult in the LORD, I will rejoice in the God of my salvation" (Habakkuk 3:17–18 NASB).

 Final Thought

Most of the women in the Bible who had trouble conceiving eventually gave birth. That can make you either hopeful or discouraged, depending on your perspective. But reading about their experiences—the level of their trust in God, the way they handled their infertility—may give you insight into your own situation.

How to Pray with Confidence concerning Military Service

In times of economic downturn, one segment of society sees a dramatic upturn of interest in its work: the military. And why not? Military service offers a steady paycheck, great training, and enviable benefits. When little other work is available, the advantages of joining the military outweigh the dangers. But military service is much more than a smart career choice. The decision to serve your country in the armed forces is not one to be taken lightly. It requires a sense of mission and patriotism, a thorough understanding of what you may be ordered to do, and clear direction from God.

Since 1973, the United States has had an all-volunteer military. Before that, young men were required to serve unless they had a legitimate reason not to. Today, young men and women alike can choose to serve, with many seeing the military as a viable option to college—or unemployment.

> *The LORD will protect you and keep you safe*
> *from all dangers. The LORD will protect you now*
> *and always wherever you go.*
>
> PSALM 121:7–8 CEV

> *You are my hiding place; You protect me from trouble.*
> *You surround me with joyful shouts of deliverance.*
>
> PSALM 32:7 HCSB

Pray about Your Decision to Serve

But a military career is service to your country rather than just another job. It's important to pray about your decision to serve. Military service may place you in dangerous situations where military leadership is recognized as the final authority.

That's a necessary component of military life. A commanding officer must have unquestioned authority. Without it, the unit would be disorganized and be ill-prepared to act. In the service, you will face difficult situations requiring your automatic and complete obedience.

How should you pray? First, be sure this is God's will for your life and not a default decision. Military service can be an honorable, rewarding career, but it's also a mission. Is the military's mission compatible with God's mission, that of defending the powerless from their enemies? If you answer yes but have misgivings, make your concerns known at the outset. Every branch of the armed forces offers opportunities to serve in ways that honor your religious beliefs. Then begin your service with enthusiasm and energy, giving it your all.

 Final Thought

You can't read very far in the Bible without coming across passages that offer assurance that God will provide safety and security and save His people from their enemies. Knowing the Scripture verses that help you in your time of military service can be a reassuring guide. Read and reflect on the following:

- *Psalm 31:15—My life is in your hands. Save me from enemies who hunt me down (CEV).*
- *Psalm 32:7—You are my hiding place; You protect me from trouble. You surround me with joyful shouts of deliverance (HCSB).*
- *Psalm 32:8—I will guide you along the best pathway for your life. I will advise you and watch over you (NLT).*
- *Psalm 33:20—We wait for Yahweh; He is our help and shield (HCSB).*

How to Pray with Focus when Starting a New Job

So—you've landed a new job. How exciting! A fresh start, a different environment, all new coworkers…everything strange and unfamiliar. Maybe it's not so exciting after all. A new opportunity carries with it some old fears and some nagging questions. How steep is the learning curve? Are you up to the challenge? Will your future colleagues like you? Will you fit in? Those answers will come in time. Right now, your job is to focus on the most important question: What does God want you to accomplish in your new position?

Be Confident in Your Purpose

You may never know why God has placed you in this new job. But if you are confident God provided the job, you can also be confident that there's a purpose for your being there. That's a good place to start—asking God to accomplish His will through you at your new place of employment.

But you still have many practical concerns and questions. It's normal to feel apprehensive before your first day in a new job. The more detailed your prayers, the less anxious you're likely to feel when that day comes.

Here are some ideas to get you started:

- Thank God for the opportunity.
- Pray God's blessing on your new colleagues.
- Trust God to give you wisdom regarding every aspect of your job.
- Ask God for patience as you seek to understand the company before suggesting changes.
- Call upon God to help you be the best employee (or boss) you can possibly be.
- Pray that God will give you a true servant's heart and attitude in the workplace.
- Give God your fears, worries, and misgivings about your ability to perform the work that's ahead of you.

> *Pay careful attention to your own work, for then you will get the satisfaction of a job well done, and you won't need to compare yourself to anyone else.*
>
> GALATIANS 6:4 NLT

> *Whatever you do, do your work heartily, as for the Lord rather than for men.*
>
> COLOSSIANS 3:23 NASB

Pray in Detail

Pray in detail about your specific job; if you are a health-care professional, for example, ask God for compassion for the patients you'll be treating.

Finally, don't forget about the joy, the excitement, and the positive challenges you'll experience. Thank God in advance for all the good things to come—including that first paycheck.

Final Thought

- *God has a purpose in placing you in this new position.*
- *Your many questions about your new workplace will be answered in time; let go of them for now.*
- *Feeling nervous about starting a new job is normal.*
- *Praying about specific concerns will help alleviate your apprehension.*
- *It's OK to enjoy this new experience; allow yourself to feel joyful and excited!*

How to Pray with Expectation when Getting Married

Engaged couples who are head over heels in love may read all the right books on marriage, go for extensive premarital counseling, and listen to lots of advice from those who are—or have been—married, but seldom does all that prepare them for the reality of married life. One reason is that marriage has to be experienced and not just talked about. Another reason is this: those head-over-heels-in-love couples secretly believe that they're different. No one can possibly understand their love; others just don't get it. But their marriage will set a new standard for marital bliss and success.

If your expectation is for yours to be a groundbreaking marriage, that would be a great concept to start praying about. You probably also have a different and larger set of expectations. It's time to start talking to God about those as well.

Wives, understand and support your husbands in ways that show your support for Christ.

EPHESIANS 5:22 MSG

A World of Two or Three

Couples often believe that all they need is each other, and that's understandable. When you first fall in love, the universe shrinks down to a world of two—or three, if you are both Christians and include God in your world. Ask God to show you how you can keep your marriage free of an unhealthy dependence on each other as your friends and coworkers gradually resume their importance in your lives.

Husbands, go all out in your love for your wives, exactly as Christ did for the church— a love marked by giving, not getting.

EPHESIANS 5:25 MSG

Since money can cause the biggest problems in a marriage, ask God to help you and your future spouse work out some ground rules now. If one of you is a saver and the other a spender, you need to come to a consensus about your financial expectations before the wedding.

Be Prepared to Fight for Your Spouse's Faith

Right now your future partner may have a seemingly unshakable faith in God, and you can't imagine your spouse walking away from God. But it happens. Begin praying that both of you will cling to God throughout your marriage, ramp up that prayer at the first hint of a problem, and be prepared to fight for your spouse's faith with everything you have.

List all your other expectations for your marriage, and pray about each one—now, before the wedding takes place.

Something to Ponder

Ephesians 5 contains several verses telling wives and husbands how they should relate to each other. Take a look at the married couples in your sphere of close relationships. Would their marriages be different if they took these verses to heart? Then set the same standard for your own upcoming marriage. How can you apply the appropriate verse to your role in the relationship?

 Final Thought

One of the greatest evidences of genuine love is wanting the best for the other person. Sometimes what is best for your spouse will be at odds with your desires, expectations, and what you think is best for you. That's when you'll come to an understanding of just how difficult sacrificial love can be. Make the sacrifice out of a loving commitment to your mate, and see what God has in store for you.

How to Pray with Excitement when Graduating

As you approach graduation, you've likely been inundated with motivational messages that can be summed up in one word: possibilities. The possibilities that lie before you are endless. You can be anything you want to be. There's no limit to all you can accomplish as you begin this next stage of your life's journey. It all sounds so exciting—and so frightening. Stepping out into a world of new responsibilities and challenges can instill as much fear as enthusiasm. What many motivational messages omit, however, is the one word that can dispel that fear—Jesus.

"Go Out and Train Everyone"

After the resurrection, the disciples came together in the presence of their resurrected Lord. Some worshipped Him without hesitation, but others held back. That didn't faze Jesus: "Jesus, undeterred, went right ahead and gave his charge: 'God authorized and commanded me to commission you: Go out and train everyone you meet, far and near, in this way of life, marking them by baptism in the threefold name: Father, Son, and Holy Spirit. Then instruct them in the practice of all I have commanded you. I'll be with you as you do this, day after day after day, right up to the end of the age'" (Matthew 28:18–20 MSG).

This is known as the commissioning of the disciples. Jesus sent them out in His power to do God's will. While their mission may have differed from yours, the final words of that passage apply to your "commission" upon graduating: Jesus will be with you as you enter this new world, every day for the rest of your life.

> *Don't let anyone think less of you because you are young.*
> *Be an example to all believers in what you say, in the way*
> *you live, in your love, your faith, and your purity.*
>
> 1 TIMOTHY 4:12 NLT

> *Be strong and courageous. Do not be afraid; do not be discouraged, for the LORD your God will be with you wherever you go.*
>
> JOSHUA 1:9 NIV

Charge to Transform Lives

Notice this as well: Jesus did not commission the disciples to go out and be all that they could be. His charge to you isn't about how you can succeed; rather, it is about how you can help transform lives. The world's motivational message is all about you. Jesus's words are all about serving others.

No matter what field you enter after graduation, you will be in a position to change the lives of others. What could be more exciting than that?

Myth Buster

"You can be anything you want to be." Those are high-sounding words that many a commencement speaker has uttered. But they simply aren't true. God gives each person certain talents and strengths, and when people use their gifts to their fullest, everyone benefits. You can be any number of things, but you will be most fulfilled when you do whatever it is that God created you to do. And that's no myth.

 Final Thought

Do you want success? Meditate on this: "God blesses those people who refuse evil advice and won't follow sinners or join in sneering at God. Instead, the Law of the LORD makes them happy, and they think about it day and night. They are like trees growing beside a stream, trees that produce fruit in season and always have leaves. Those people succeed in everything they do" (Psalm 1:1–3 CEV).

How to Pray in Sympathy when Someone Has Died

At some point in your life, you may have been on the receiving end of condolences when a loved one died. What do you remember about the expressions of sympathy you received? Most likely, the ones you recall fall into one of two categories: unbelievably insensitive or incredibly helpful. What does that tell you about the best way to show your sympathy when a friend or acquaintance is grieving? For one thing, it tells you that being incredibly helpful has a lasting positive effect on the one in mourning.

Many people are at a loss when it comes to expressing their condolences when someone they know has lost a loved one. They're so afraid of saying the wrong thing that they end up doing just that. "I know just how you feel," a neighbor may say to a woman who just lost her mother. "My cat died last month." That kind of comment is memorable, but only for being entirely inappropriate.

For Christians, the standard sympathetic comment is this: "I'll be praying for you." There's nothing wrong with that on the surface; mourners often appreciate knowing others are praying for them, and it helps smooth over the awkwardness of the situation.

But what if you want to go deeper than the surface? What would your prayer sound like then?

> *Rejoice with those who rejoice, and weep with those who weep.*
>
> ROMANS 12:15 NKJV

> *Bear one another's burdens, and so fulfill the law of Christ.*
>
> GALATIANS 6:2 NKJV

Add God-Acts to God-Talk

Here is a good place to start. For a different kind of prayer, look to the book of James: "Dear friends, do you think you'll get anywhere in this if you learn all the right words but never do anything? Does merely talking about faith indicate that a person really has it? For instance, you come upon an old friend dressed in rags and half-starved and say, 'Good morning, friend! Be clothed in Christ! Be filled with the Holy Spirit!' and walk off without providing so much as a coat or a cup of soup—where does that get you? Isn't it obvious that God-talk without God-acts is outrageous nonsense?" (2:14–17 MSG). Place that in the context of grief, and ask God how you can add some God-acts to your God-talk.

People experiencing grief often have many practical needs, but they can be so focused on their loss that they find it impossible to articulate those needs. Telling your friend something along the lines of "Let me know how I can help" may sound like the right thing to say, but it places the burden on the mourner to think clearly and try to remember what needs to be done. But when you utter those same words to God, they become a prayer that results in God-talk in action.

Offer Practical Help without Being Intrusive

John 11 tells of people coming from all around Jerusalem to comfort Mary and Martha when they learned of their brother's death. That way of expressing sympathy hasn't changed in two thousand years; friends, neighbors, and acquaintances want to do something, which often means bringing the grieving person a casserole to eliminate the need to cook. But it also means that mourners often find themselves overwhelmed with company. As you're praying that God will comfort your friend, pray also that God will show you how you can provide practical help without being intrusive. That could mean cleaning her house while she's at the funeral home making arrangements, but it could also mean forgetting about the house and going to the funeral home with her.

Throughout this time of mourning, continue praying in the same way. If you've lost a loved one, you know how lonely you can feel weeks and months later, when the cards and company have stopped arriving. Seek God's wisdom on how you can continue to serve and help the one who is still in mourning long after the other people in his life have become busy with their own lives. God may choose to use you to show his continued love and compassion toward your grieving friend.

> *Many people had come from the city to comfort Martha and Mary because their brother had died.*
>
> JOHN 11:19 CEV

Walk Alongside Your Friend

Most of all, your friend will need someone who is willing to "come alongside" and quietly walk with her on the difficult path of mourning. Pray that God will give you that willingness, along with His wisdom and the right words of comfort at the right time, so you can be a true representative of Christ in her life.

Something to Ponder

Not everyone feels comfortable being prayed for by others. Someone who is grieving a loss will seldom be able to say no when asked if it's OK to pray with him. If you sense that the person would prefer that you not pray, remember that there's nothing wrong with simply sitting with her and praying silently. God will still hear your prayer.

 ## Check Your Understanding

- **What's wrong with saying, "I know just how you feel"?**

  Everything. Each person's grief is intensely personal, and each person's relationship with the one who died is unique. Even if your losses are similar—her mother just died, and yours died recently—you can't possibly know just how she feels.

- **What's wrong with saying, "I'll be praying for you"?**

  Nothing. It is something of a default comment, though, and it's much more helpful when you customize your prayers specifically to the person's needs.

- **What's wrong with saying, "Let me know how I can help"?**

  It's an open-ended offer that forces a grieving person to divert his thinking in a whole different direction. It's much better for you to do the thinking for him by asking God how you can help and then going to the person with specific, practical suggestions.

 ## Final Thought

In years past, it was a common practice for people to write a note or a letter to a person in mourning. As greeting cards became commonplace, that practice fell by the wayside. In today's culture of emails and instant messaging, receiving a handwritten letter is a memorable occurrence. Consider reviving that practice. Your friend will no doubt appreciate a condolence letter that recounts fond memories of the one who has died.

How to Pray when You Are Afraid

Terrorist attacks. Terminal illnesses. Plane crashes, car crashes, stock market crashes. Things that go bump in the night. And landing in the number-one spot on many polls, public speaking. There seems to be no limit to things people fear. Throughout the Bible, God told His people to not be afraid. How can you not be afraid when terrible things happen every day? The nightly news and personal experience confirm that. Is there some secret formula for making fear disappear?

Controlling Your Fears

Your fears may never disappear entirely, but you can learn to control them instead of allowing them to control you. God's formula for letting go of fear is no secret, though. It's written on page after page in the Bible, in passages as clear and direct as this one: "Do not fear, for I am with you; do not be dismayed, for I am your God. I will strengthen you and help you; I will uphold you with my righteous right hand....For I am the LORD your God who takes hold of your right hand and says to you, Do not fear; I will help you" (Isaiah 41:10, 13 NIV).

Look closely at those verses. Stop and meditate on the precise language God used: God is with you. He is your God. He will make you strong. He will come to your aid, grasping your right hand and keeping you standing with his own right hand—His righteous right hand. And He will tell you, directly and in no uncertain terms, not to be afraid. He will help you.

The LORD is my light and my salvation; whom shall I fear?
The LORD is the strength of my life; of whom shall I be afraid?

PSALM 27:1 NKJV

What then? I will pray with the spirit, and I will also pray
with my understanding. I will sing with the spirit, and I will
also sing with my understanding.

1 CORINTHIANS 14:15 HCSB

Weapons in Your Spiritual Arsenal

Those are more than words of comfort. Countless Christians can attest to the very real presence of God in the face of unspeakable horror as well as everyday fears. When fear threatens to overwhelm you, pull out two of the most powerful weapons in your spiritual arsenal—the Bible and prayer—and fight fear head-on. You may find yourself above it, no longer cowering under its tyranny.

Something to Ponder

How you answer these questions may help you better understand your relationship with fear: What are you really afraid of? Is this a legitimate or an irrational fear? Do you believe God will see you through this, regardless of the outcome? Have you prayed to the point of experiencing genuine peace? Why do you think God has allowed this fear-inducing situation to continue? How has your fear helped the situation?

 Final Thought

Remember that fear can be beneficial, warning you of real dangers—but God's admonition to not be afraid still applies. Violent-crime survivors often describe feeling fear immediately before an attack, as do would-be victims who responded to fear and escaped unharmed. The key is acting on the warning rather than remaining afraid. Discerning the difference between legitimate and irrational fear requires spiritual vigilance—a continual alertness to God's direction.

Another driver cuts you off in rush-hour traffic, a coworker sabotages your chance to get the recognition you deserve, the city increases your property tax by 20 percent, your daughter manages once again to leave the house without cleaning her room—and that's all in one day. It's enough to make anyone see red. Before you vent your anger inappropriately—giving in to road rage, undermining your colleague, calling the mayor at home at 3:00 a.m., grounding your firstborn for the rest of her life—stop a minute and think. Think about how God wants you to respond.

The Bible frequently addresses the problem of anger. In some cases, the anger is justified, as when Jesus overturned the tables of the temple moneychangers (Matthew 21:12–13). But when the Bible addresses the problem of not-so-righteous anger, it's clear that such anger needs to be dealt with.

> *Stop being angry! Turn from your rage! Do not lose your temper—it only leads to harm. For the wicked will be destroyed, but those who trust in the LORD will possess the land.*
>
> PSALM 37:8–9 NLT

> *My dearly loved brothers, understand this: Everyone must be quick to hear, slow to speak, and slow to anger, for man's anger does not accomplish God's righteousness.*
>
> JAMES 1:19–20 HCSB

Not-So-Righteous Anger

The ideal method is to ask God to calm you down, resolve the problem that caused your rage, and restore relationships that were damaged in the heat of your anger. All that can come to pass, but it often doesn't. Thankfully, God has provided a way for you to release your anger when your thoughts are so clouded you can't pray as you normally would and you feel as if your fury is eating you up inside.

The way He has provided is found in the Psalms.

Right there, amid lovely passages about green pastures and still waters, you'll find psalms in which the writers lashed out in anger. Christians through the centuries have found value in venting their feelings by praying these "angry psalms" (Psalm 7, 13, and 55, for example) back to God. Instead of verbally attacking the people who angered them, they expressed themselves honestly to someone who already knew how they felt.

 Final Thought

Some of the Psalms are challenging to modern sensibilities; use discernment in deciding which to pray. In most cases, the psalmist's anger eventually dissipates, and he places his trust in God—not a bad way for an angry prayer to end.

Many people have found it helpful to ward off anger by learning and practicing ways to control their emotions in advance. Look to God for ways to handle your own anger. And like the psalmist, trust in His ability to help you through each situation.

How to Pray when You Are Depressed

Depression is a serious, paralyzing disorder so complex that the medical community continues to learn more about it, thousands of years after it was first described in ancient writings. But one thing they learned long ago is this: no one is immune to depression, and that includes Christians. If you are suffering from depression, you know how crippling it is. You're vaguely aware that help is available, but you can't take the first step toward getting help. God seems so far away that you doubt He could hear your prayers, if you could even find the will to pray them.

Frustrating Aspects of Depression

One of the most frustrating aspects of depression is the fact that the steps depressives can take to get better are the very things they find impossible: changing their thought patterns, seeking medical attention, enlisting the support of family and friends, establishing healthy routines—and praying. Medical professionals recognize the power of prayer to help overcome the debilitating effects of depression, even if the depressed patient isn't the one praying; the prayers of the patient's circle of relationships can have a profound effect on her recovery.

Still, for any treatment to be fully effective, the depressed person—you—must be actively involved. So how do you take that first step? Take a cue from some prominent figures in Israel's history—David, Elijah, and Jeremiah, among others.

All three suffered from depression, but their means of dealing with it may be a lesson to twenty-first-century believers. They didn't deny it; they acknowledged it and at times lashed out at God in the midst of their pain. That may not seem very nice, but their railing at God was an honest expression of prayer.

> *I am convinced that neither death, nor life, nor angels, nor principalities, nor things present, nor things to come, nor powers, nor height, nor depth, nor any other created thing, will be able to separate us from the love of God, which is in Christ Jesus our Lord.*
>
> ROMANS 8:38–39 NASB

Tell God about Your Suffering

Are you suffering? Tell God all about it. He already knows, but He's waiting to hear from you; He wants a restored relationship with you so your healing can begin. Venting your anger, your pain, your hopelessness, your despair may not seem like praying, but it may be one of the most important prayers you will ever utter.

> *The LORD is my rock, my fortress and my deliverer; my God is my rock, in whom I take refuge.*
>
> PSALM 18:2 NIV

Something to Ponder

Author Sheila Walsh once said of her period of severe depression, "I never knew God lived so close to the floor." Lying on the floor in a mental-health facility and discovering that God was right there with her helped reverse the downward progression of the disorder for her. Wherever depression has led you—isolated, unable to leave the house, unable to relate to anyone—imagine that God is right there with you, because He is.

 Final Thought

You may think that no one at church will understand. Christians are half as likely to become depressed as the general population, but that means it is likely that some in your own faith community have had firsthand experience with depression and will understand. Some Christians believe that taking antidepressants shows a lack of faith. Taking medication, however, shows you have faith that God has revealed to medical researchers the ideal chemical balance the brain needs to function properly.

Doubt is a vexing problem for many Christians. They wonder how they can be true Christians if they have doubts, so they resist seeking the counsel of more mature Christians. They wonder what their pastors would think of them. And they wonder if their friends would brand them as "nonbelievers." From Abraham and Peter to Billy Graham and Mother Teresa, stalwarts of the faith have expressed doubt. Some, like Abraham, had their doubts erased after witnessing a genuine miracle. Others found their faith restored by tenaciously pursuing the answers to their questions. They discovered that doubt strengthened their faith.

An Astonishing Secret

Ten years after Mother Teresa's 1997 death, the world learned an astonishing secret about her. This loving, compassionate nun who had devoted her life to the poorest of the poor experienced such intense spiritual pain that she doubted the existence of God and heaven throughout the latter years of her ministry. So shocking was this revelation that it made headlines around the world; major news services, networks, and newsmagazines gave the story prominent play, a rarity for news about a religious figure.

Meanwhile, many Christians around the world breathed a nearly audible sigh of relief. After years or decades of harboring their own doubts about God, they learned they were neither inferior nor alone. In her private correspondence, Mother Teresa, one of the most admired personalities of the twentieth century, admitted to experiencing a great "silence and emptiness"; her letters exposed the interior life of a believer in crisis who confessed that spiritual dryness, darkness, loneliness, and torture characterized her days.

Jesus said..., "If you can believe, all things are possible to him who believes." Immediately the father of the child cried out and said with tears, "Lord, I believe; help my unbelief!"

MARK 9:23–24 NKJV

The Nature of Religious Doubt

In the wake of these revelations, prominent Christian leaders weighed in on the nature of religious doubt. What emerged from this public discussion about a controversial theological concept provided even greater relief for doubting Christians everywhere. Perhaps for the first time, they heard theologians make the crucial distinction between doubt and disbelief, affirm the importance of doubt as an integral part of the faith journey, and describe doubt as the fertilizer that enables faith to grow.

Let him ask in faith without doubting. For the doubter is like the surging sea, driven and tossed by the wind.

JAMES 1:6 HCSB

What does all this mean for you? Doubting God means you are thinking about Him—who He is, if He is, what He's like, why He doesn't do what you expect Him to. This exploration proves you haven't dismissed Him as nonexistent or irrelevant; He is important to you, even if you're not so sure about everything you've been taught to believe about Him. Where there is doubt, there is also hope.

Questions as a Springboard to Faith

With that in mind, you can begin to look at your questions about God as a springboard to faith. Even in her darkest days, Mother Teresa never stopped serving or praying to the God she wasn't so sure of. Despite your doubts, continue to do the same. Talk to God about every one of your concerns, even if it feels as if you're talking to the walls that surround you. Be honest and open and real with God. If this is the genuine cry of your heart, begin with the words from the gospel of Mark that have given many Christians a prayer to pray when no other words would come: "Lord, I believe; help my unbelief!" (9:24 NKJV).

As you continue to hold out hope that your faith will be restored and you'll find at least some of the answers you're seeking, enlist the support of trustworthy believers. They will encourage you to examine the biblical evidence of Who God is, and they will pray for you as you walk this path of uncertainty. You may be surprised to discover that many people who are so strong in their faith today got to that point after a long and intense struggle over what they truly believed.

You Are in Good Company

Regardless of how alone you may still feel, remember that you are in good company. Jesus Himself felt as if God had abandoned Him as He cried out on the cross, "My God, My God, why have You forsaken Me?" (Matthew 27:46 NKJV). Martin Luther echoed those same words after the Roman Catholic Church excommunicated him for renouncing certain doctrines. "My God, my God, do you hear me? Are you dead? Are you dead? No, you can't die. You can only hide yourself, can't you?" Luther asked, questioning the reality of God's presence.

Confess your doubt to the God you're not so sure of. He has heard it all before, and He has given some of His greatest doubters a reason to believe. Allow Him to do the same for you.

> *[Jesus] said to Thomas, "Put your finger here; see my hands. Reach out your hand and put it into my side. Stop doubting and believe." Thomas said to him, "My Lord and my God!" Then Jesus told him, "Because you have seen me, you have believed; blessed are those who have not seen and yet have believed."*
>
> JOHN 20:27–29 NIV

Digging Deeper

If you have serious doubts about God—His existence, His love for you and humanity, His willingness and ability to make things right in a world gone wrong—spend time in deep reflection thinking about what you actually do believe. Then turn to the gospels and read what Jesus said about faith and doubt, praying as you do that God will reveal Himself to you and help you to have faith in Him once again.

Check Your Understanding

- **Does your doubt about God mean that you are no longer a Christian?**

  Absolutely not. It means only that you are a Christian who has questions that need to be answered. The fact that you are concerned about the authenticity of your faith underscores your desire to find those answers and have your assurance in God restored.

- **Is it possible to have complete certainty about everything relating to God, Jesus, and the Bible?**

  Some people seem to, but this side of heaven it's unlikely. God has revealed a great deal, but He has also withheld much. Certainty leaves little room for faith. God wants you to trust Him for the things you don't understand and rely on Him to give you greater understanding when the time is right.

 ### Final Thought

- *Doubt is not the same as disbelief.*
- *You can continue to serve God during a time of questioning.*
- *Doubt is the fertilizer that causes faith to grow.*
- *Your uncertainty about God is a healthy sign that you are thinking deeply about Him.*
- *Your doubts will never separate you from the love of God.*
- *Times of doubting are a normal component of faith.*
- *Many well-known Christian leaders have experienced extended periods of doubt.*

If ever there was a perfect setup for a lifetime of jealousy and ill will, it was the plan hatched by a man named Laban. After promising that Jacob could marry his beautiful daughter Rachel, Laban pulled a fast one and tricked Jacob into marrying his homely daughter Leah. When Jacob got angry with him, Laban shrugged it off but wanted to make it right—so he let Jacob marry Rachel as well. Do you see the potential for maximum jealousy here? But wait. The story actually gets worse.

Jacob's love for Rachel was obvious to everyone. That made Leah jealous—until she became the favored one in the culture of the time by bearing seven children and using them to win over Jacob. Rachel would have none of that. In a jealous rage, she demanded that Jacob give her children as well.

> *Wherever there is jealousy and selfish ambition, there you will find disorder and evil of every kind.*
>
> JAMES 3:16 NLT

Deadly Consequences of Jealousy

Rachel got her demand at the price of her own life. After delivering a healthy child, Joseph, she died giving birth to a second child. Jealousy can have deadly consequences, and it can be passed from one generation to another. Jacob not only preferred one wife over another; he also preferred one child over others. Of all his children, he loved Joseph the most. And Joseph's siblings hated him for it.

> *Let us walk with decency, as in the daylight: not in carousing and drunkenness; not in sexual impurity and promiscuity; not in quarreling and jealousy.*
>
> ROMANS 13:13 HCSB

If you are struggling with jealousy, turn to God immediately. When jealousy is allowed to fester, it breeds bitterness, resentment, and hatred. It will hurt you far more than it will hurt the other person. Nothing good can come from a spirit of jealousy.

 Final Thought

The antidote is simple, but not easy. It begins with a prayer of blessing for the person. That may seem difficult, even impossible, but ridding your life of jealousy requires bold, tough action. Ask God to give you power over your negative feelings. Ask Him to open your eyes to His work in the life of the person you envy so you may begin to have compassion on him or her—and maybe even love the person.

Jealousy is nothing new. God's people have been dealing with it since the family of Adam and Eve.

How to Pray when You Feel Exhausted

Are you among the millions of Americans who hurry from one activity to another, working day and night, living lives of constant exhaustion? Maybe you are also involved in ministry; whether it's full-time or part-time, paid or voluntary, ministry can be more draining than any other activity. You're weary, run-down, and so overtired that the little sleep you get doesn't revive you. You need a break. What if someone offered you a free, fail-proof, guaranteed opportunity to take that break? You would take it, right? Well, Someone has, and you would do well to take it. It's called the Sabbath.

Understanding the Sabbath

Keeping the Sabbath begins with understanding what that means. In some Jewish and Christian traditions, it is characterized by a long list of rules governing what can and cannot be done on the day recognized as the Sabbath. If that's your context for understanding the Sabbath, it's no wonder you don't observe it; following all those rules is hard work and is not exactly a break from your routine.

Jesus never encouraged that kind of Sabbath-keeping. Instead, He considered the Sabbath to be a gift from God: "The Sabbath was made to serve us; we weren't made to serve the Sabbath," he said (Mark 2:27 MSG). The Sabbath provides us with a priceless opportunity to stop, catch our breath, and experience a day unlike any other in the week.

> *Those who trust in the LORD will find new strength. They will soar high on wings like eagles. They will run and not grow weary. They will walk and not faint.*
>
> ISAIAH 40:31 NLT

> *Come to me, all of you who are weary and carry heavy burdens, and I will give you rest. Take my yoke upon you. Let me teach you, because I am humble and gentle at heart, and you will find rest for your souls. For my yoke is easy to bear, and the burden I give you is light.*
>
> MATTHEW 11:28–30 NLT

Stopping for a Full Day

How can you stop for a full day? The need never stops; how can you? Interestingly, studies have shown that people are more productive when they work six days and take an entire day off than if they spread their work over seven days. A day of rest, relaxation, and life-enriching activities makes people more creative, energized, and effective at what they do on the other six days. (If you work on Sunday, keep the Sabbath on another day.)

Thank God for the precious gift of a day of rest. Ask Him how you can rearrange your life to take advantage of the Sabbath—and how to rearrange the other six days to take advantage of the life He has given you.

Points to Remember

- Reducing your responsibilities is not an indication of weakness; it's a sign of wisdom.
- If you think your work is indispensable, you are taking your work too seriously.
- Fatigue is not a fruit of the Spirit (Galatians 5:22–23).
- Taking a walk and breathing deeply are two of the best physical remedies for exhaustion—and both are free.

 Final Thought

With few exceptions—say, a single parent working two jobs to survive—people end up exhausted because they overcommit or can't say no when others make demands on their time. Their choices may be well-intended, but the results can be harmful. Instead of wondering why you are so tired, you'll find it more beneficial to reflect on the answer to this question: Why do you choose to live the way you do?

How to Pray during Illness

Everyone gets sick from time to time. Illness is never pleasant, but temporary illness is generally tolerable. You rest for a while, maybe take some medication, pray for a speedy recovery, and eventually you're back on your feet again. But chronic illness? That's another matter entirely, one that requires an often extraordinary amount of medical attention, patience, faith, and support. The prayers you pray take on a dramatically different tone. You would certainly appreciate a speedy recovery, but you find yourself praying instead to simply make it through the day.

The Centers for Disease Control and Prevention estimates that nearly one-third of all Americans—not just adults, but children as well—suffer from some kind of chronic disorder. Despite medical advances, that proportion is expected to rise, given the often unhealthy lifestyles of Americans and the high number of people who lack health insurance and can't afford to pay for the medical care they need.

For you who fear My name, the sun of righteousness will rise with healing in its wings; and you will go forth and skip about like calves from the stall.

MALACHI 4:2 NASB

Don't consider yourself to be wise; fear the LORD and turn away from evil. This will be healing for your body and strengthening for your bones.

PROVERBS 3:7–8 HCSB

Chronic Illness

That means it's likely that you or someone close to you is suffering from chronic illness. "Chronic illness," of course, is a relative term; a person with progressive multiple sclerosis may not agree that someone with environmental allergies is "suffering." But even though the severity of chronic disorders may vary considerably, those hundred million Americans with persistent ailments share one thing in common: the every-dayness of their care.

Whether you are a diabetic facing insulin injections, a cancer patient on chemo treatments, or a victim of celiac disease for whom a grain of wheat could have debili-tating consequences, the attention your illness requires begins to rule your life, and the illness itself comes to define who you are.

Bigger than Illness

But you are much bigger than your illness, and the primary definition of who you are lies in these words: *child of God*. Every aspect of your life is important to God. So while He cares about the pain, discomfort, progression, and even cost of your illness, He sees the bigger picture of who you are. Understanding this is critical to deciding how you should pray about your present condition.

There is no question that praying for healing is appropriate. Healing was central to Jesus's earthly ministry, and the Bible encourages praying for healing and having faith that you will be healed. Praying only for healing, however, places your focus on your illness. By contrast, praying for the presence of God as you endure this ordeal places the focus on God and your relationship with Him—a focus that transcends your physical condition and encompasses all that you are.

Healing-Centered Prayer

In fact, healing-centered prayer is a fairly recent development in church history. Previous generations of believers accepted illness as a part of life and prayed that their suffer-ings would draw them closer to God, deliver them from a complaining spirit, and instill in them the virtue of patience, among other outcomes. Today, people joke that praying for patience carries with it the danger that God will place you in some terrible, patience-trying circumstance, but in earlier times Christians considered patience a vir-tue critical to their moral development and ability to please God. The need to pray for that virtue simply came with whatever disorder they suffered from.

Here are some other ways you can pray in the face of serious illness:

- Tell God your fears: This is not a time to pretend that all is well. Besides, God knows that isn't the truth.
- Ask God for the strength to endure the everyday complications your illness creates as well as the major events like surgery or dialysis treatments.
- Pray for God to surround you with a team of friends, family, believers, and pastoral and health-care professionals who will come alongside you and help you through this trial.
- Call upon the Holy Spirit to become the comforter you need; ask Him to give you the peace, the power, and the grace to make it through each day and each night.

🍃 Final Thought

Don't allow the everydayness of your chronic condition to define who you are. Instead, allow the everydayness of your prayer life to bring you into a more intimate relationship with God, the One Who made you in His own whole, complete, and perfect image.

Carry that image with you throughout each day. In God's sight, you are the healthy person He made you to be.

References to healing appear throughout the Bible. Examples of healing in the New Testament show the many facets of the healing ministries of Jesus and the apostles.

"Your healing shall spring forth speedily, and your righteousness shall go before you" Isaiah 58:8 (NKJV).

How to Pray when under Financial Distress

In the summer of 2008, people in the United States agonized over the skyrocketing cost of gasoline. Within months, though, a much bigger problem hit—a global financial crisis the likes of which few people alive today had ever seen. Many had to face some challenging and painful questions: Where had they placed their trust? Was it in the stocks they owned? The equity in their home? A steady paycheck? A steady job? All were in jeopardy, if not already gone. Or did they genuinely trust God, as many had once claimed?

Where Is Your Trust?

There's nothing like financial loss to reveal where you have placed your trust. In the wake of any economic problem, many Christians who think they have been relying on God discover they were actually counting on a certain measure of stability. As long as they had a steady income, a decent roof over their heads, and some money in the bank, it was easy to believe they were trusting God with their finances.

But when things happen that change all that—like a job loss or an emergency that depletes their emergency fund—Christians are sometimes forced to face the reality that they weren't trusting God; they were trusting God to keep things normal. They had relied on money, but as author Max Lucado put it, "Money is a fickle lover, and we just got dumped."

My God shall supply all your need according to His riches in glory by Christ Jesus.

PHILIPPIANS 4:19 NKJV

The Spirit of the Lord is on me, because he has anointed me to proclaim good news to the poor. He has sent me to proclaim freedom for the prisoners and recovery of sight for the blind, to set the oppressed free, to proclaim the year of the Lord's favor.

LUKE 4:18–19 NIV

It's Never Too Late to Trust God

The good news is that it's never too late to start trusting God. But what will you trust Him for? Will you trust Him only for a windfall? Nothing is impossible with God, but the greater likelihood is that He wants His people to learn a thing or two through any crisis. Pray instead that God will reveal to you His greater purpose in whatever type of financial distress you are experiencing.

 Final Thought

Remember God has infinite love for you. Your finances are important to Him, and He wants you to trust him to provide (Philippians 4:19). Take heart and know God is not fickle, and He is much more steady than the economy.

How to Pray in the Midst of Family Strife

Every family has problems—every family. But when your own family is in crisis, it's tempting to look at other families and convince yourself that they have it all together. The parents are as much in love today as they were on their wedding day, the children obediently clean their rooms and do their homework and never talk back, and there's never any interference from extended family members. Don't kid yourself. You don't know what goes on behind closed doors. But that doesn't matter. What matters is what's going on behind the closed doors of your own home.

Coping with Problems

Is your family in trouble right now? The nature of that trouble can take many forms. Every family has its own dynamic, with its members relating to one another in ways that are unique to that family. That can create a special bond, but it can also present challenges when it comes to coping with family problems or resolving them.

Equally challenging is praying for your family when turmoil seems to rule every day and when you're the one bearing the brunt of the strife, perhaps even the most direct victim of it. You may not feel like praying, particularly for those who stirred up the strife. You may feel as if there's no point; your spouse already left, your children blame you for the split, and it's too late to make a difference.

Always be humble and gentle. Be patient with each other, making allowance for each other's faults because of your love.

EPHESIANS 4:2 NLT

Don't use foul or abusive language. Let everything you say be good and helpful, so that your words will be an encouragement to those who hear them.

EPHESIANS 4:29 NLT

Never Too Late to Pray

It's never too late to pray, but it's not always easy. Regardless of the current conflict, God has placed each person where he or she is for a reason. Go to God in prayer and thank Him for each and every one—no matter how difficult or disobedient or unfaithful he or she may have been—and seek God's wisdom for the situation. Pray that peace will descend on your household so you may resolve the conflict together, as a family. Most of all, pray that God will reveal Himself and His love to every member of your family. Trust Him to settle the conflict—and keep on praying.

Digging Deeper

Abigail was a woman of good reputation who was married to an evil and amazingly foolish man named Nabal. When Nabal brusquely dismissed David's men, refusing their request for food and drink, David and four hundred of his soldiers sought revenge. Abigail learned what had happened, but instead of blaming and dishonoring her husband, she acted wisely to prevent bloodshed. You can read how she defused this potentially disastrous situation in 1 Samuel 25.

 Final Thought

There are no perfect, problem-free families.

The focus needs to be kept on your own family.

It's never too late to pray about a family problem.

God loves each member of your family, regardless of what anyone has done to cause trouble.

God wants each member of your family to be in relationship with Him.

Peaceful resolution is one goal, but the greater goal is seeing God's purpose come to pass.

How to Pray when You Are Worried

Are you a worrier? Lots of people are, including Christians who believe they have placed their faith and trust in God. Worry has become so tightly woven into the fabric of their lives that they don't recognize their fretting as a betrayal of the faith they profess. Think about your typical prayer time and then answer this question: When you pray, do you cast your cares on God and experience the peace of knowing they're all in His hands?

For some people, prayer has become simply worrying out loud. You hear it in their voices when they pray aloud in a group; you see it in their expressions when they utter their prayer requests. Worry lines are so deeply etched on their faces that it's evident that anxiety and dread are equally entrenched in their lives.

> *Can all your worries add a single moment to your life? And why worry about your clothing? Look at the lilies of the field and how they grow. They don't work or make their clothing, yet Solomon in all his glory was not dressed as beautifully as they are.*
>
> MATTHEW 6:27–29 NLT

> *Don't fret or worry. Instead of worrying, pray. Let petitions and praises shape your worries into prayers, letting God know your concerns. Before you know it, a sense of God's wholeness, everything coming together for good, will come and settle you down. It's wonderful what happens when Christ displaces worry at the center of your life.*
>
> PHILIPPIANS 4:6–7 MSG

Time to Gain Control

Maybe you aren't a chronic worrier, but you've experienced enough apprehension about the terrible possibilities in life to know that anxiety is jeopardizing your faith relationship with God. You know it's time to gain control over the anxiety that has crept into your life.

You also know how to do that. You need to cast your cares on Jesus, because He cares for you (1 Peter 5:7). But knowing that and doing that aren't the same thing. Maybe you need a fresh way of understanding how that happens.

Peace-Producing Prayer

"Let petitions and praises shape your worries into prayers" (Philippians 4:6 MSG). That's how a popular paraphrase of the Bible describes the process of casting your cares on God in prayer. Ask God for what you need, praise God for Who He is, and watch as those constant worries become transformed into peace-producing prayer.

Faith in God cancels out worry, but the opposite is also true: worry cancels out faith in God. Don't allow worry to displace your faith in God—you've come too far to let that happen now.

Something to Ponder

Some negative aspects of life have a positive benefit. Fear may alert us to danger; pain may alert us to an infection. But think for a while about worry. What benefit have you ever derived from worrying? How has it enhanced your life? How has it changed a situation you were worried about? Can anything good come from worrying?

 Final Thought

You've likely heard the expression "Prayer doesn't change things; prayer changes you." The first part is questionable—many people attest to the power of prayer in changing situations—but the second part is most certainly true. Private prayer brings people closer to God. Corporate prayer brings people closer to one another in the presence of God. And all genuine prayer has the power to transform you. May you continue on this journey of learning to pray—its life-giving lessons never end.

Practical Matters of Prayer

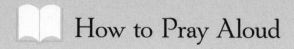

How to Pray Aloud

Glossophobia is the fear of speaking in public. Some surveys contend that more than 70 percent of Americans fear speaking in front of others more than they fear dying. As Christians, this social fear shows up when praying aloud in the presence of other believers. Don't let your fear keep you away from experiencing the great joy. Whether praying with a small group or opening a meeting in prayer, keep these things in common.

Pray for God's Ears Alone

Even though there may be a few—or a few dozen—others in the room, direct your words to the ears of God alone. Avoid the temptation to perform. Christians in South Korea pray aloud, but they don't take turns the way Christians in America do; everyone prays aloud simultaneously. This practice helps focus their prayers toward heaven and tamps down ego.

Avoid Using Prayer to Curse Others

When David was fighting war after war, he often prayed against his enemies. These petitions (such as Psalm 35) are called imprecatory (i.e., cursing) prayers. While most prayers are good models, imprecatory prayers should never be heard in public. Conflict exists in every group, but the prayer circle is not an appropriate place to air your grievances.

Avoid Verbal Traps

Praying aloud is a unique speaking experience. In public speaking, some people fall on such verbal crutches as *um, you see, and, etc., and all that*. When praying aloud, some use these crutches and add others, like using God's name to begin or connect sentences. Remember to speak as naturally as possible.

Something to Ponder

Moses suffered from a fear of public speaking. He complained to God about the task, his lack of eloquence, and even the sound of his voice. God's response to Moses is a great reminder when you worry about praying in public. "Who gave human beings their mouths? Who makes them deaf or mute? Who gives them sight or makes them blind? Is it not I, the LORD?" (Exodus 4:11 NIV).

 Final Thought

Have you heard that women aren't allowed to pray aloud if men are present? Christian traditions debate the roles of men and women in public worship. Some advocate for a woman's silence by quoting 1 Corinthians 14:34: "Women should remain silent in the churches. They are not allowed to speak, but must be in submission" (NIV). A more complete reading of the New Testament gives women great freedom in public worship—including praying aloud—but reserves teaching for men only. Everyone can bring forth a word of praise or prayer of thanksgiving to God. We are encouraged to pray our concerns and silence and aloud.

Holding Hands for Mealtime Prayers

Today's mealtime prayers look less like a Norman Rockwell painting and more like a television commercial for a casual dining restaurant, and yet families are united throughout the ages by the prayers they've prayed before breaking bread. Food is a consistent part of every day. Our bodies require food to survive. Praying before meals reminds us Who provided the food and gives us at least one opportunity each day to express our dependence on the Provider.

An Old Testament Tradition—Thanksgiving

Agriculture fueled much of Israel's calendar. Thanksgiving was integral to the many feasts celebrated each year. They brought sacrifices from their crops and herds to the temple out of thanksgiving and worship. Many of the Psalms repeat the refrain of thanksgiving and gratitude.

New Testament Model—Blessing

Jesus modeled a lifestyle of praying before meals. Before two fish and five loaves became an all-you-can-eat buffet, Jesus thanked God for the provision and blessed the food. In the upper room during the Last Supper, Jesus thanked God for the bread and the wine.

Practical Matters

Singing Table Prayers. Many families enjoy singing their premeal prayers. Enjoy the process and laughter, and know that the practice will help rutabagas taste a little better.

Praying in a Restaurant. While singing isn't recommended, your family's routine is portable to fast-food and sit-down restaurants alike. Prayers should be shorter than at home. If the restaurant isn't teeming with the sounds of clatter, music, and conversation, keep your volume low to avoid distracting other diners.

Teaching Opportunity. Your children can learn to pray in short, fun spurts by praying for your family's meal. Invite the child to do so before you arrive at the table to avoid stage fright. Model how to participate in prayer while your child prays, and thank the child after the prayer. You'll build a spiritual discipline and confidence in your child.

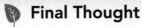 Final Thought

The simple act of holding hands transforms mealtime into a solemn, special, and memorable time. In one family, Dad prays while the other members of the family gently squeeze the hands of those next to them to indicate agreement with the prayer. Another family created "shake the love." After the amen, everyone raises held hands above their heads and says, "Johnson family: shake the love!" The giggles and smiles lighten even the heaviest days.

Kneeling for Bedtime Prayers

Parents worldwide have struggled with bedtime prayers for generations. Many feel empty merely praying, "Now I lay me down to sleep." They worry that the rote repetition will lead to a lack of interest in spiritual matters as they grow older. Others wonder about the nuts and bolts. They wonder how they can teach their children to pray if they barely know how to pray themselves. Many parents question if bedtime prayers do any good. Bedtime prayers offer six benefits to your child.

Bedtime prayers quiet your child before bedtime. It's hard to fall asleep when you're bouncing on your bed or playing with a toy. Prayer time offers a chance to settle down, be still, and be quiet right before bedtime. The heart rate will slow and, hopefully, the eyelids will begin to droop. This benefit is more practical than spiritual, but it is important nonetheless. For better results, dim the lights and speak in soft tones for a few minutes before prayer time to start the descent.

Bedtime prayers offer you an opportunity to speak into your child's life. Most parents fall into a rut of praying shortsighted prayers, that is, prayers for a good night's sleep or for a good day tomorrow. The prayer model in the Bible asks God for growth in aspects of character over a lifetime. As your child hears you asking God for higher things, you are training your child to desire higher things. C. S. Lewis observed, "We are half-hearted creatures fooling about...when infinite joy is offered us, like an ignorant child who wants to go on making mud pies in a slum because he cannot imagine what is meant by the offer of a holiday at the sea. We are far too easily pleased." Pray specifically for traits under development. For instance, if your child is lying, pray for a truthful heart and an end to the lies.

Bedtime prayers give a blanket of godly—and parental—protection. Some children are afraid of the dark. Some are afraid of storms that might stir up overnight. Others are afraid of imaginary creatures tucked away in their closets. Parents fear wars and the rumors of wars, financial stress, traffic accidents, and the unknown. Bedtime prayers remind us that God is in control and help us to look to Him for protection and comfort. When your children hear you casting your cares upon the Lord, they will follow with their cares. When you hear yourself casting your cares upon the Lord, your faith will grow.

Bedtime prayers program your child's dreams. Sleep scientists and psychologists report that children dream three or four times every night. Your child will dream most often about his worries or the last thing on his mind before going to sleep. Bedtime prayers provide tremendous power to shape children's dreams. As you pray with your children, you can help them see how God answered their prayers, protected them on the playground, and made their scrapes better. Your prayers for peace will be answered by God and allow your child to experience more dreams than nightmares. If your child does wake up from a bad dream, your prayers can also be the key to getting your child back to sleep.

Bedtime prayers allow you to hear from your child's heart. As your child develops language, encourage your child to pray along with you. Start with a written prayer like "Now I lay me down to sleep" or the Lord's Prayer. Once your child is comfortable praying aloud with you, coach your child how to talk with God the way your child talks with you. The text of your child's prayer will surprise you and sometimes break your heart. Consider keeping a journal of prayers your child makes and the answers God brings.

Bedtime prayers build family memories. Think back to your own childhood. What do you remember more—the things your family did repeatedly or only once? Many children will remember your family traditions—both good and bad—far more vividly than landmark vacations. Pray as consistently as possible. Some families ask babysitters to keep the tradition going when they can't be at home. Don't rush. Bedtime prayers are an important part of Christian parenting, not just an item on the day's checklist. Linger for a few seconds after the *amen*. If the prayer time generates a question, listen carefully and quietly answer.

Myth Buster

Is it true that children use bedtime prayers to manipulate their parents into staying up later? Many parents struggle to discern whether their children's questions are the genuine thoughts of spiritual growth or a stalling technique. Clear boundaries can aid you. If your child's bedtime is 8:00 and you typically spend five minutes in prayer, begin your prayers at 7:50 so you have time to pray and field questions. When 8:00 comes, remind your child of the family rule. Use discernment if your child seems to be stalling.

Something to Ponder

Don't be afraid to make bedtime prayers fun.

- Does your child sleep with a toy? Add the bear or doll to your prayer circle. Take one hand and ask your child to take the other. Don't forget to pray for the toy by name.
- Sing your prayers by making up your own words to a simple song like "Twinkle, Twinkle, Little Star."
- Hide under a blanket with a flashlight and whisper your prayers.

 ## Check Your Understanding

- **Can prayer help prevent my child's nightmares?**

  Prayer can ward off nightmares in several ways. By making prayer your child's last activity of the night, you make it more likely her dreams will reflect what you prayed about. Praying creates a peaceful atmosphere more conducive to pleasant dreams.

- **Won't my child see this as just another routine in his day?**

  If you treat this as a special time and avoid making the prayers themselves routine, your child will likely carry into adulthood precious memories of this family tradition.

 ### Final Thought

Do you pray before your bedtime? The same reasons that prayer makes sleep time better for your children will make the evening better for you. Don't allow a stand-up comedian's monologue, an infomercial, or a black-and-white movie to be the last thing on the screen of your mind when you turn out the lights.

Have you ever heard yourself say, "God doesn't have time for my prayers" or "God doesn't care about my prayers"? Questions like these—the "God" barriers—often arise from past disappointment or misunderstanding. You can get past the "God" barriers by realigning your view of God. Imagine your perception of God as the Leaning Tower of Pisa. You must get under the foundation and repair the balance in order to move forward and into a deeper relationship with God through prayer.

God Wants to Listen to You because He Loves You

When God instructed Moses to bring His laws to Israel, Moses shared some opening remarks. He said, "The LORD loved your ancestors and wanted them to belong to him. So he chose them and their descendants rather than any other nation, and today you are still his people" (Deuteronomy 10:15 CEV). Inspirational author Max Lucado explained the meaning of the Hebrew word for *love* used here. "This passage warms our hearts. But it shook the Hebrews' world. They heard this: 'The Lord binds [*hasaq*] himself to his people.' *Hasaq* speaks of a tethered love. God chained himself to Israel. Because the people were lovable? No. God loves Israel and the rest of us because he chooses to."

God Wants to Listen to You because He Prays for You

Have you ever had a friend reach out his hand to your shoulder, bow his head, and pour out prayers to God on your behalf? This hopeful and encouraging act of friendship is trumped by only one thing: Jesus Himself praying for you. The apostle Paul told the Romans that Jesus "is at God's right side, speaking to him for us" (Romans 8:34 CEV). Jesus is leaning toward His Father, His hands are cupped around His mouth, and He is talking about you directly into God's ear. God listens to you because He listens to His Son.

Something to Ponder

In his teens, George Matheson's eyesight began failing. University and seminary were excruciating. He was blind by graduation. His fiancée returned the engagement ring. He enjoyed a full career as a pastor, but he suffered from a broken heart. Reflecting on God's love, he penned this hymn: "O Love that wilt not let me go, I rest my weary soul in thee; I give thee back the life I owe, that in thine ocean depths its flow may richer, fuller be."

 Final Thought

Ambrose (339?–397), a leader in the early church, mused that praying is like a little child who gathers flowers to present to his or her father. The child picks as many weeds as flowers. The mother snags the child and transforms the bunch into a beautiful bouquet. The prince of preachers, Charles Spurgeon, commented on Ambrose's analogy: "If we could see one of our prayers after Christ Jesus has amended it—we would hardly recognize it."

"How Do I Pray to God when He Knows Everything?"

Ken Jennings is probably the only person in history who deserves the title "know-it-all." He reigned as champion on the television game show *Jeopardy!* for seventy-four programs and won more money than any regular-season contestant. Some Christians feel as if life is a game of *Jeopardy!* played against the God of the universe. They wonder why they should play when God knows all the answers on the board. His infinite knowledge is an invitation to move you closer to Him.

God Does Know It All

God is *omniscient*. This theological term means "all knowing." The Bible says that God knows such things as the number of hairs on your head, the stars in the sky, and the grains of sand.

God knows far more than trivial facts about you. He knows your thoughts, plans, and emotions. Jesus traveled on a journey from Judea to His hometown of Galilee. He paused to rest beside a well in Samaria. A woman came to the well, and Jesus spoke to her. Her jaw scraped the sand as Jesus told her about her life and her mistakes and then helped her see Him as the Messiah. After her encounter, she ran into town, telling everyone, "Come, see a man who told me everything I ever did! Could this be the Messiah?" (John 4:29 HCSB).

God Does Know Everything, but You Don't

A wise man once said, "God does not tell you everything you will encounter in life. If He did, you would go off and do it without Him." God wants a relationship with you. Keep in mind that prayer is dialogue, not monologue, so approach it like a conversation. When you pray, you tell God the things you want Him to hear. You ask for the things that you need. In reply, God tells you about Himself and outlines His plans for you.

 Final Thought

Pray in times of doubt and fear. Ask God every question you've ever wondered about. Stay close to Him. If life is a test, He knows the answers. Trust in His omniscience.

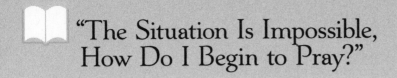

"The Situation Is Impossible, How Do I Begin to Pray?"

Old scholars trying to trip up those who believe in the Bible used to ask, "If God can do anything, can He make a rock so large that he cannot move it?" The answer to this riddle helps us understand the nature of prayer: God can do nothing against His nature. For example, God cannot allow a sinner who has not repented into heaven. The converse is also true; God cannot prevent a sinner who has repented from entering heaven. Rejoice because God's nature includes miracles, wonders, and doing the impossible.

Pray to Feel the Comfort of God

King Saul hunted David like an animal. The future king hid in the brush or rocks, dodging soldiers who came within a spear's length of finding him. For months, the Lord preserved him. David composed Psalm 31 to celebrate God's protection and safety. When life feels impossible and storms rage around you, go to God in prayer for His protection and comfort.

Pray Because God Weeps with You

Where was Jesus? Sisters Mary and Martha were losing their patience. Their brother was dying, but Jesus was busy in the neighboring town. Didn't Jesus care? Wasn't Lazarus His friend? When Jesus finally arrived, the sisters met Him with the news: Lazarus was dead. Jesus wept with them. In a matter of minutes, Jesus would raise Lazarus from the grave. Nevertheless, Jesus wept. When your grief and sorrow are at their worst, go to God in prayer because He weeps with you.

Pray Because God Can Do the Impossible

Moses passed the mantle of leadership to Joshua. It was then up to him to lead Israel into the Promised Land. Could God do the impossible again? Five times, God told Joshua to be strong and courageous. God prepared him for challenges and difficulty. Then God did the impossible—He divided the Jordan River. A second crossing. A second miracle. When the impossible stares you in the face, pray because God can do the impossible.

Jesus is the Lord of the impossible. When you're facing the impossible, find encouragement in Jesus's miracles.

 Final Thought

Throughout the Bible, there are examples of God working through, erasing, and resolving impossible situations. There is a great confidence among Christians who believe in the power of His might. Look to the Scriptures that tell us about His works and know He can do all things. Trust in these truths.

The Prayers of the Bible

Jesus's Prayer for All Believers—
How to Find Unity

It's been called the greatest prayer in the Bible—the words Jesus prayed in John 17 that have come to be known as the High Priestly Prayer. Of the approximately six hundred and fifty prayers in the Bible, this prayer stands apart as Jesus's expression of love and concern for those who believe in Him. In this prayer, Jesus's role as High Priest, which is thoroughly defined in the book of Hebrews, is evident. He continuously intercedes for the people of God. But instead of presenting a sacrifice to God, as the Jewish high priests did, He became the ultimate sacrifice.

The words of John 17 have offered comfort and assurance to Christians over the course of two millennia. But they've also caused many Christians to mourn the lack of unity in the church. After all, Jesus prayed not just that His followers would be "one," but also that their unity would mirror the oneness of the Trinity: "I am no longer in the world; and *yet* they themselves are in the world, and I come to You. Holy Father, keep them in Your name, *the name* which You have given Me, that they may be one even as We *are*" (John 17:11 NASB).

Thousands of Denominations

Numerous sects claiming to be "Christian" existed following the resurrection, and even after the Roman Catholic and Orthodox churches unified believers to some extent, various smaller groups existed and at times flourished. But never in the past has the number of Christian denominations rivaled that which exists today. Depending on the method used to count and define denominations, the total may be as high as thirty-four thousand. Even the most conservative estimates top twenty thousand.

How does this square with Jesus's prayer for unity? Was Jesus's prayer ineffective? Did God not honor His Son's request? Jesus's plea is recorded several verses later: "I do not ask on behalf of these alone, but for those also who believe in Me through their word; that they may all be one; even as You, Father, *are* in Me and I in You, that they also may be in Us, so that the world may believe that You sent Me. The glory which You have given Me I have given to them, that they may be one, just as We are one; I in them and You in Me, that they may be perfected in unity, so that the world may know that You sent Me, and loved them, even as You have loved Me" (John 17:20–23 NASB).

Understanding of Unity

Jesus expanded the purpose of His request. He didn't want only for believers to experience the wonderful unity He and His Father shared; He also wanted their unity to testify to his identity as the Son of God. Many would say Christians have failed Jesus in this regard. It's hard to argue with those who point to denominations as evidence of Christians' disunity—unless unity is to be understood in a much broader sense.

Here's a major distinction to remember when the topic of Christian unity—or disunity—comes up: unity does not equal complete agreement. If it did, ministers would find it impossible to "unite" any couple in marriage. If you are married, or if you have observed your parents or other married couples, you know two spouses don't agree on everything. But they are still "one," according to the biblical definition of marriage (Genesis 2:24).

Think, too, of the unity found in the Trinity. The three persons of the Trinity are one, yet they have distinct roles. Their roles in no way interfere with their oneness.

But neither a lack of agreement in marriage nor the distinct roles in the Trinity justify the high number of denominations, especially those that disagree on basic doctrines. Two responses to this are the ecumenical movement, which seeks to unite certain Christian denominations, and the interfaith movement, which fosters respect for all faiths. Many Christians, however, are uncomfortable with those efforts and feel powerless to overcome denominationalism.

Unity

Believers who trust in Christ are already one, regardless of denominational label. And many have found unity across whatever lines may exist by praying together, thanking God for the unity they do have. When you focus on common ground, you begin to discover the unity that exists, often in surprising places.

Better yet, by dwelling in that place of common ground with other believers, you become something you probably thought you could never be: an answer to Jesus's High Priestly Prayer.

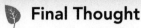 ## Final Thought

Throughout the New Testament, Jesus and the writers of the Epistles emphasized the need for love, respect, care, harmony, and peace among believers—in short, unity. Many verses encourage Christians to offer ways we should "be" with one another:

Be devoted to one another, Acts 2:42–47.
Be harmonious, brotherly, 1 Peter 3:8.
Be like-minded and live in peace, 2 Corinthians 13:11.
Be united in mind, love, spirit, and purpose, Philippians 2:1–4.

Paul's Prayers for the Churches— How to Grow in Faith

The apostle Paul is considered among the greatest spiritual writers in all of history, and for good reason. His letters to the people of the early church who were scattered throughout the Mediterranean area reveal the mind and heart of an educated wordsmith devoted to Jesus. Even many of his detractors admit that while they may not always like what he wrote, particularly about women's roles in the church, they recognize him as a brilliant communicator. And few passages from his letters surpass the expression of his mind and heart that he revealed in his prayers for the church.

A Man Who Used Talent from God

Upon Paul's conversion, God transformed the apostle's former zeal for persecuting the church into a passion for serving the church. Because the New Testament includes so many of Paul's writings, with thirteen letters attributed to him, today's believers have a clearer picture of who he was than they have of most of the other apostles. The picture that emerges is of a man who used the talent God gave him in service to the church. For Paul, that gift from God was one of communication.

In addition to communicating the gospel to the world around him, Paul expressed his deepest longings for the church to God and to the church itself. Those longings frequently centered on his desire to see Christians grow in the faith, acquiring not only knowledge (fact-based information about the truth of God) but also wisdom (the life application of that knowledge of God): "*I pray that* the eyes of your heart may be enlightened, so that you will know what is the hope of His calling, what are the riches of the glory of His inheritance in the saints, and what is the surpassing greatness of His power toward us who believe" (Ephesians 1:18–19 NASB).

Knowing the Fullness of God

But even as he prayed for the church to grow in faith, Paul bowed his knees before God and prayed that the followers of Jesus would gain an even greater knowledge—a deeper understanding of the love of God. Later, in his letter to the Ephesian church, he wrote that it was his prayer that believers would "be able to comprehend with all the saints what is the breadth and length and height and depth, and to know the love of Christ which surpasses knowledge, that you may be filled up to all the fullness of God" (Ephesians 3:18–19 NASB). Paul understood that even as he prayed for Christians to grasp the dimensions of Christ's love, the full magnitude of that love was beyond human comprehension. He wanted the followers of Christ to continually aim higher in their efforts to know God and His love.

In nearly all his prayers, Paul expressed his thankfulness to God for all who have come to Christ. Repeatedly in his epistles, he assured the Christians to whom he was writing that he prayed for them without ceasing; Paul fully understood the persecution, temptations, and challenges they faced.

Broad Needs of the Church

Few people have the gift of eloquence that Paul had, but his prayers for the church can still serve as a model for Christians today. Throughout his epistles, Paul prayed at times for the more practical needs of the church, and those are not to be ignored. But there was also a place for prayer for the broader needs of the church—the need to get to know God, grow in faith, know the love of Christ, have the eyes of the heart enlightened, know the hope of His calling, and be filled with the fullness of God.

Praying for healing, financial blessing, comfort, reconciliation, salvation, and so many other concerns is crucial to the faith and functioning of the body of Christ. Next time you pray about those needs, consider praying also for the church as a whole, the entire body of Christ. You can start by praying Paul's prayers for the church directly to God. Soon enough, you'll likely progress on to your own concerns for the universal church—and for all of the ways the church can continue to grow in order to become a powerful witness for Christ, an example to all of the "breadth and length and height and depth" of His love.

Digging Deeper

Paul prayed for the church throughout his letters, which are peppered with expressions of his hopes for believers. Here is a short list of his prayers:

- Prayer for endurance amid trouble (Colossians 1:9–14)
- Prayer for power to be strong in love and faith (Ephesians 3:14–21)

- Prayer for purity and wisdom to make right choices (Philippians 1:3–11)
- Prayer for the ability to do good works (2 Thessalonians 1:11–12)
- Prayer for wisdom, revelation, and understanding of the truth (Ephesians 1:15–23)
- Prayer of thankfulness for the believers' hope in Christ (Colossians 1:3–6)

 ## Check Your Understanding

- **Paul prayed that Christians would grow in both knowledge and wisdom. What is the difference between the two?**

  In a Christian context, knowledge is information about God—who He is, what has been His plan of redemption throughout history, why Jesus came, what the Scriptures say. Wisdom is applying all of that knowledge to daily life.

- **Paul prayed such lofty prayers for believers, both in content and in style. How can his prayers serve as a model for others?**

  Paul had a God-given talent for communication. His eloquence should never hinder Christians from praying. But the content of his prayers for the church is an example of how believers might want to pray.

- **Above all else, what did Paul want the church to have?**

  Paul wanted believers to comprehend the measure of God's love for the church— and the power contained in that love to bring others to Christ.

 ## Final Thought

God wants all Christians to share the gospel with others. But Paul's gift of communication can seem daunting to those who feel they don't have a way with words or may be introverted. If that's you, take a look at the gifts you do have and think about the ways God can use those gifts to help you share your faith with others.

Nehemiah's Prayer Project—
"Have Mercy and Answer My Prayer"

If you've ever been far from loved ones when catastrophe has struck, you know how helpless you can feel. You want to go and help, but for whatever reason, you can't leave where you are. Nehemiah found himself in just such a situation. News reached him in Persia that Jerusalem lay in ruins, and he left this record of his reaction: "When I heard this, I sat down and cried. Then for several days, I mourned; I went without eating to show my sorrow, and I prayed" (Nehemiah 1:4 CEV).

Crying Out to God

Nehemiah's heart ached for the exiles who had returned to Jerusalem only to discover that the city had deteriorated into a pile of rubble. He cried out to God, but he didn't begin by making a request.

Instead, he affirmed his commitment and subservience to God, establishing his right to seek God's mercy and expect an answer to his constant prayers for the people of Israel (Nehemiah 1:6). He continued with a confession that is both personal and corporate; he and the Israelites had sinned by disobeying God and the law of Moses (v. 7). Only then did he make his petition, asking God to remember the promises He had made to the Israelites through Moses: "You told him that if we were unfaithful, you would scatter us among foreign nations. But you also said that no matter how far away we were, we could turn to you and start obeying your laws. Then you would bring us back to the place where you have chosen to be worshiped" (Nehemiah 1:8–9 CEV).

Pleading for God's Mercy

Notice how he prayed. As a servant of God, he pleaded for God's mercy and for answers to his prayers. He confessed the sins of his family, himself, and the people of God, and he reminded God of his promises.

Nehemiah did what he could do: He asked. He confessed. He reminded. When you feel helpless, remember Nehemiah. From a distance, he cried and fasted, but he also prayed. And God was faithful to answer; the king granted him permission to return to Jerusalem to help the people of God rebuild the city.

Digging Deeper

As cupbearer to the Persian king, Nehemiah held a position of great responsibility. The position involved not only preventing the king from being intentionally or accidentally poisoned but also serving as a trusted adviser, similar to a prime minister. Nehemiah was the third man in Jewish history to serve as cupbearer to a foreign king; Joseph held the position of cupbearer in Egypt, while Daniel did the same in Babylon.

 Final Thought

Nehemiah's sorrow was evident. When King Artaxerxes asked why he was sad, Nehemiah feared that if his answer displeased the king, he could lose his life. He prayed, and he related his desire to rebuild Jerusalem. Instead of beheading him, Artaxerxes asked him to make his request specific: How long would he be gone? When did he expect to return? As a servant of God, he had nothing to fear.

Elijah's Prayer—"God, Reveal Yourself to Me"

The people of God had been led into error, leaving the one true God in favor of worshipping an idol—Baal. Only one prophet of God remained. But if you can have only one prophet, you would want a prophet like the one who survived: Elijah the Tishbite. Elijah confronted the people with a challenge: he would pit his God against any other any day. It was time for a showdown. If God won the challenge, the people would follow Him; if Baal won, the people would follow him. Elijah, the lone prophet of God, prepared to face the prophets of Baal—all four hundred and fifty of them.

The Prophets of Baal

The rules were these: both Elijah and the Baal prophets would slaughter an ox, place it on a wooden altar, and pray for their respective deities to ignite the fire. Elijah let his opposition go first. The prophets of Baal prayed all morning long and began jumping on the altar, but nothing happened.

"About noontime Elijah began mocking them. 'You'll have to shout louder,' he scoffed, 'for surely he is a god! Perhaps he is daydreaming, or is relieving himself. Or maybe he is away on a trip, or is asleep and needs to be wakened!'" (1 Kings 18:27 NLT). This enraged the prophets further, and they began praying louder and cutting themselves as part of a religious ritual.

Elijah's Prayer to the True God

Elijah had enough and called an end to the prophets' petitions. He rebuilt the altar, placed his slaughtered ox on it—and drenched the whole works with bucket after bucket of water. And then he prayed: "O God, God of Abraham, Isaac, and Israel, make it known right now that you are God in Israel, that I am your servant, and that I'm doing what I'm doing under your orders. Answer me, God; O answer me and reveal to this people that you are God, the true God, and that you are giving these people another chance at repentance" (1 Kings 18:36–37 MSG).

The result? The people believed what was right before their eyes, the evidence that there is only one true God—and His name is not Baal.

- **Why did Elijah challenge the prophets of Baal?**

  The Israelites had been enticed into worshipping Baal. The burden of returning them to God fell to Elijah, the last remaining prophet. So sure was his faith in God that he issued the challenge to prove that there was only one powerful God.

- **How did Elijah give the prophets of Baal an advantage?**

  Elijah drenched the altar with water to make the challenge more difficult. Baal's prophets had already lost, but Elijah would not have won; a stalemate would have resulted. But God proved Himself to be all-powerful.

 Final Thought

When Elijah rebuilt the altar that had proven to be a failure for the prophets of Baal, he performed a symbolic gesture on behalf of the nation of Israel. After gathering twelve stones, he placed them in the wood on the altar. The stones represented the twelve tribes of Israel, and Elijah's gesture was his way of showing honor to God.

David's Prayer of Protection—"Hide Me"

The book of Psalms is among the best known and most loved in all of Scripture. The poetry is often of the highest quality, but the cry of the human heart found in the individual psalms sets the poems apart as expressions of a deep hunger for God. The poems, prayers, and songs of praise found in this book cover the spectrum of human need. And because he was so relentlessly pursued by so many enemies, the psalmist David often called out to God to meet one need in particular: the need for protection.

David's Images of God's Protection

When it came to describing the way God defended him, David abandoned the abstract in favor of visual imagery. When he needed God's protection, David saw God as a shield, a fortress, a refuge, a shelter, a high and strong tower—even as wings. In Psalm 57, that was the protection he sought when his archenemy, Saul, entered the cave David was hiding in: "God Most High, have pity on me! Have mercy. I run to you for safety. In the shadow of your wings, I seek protection till danger dies down" (v. 1 CEV).

Even though he had sought refuge in a cave, David needed more than mere limestone to protect him. He needed the shadow of God's wings—a comforting image for you to carry with you and call upon whenever you are fearful or exposed to danger.

Power of David's Words

David also sought protection from danger of a different kind: "Hide me from the conspiracy of the wicked, from the plots of evildoers. They sharpen their tongues like swords and aim cruel words like deadly arrows" (Psalm 64:2–3 NIV). David the poet was well aware of the power of words—and the power of God to "turn their own tongues against them and bring them to ruin; all who see them will shake their heads in scorn" (Psalm 64:8 NIV).

Whatever you need protection from, God is there to hide you from your enemies—whether as a mighty fortress or as a wing-shaped shadow.

In the Psalms and elsewhere, biblical writers used imagery to convey the way they visualized God's protection.

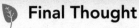 Final Thought

David said in Psalm 27, "For he will hide me in his shelter in the day of trouble; he will conceal me under the cover of his tent; he will lift me high upon a rock" (v. 5 ESV). He spoke with confidence about God being his safe haven. He believed God would be merciful and shield him from harm. God alone has the power to aid us, provide for us, and protect us from everything that we encounter in life.

Solomon's Humility—"Grant Me Wisdom"

What is the first quality that comes to mind when you hear the name of Solomon? Most likely, it's wisdom. Solomon's request that God grant him wisdom to rule Israel is known even among those who have little knowledge of the rest of the Bible. The "wisdom of Solomon" is legendary. The irony, of course, is that Solomon even thought he had to ask for wisdom—because Solomon already had the wisdom to ask for wisdom.

Conflict on a Number of Fronts

Solomon was a son of David who had been appointed king over Israel as David lay dying. As he assumed his royal position, he faced conflict on a number of fronts. He faced opposition from two factions that believed someone else should be king: the followers of the high priest Abiathar, who had been deposed; and the followers of Solomon's brother Adonijah, who was later executed. Solomon knew both factions would continue to cause unrest once he ascended to the throne.

Solomon's request for wisdom came in response to a question God asked him in a dream after he became king: "What can I give you?"

Youthful Inexperience

After recounting God's love and faithfulness to his father, David, Solomon admitted to his youthful inexperience in light of the enormous task of reigning over the nation of Israel, a nation so large that its population was too high to record (1 Kings 3:7–8). Only then does he make his request: "Give Your servant an obedient heart to judge Your people and to discern between good and evil. For who is able to judge this great people of Yours?" (1 Kings 3:9 HCSB).

Bear in mind that Solomon was all of twenty years old when he became king. Solomon's request revealed another quality: humility. His humble request reveals his insecurity over whether he was mature enough to be equipped to discern between good and evil.

Solomon's response was pleasing to God, Who pointed out all the things Solomon could have asked for: a long life, personal wealth, revenge against his enemies—who were already threatening his kingdom. But because Solomon considered the welfare of God's people above his own desires, God rewarded him by promising to give him much more than he requested.

Wisdom, Understanding, Wealth, and Honor

God not only gave Solomon wisdom and understanding but He also showered him with wealth and honor and a singular place in history (1 Kings 3:11–13). Not only would there never be another person like Solomon but God also assured him there would be no other king like him as long as he lived.

Humility is always pleasing to God. Praying with humility shows an acknowledgment of God's sovereignty; when you humble yourself before God, you own up to your position of subservience. A humble heart recognizes God as Lord, and such a heart is rewarded: "For Yahweh takes pleasure in His people; He adorns the humble with salvation" (Psalm 149:4 HCSB).

Solomon's Reward

After promising Solomon riches and honor, God rewarded him for his humble request:

- Solomon ruled over an enormous kingdom, from Egypt to the Euphrates.
- During his lifetime, peace reigned throughout his kingdom; the borders were kept safe.
- Every family in his kingdom enjoyed security and some measure of prosperity.
- Solomon's prosperity was unrivaled in the known world.
- His fame was known among the surrounding nations; ambassadors came from far and wide to partake of his wisdom.
- His intellect was also legendary; he was well versed in both botany and zoology and was a prolific writer, composing three thousand proverbs and more than one thousand songs.

And the wisdom God promised him? Solomon became known throughout the region for his wisdom, knowledge, and understanding; 1 Kings 4:29–31 indicates that his wisdom was greater than that of all the wisdom teachers from Babylon to Egypt, including some of such renown that their names were recorded in the Bible.

Indeed, no other king was like him as long as he lived, just as God had assured him. By humbling himself, acknowledging his shortcomings, and asking God to give him a heart willing to listen to the voice of God, Solomon received far more than he asked for—and nearly everyone under his authority benefited.

Digging Deeper

One of the greatest of Solomon's achievements was construction of the temple. Though many attempts have been made to create an accurate model of the temple based on biblical dimensions, the unit of measure, the cubit, represented different lengths in different cultures. Regardless of its size, it is generally agreed that gold played a prominent role, with an estimated twenty tons used in its construction. In addition, King Solomon received an annual revenue in excess of $256 million in gold over a period of forty years.

 Points to Remember

- God chooses the way He communicates; He spoke to Solomon in a dream.
- Solomon humbled himself before God.
- Acknowledging his inexperience, he asked for a heart willing to listen to God's wisdom.
- Solomon's request pleased God, Who promised more than he asked for.
- Humility indicates an attitude of respectful subservience to God.

 Final Thought

Despite his auspicious beginning, Solomon's later years were marked by moral failure. With some seven hundred women in his life, he became distracted and abandoned the things of God. In fact, he began worshipping other gods. His wealth and power had taken their toll. God had promised him a long life if only he would serve Him with his whole heart. Solomon, who was sixty when he died, did not live a particularly long life.

Jude's Praise—Worshipping through Prayer

Every week in liturgical churches, those that follow a formal ritual, the congregation sings or chants a particular form of praise to God. Among the most familiar are the Gloria Patri ("Glory Be to the Father") and the Doxology ("Praise God from Whom All Blessings Flow"). Less familiar is the doxology found at the end of the epistle of Jude, a letter possibly written by a brother of Jesus and intended to be circulated among all the churches. What sets Jude's doxology apart is the context in which it was written.

Unique among New Testament Letters

Jude's brief letter consisting of just twenty-five verses is unique among New Testament letters, not only for its brevity but also for its harsh tone. Jude begins on a note of regret; he had wanted to write about their shared salvation, presumably a more uplifting topic, but he felt led to issue a warning instead. Evildoers guilty of sexual sin had infiltrated the church.

Jude minced no words in describing these wicked people: they had "given themselves over to sexual immorality" (Jude 7 NKJV), rejected authority, and spoken evil of things they knew nothing about. Moreover, they were a blemish on the communal meals that Christians shared, sinners who were "twice dead…foaming up their own shame" (Jude 12–13 NKJV), who lived by their lust, and who caused division in the church.

Troublemakers in Their Midst

Jude left little doubt how he felt about the troublemakers in their midst.

But then, when he reached the end of his diatribe, Jude remembered the One Who makes everything right, and he broke out into praise: "To Him who is able to keep you from stumbling, and to present you faultless before the presence of His glory with exceeding joy, to God our Savior, who alone is wise, be glory and majesty, dominion and power, both now and forever. Amen" (Jude 24–25 NKJV).

Jude left the matter of the infiltrators where it belonged: in the hands of the only wise God, Who alone could keep those under Jude's care pure and blameless.

Digging Deeper

Biblical writers who railed against the wicked frequently ended on a note of praise or humility; you can almost hear a sigh of relief when their thoughts turned toward God. In Psalm 139, for example, after writing an eloquent and memorable poem about God, David suddenly expressed his hatred for the wicked. But he ended by turning back to God: "Look deep into my heart, God, and find out everything I am thinking. Don't let me follow evil ways, but lead me in the way that time has proven true" (vv. 23–24 CEV). As you read through the Psalms, note how often the writers did this.

 Final Thought

Jude reminded Christians that God is able to keep them from "stumbling," which means much more than simply getting tripped up by sin now and then. It means falling away from the faith completely. Jude's choice of words was no coincidence. After issuing a stern warning about former believers wreaking havoc on the church, Jude underscored the importance of relying on God to keep your life and faith pure.

Hannah's Heart—"He's My Child"

For years, Hannah suffered the derision of Peninnah, her husband's other wife, during their journeys from their hometown of Ramah to Shiloh to observe the annual religious feasts. Peninnah, the mother of Elkanah's children, was well aware of Elkanah's preference for Hannah. Out of jealousy, she taunted Hannah because she was childless. One year, Hannah could not take Peninnah's torment any longer. She finished her meal and ran to the tabernacle, where the high priest Eli observed her behavior—and accused her of drunkenness.

Hannah in Anguish

But Hannah was pouring out her anguish to God: "Lord All-Powerful, I am your servant, but I am so miserable! Please let me have a son. I will give him to you for as long as he lives, and his hair will never be cut" (1 Samuel 1:11 CEV).

Eli could see her lips move, but no sound came out of her mouth. He assumed she was drunk. Hannah denied that and explained her sorrow: "'Sir, please don't think I'm no good!' Hannah answered. 'I'm not drunk, and I haven't been drinking. But I do feel miserable and terribly upset. I've been praying all this time, telling the Lord about my problems.' Eli replied, 'You may go home now and stop worrying. I'm sure the God of Israel will answer your prayer'" (1 Samuel 1:15–17 CEV).

God Honored Prayer

God honored Hannah's prayer and Eli's blessing. In due time, she gave birth to a son—Samuel, who would be the last judge of the Israelites. As she promised, Hannah gave Samuel to God; when he was three, she took him to live with and learn from Eli.

Leaving Samuel behind must have been difficult. But instead of mourning, Hannah praised God for his Goodness: "You make me strong and happy, Lord. You rescued me. Now I can be glad and laugh at my enemies" (1 Samuel 2:1 CEV).

Hannah's song of thanksgiving lives on in Scripture—a tribute to a woman who trusted God completely and fulfilled her vow to Him.

Digging Deeper

Hannah vowed that no razor would be used on her future son's head (1 Samuel 1:11). This refers to the Nazirite vow, through which a man was consecrated to God. Nazirites could not consume wine, beer, vinegar made from either beverage, or any product of a grapevine (grapes, raisins). They also could not cut their hair; thus, no razor would be used on their heads. Both Samson and John the Baptist were Nazirites.

 Final Thought

In Israelite society, a barren woman was a scorned woman. Conceiving and giving birth to Samuel was undoubtedly the high point of Hannah's life. But she had made a vow to God, which was a serious act; no honorable person would break such a vow. Think about what you would do if you made a difficult vow and then had to make good on it.

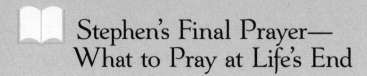

Stephen's Final Prayer—
What to Pray at Life's End

It isn't unusual for the dying to have visions or to cry out to God with their last breaths. What is unusual is for a dying person to see the heavens open or to see the Son of Man standing at the right hand of God. Stephen saw both. But as dramatic as that was, that vision didn't provide the only extraordinary moment as he neared death. A second striking event occurred when Stephen cried out to God, with his last breath, to forgive the very people responsible for his death.

Remarkable Spiritual Gifts

Stephen was among seven apostles chosen to distribute food to the widows among the Christians in Jerusalem. That may not sound like an important job, but the seven were chosen precisely because of their remarkable spiritual gifts. The widows needed their wisdom and compassion.

Stephen also distinguished himself by performing "signs and wonders," which attracted crowds and the attention of the synagogue leaders. The leaders leveled numerous accusations against him, started rumors about him, and tried to turn the people against him. Eventually, Stephen was brought up on charges of blasphemy.

Stephen's Accusation

At his trial, Stephen stood before the religious council and began preaching about God's plan of redemption. He finished with an accusation: "You stubborn people! You are heathen at heart and deaf to the truth. Must you forever resist the Holy Spirit? That's what your ancestors did, and so do you! Name one prophet your ancestors didn't persecute! They even killed the ones who predicted the coming of the Righteous One—the Messiah whom you betrayed and murdered" (Acts 7:51–52 NLT).

At that, the Jewish leaders became enraged. They rushed at him, dragged him outside the city, and began stoning him. Among the angry crowd that day was Saul of Tarsus, who would need the forgiveness Stephen prayed about.

Something to Ponder

There are times when forgiveness seems to be in short supply, and at other times tragic events—such as the schoolhouse massacre of Amish children in 2006—are marked by an outpouring of forgiveness. Experts in the field say forgiveness needs to be practiced on a daily basis so it becomes an automatic but genuine response when it is most needed. How can you practice forgiveness in your everyday life?

 Final Thought

Stephen's trial proved to be a turning point in the history of the fledgling church. The Jewish leaders ramped up their persecution of the Christians, and soon only the apostles were left in Jerusalem. But as the persecuted Christians fled to the surrounding countryside, they took with them the good news about Jesus Christ. The stoning of Stephen, the church's first martyr, was the catalyst that caused the gospel to be spread far beyond Jerusalem.

Lord, Teach Us to Pray
the Lord's Prayer

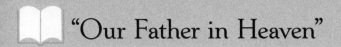

The first rule of communication is to know your audience. Broadcasters, public speakers, pastors, and teachers all face the ongoing task of learning about their audiences. In prayer, you have an audience of One. To understand your audience, it is important to understand where He lives. Heaven is a mystery that has been misunderstood and misrepresented for as long as poets and pundits have tried to define it. While it will remain mysterious until you see it with your own eyes, you can try to understand the fundamentals.

God Lives in Heaven

God told Moses to create a tabernacle—a tent in which God's people could worship. Many years later, Solomon built a permanent structure, the temple, and dedicated it with a powerful prayer. Solomon acknowledged that neither a building nor the entire earth could hold God. He prayed, "Hear the humble and earnest requests from me and your people Israel when we pray toward this place. Yes, hear us from heaven where you live, and when you hear, forgive" (1 Kings 8:30 NLT).

While God dwells in heaven, He is also "close to the brokenhearted and saves those who are crushed in spirit" (Psalm 34:18 NIV). The paradox of majesty and proximity is wrapped up in the title Father. When you pray to the Father, you are praying to One Whose wholeness cannot be contained but Who is as close to you as your skin.

Heaven Is Your Ultimate Home

Author and apologist Randy Alcorn wrote a landmark book titled *Heaven*. He wrote, "When Jesus told his disciples, 'In my Father's house are many rooms.... I am going there to prepare a place for you' (John 14:2), he deliberately chose common, physical terms (*house, rooms, place*) to describe where he was going and what he was preparing for us. He wanted to give his disciples (and us) something tangible to look forward to—an actual place where they (and we) would go to be with him."

Final Thought

Christians are ambassadors—emissaries from another country. The ambassador's permanent citizenship is in his own country. Here he is merely representing his native land on foreign soil. You are an ambassador from heaven. When you pray to God in heaven, you are sending a letter home or asking for more supplies for your outpost.

"Hallowed Be Your Name"

Reginald Heber wrote the lyrics for the majestic hymn "Holy, Holy, Holy." John Dykes's transforming melody made this song an enduring anthem to God's most wondrous attribute: holiness. "Holy, holy, holy! Though the darkness hide thee, though the eye of sinful man thy glory may not see; only thou art holy; there is none beside thee, perfect in power, in love, and purity." Holiness is the state of being wholly other, separate, or set apart. If God is holy, why do we pray, "Hallowed be thy name"?

The Intent of Jesus's Words

Theologian and author R. C. Sproul pointed out that many of us miss the intent of Jesus's specific words: "The first line of the prayer is not a petition. It's a form of personal address. The prayer continues: 'hallowed be your name, your kingdom come' (Matthew 6:9–10).

"We often confuse the words 'hallowed be your name' with part of the address, as if the words were 'Hallowed is your name.' In that case, the words would merely be an ascription of praise to God. But that is not how Jesus said it. He uttered it as a petition, as the first petition. We should be praying that God's name be hallowed, that God be regarded as holy."

The Name of God Is Holy

Sproul continued: "There is a kind of sequence within the prayer. God's kingdom will never come where His name is not considered holy. His will is not done on earth as it is in heaven if His name is desecrated here. In heaven the name of God is holy. It is breathed by angels in a sacred hush. Heaven is a place where reverence for God is total. It is foolish to look for the kingdom anywhere God is not revered."

The name for God in the Old Testament was so holy that most would not say it aloud. The scribes would not write it down. Jesus was considered blasphemous when He uttered it during His trial: "I Am." Jesus's name itself also meets the standards of holiness.

There are two types of holiness: (1) being set apart for a special purpose, and (2) set apart from evil and sin. Jesus's name meets both criteria. Jesus was set apart for a special purpose by being named in heaven. Gabriel shocked young Mary. He told her that she would conceive and deliver a son. He instructed her to name Him Jesus. Then he described what this Son would become: "He will be great, and will be called the Son of the Highest; and the Lord God will give Him the throne of His father David. And He will reign over the house of Jacob forever, and of His kingdom there will be no end" (Luke 1:32–33 NKJV).

Joseph was upset. His future wife was pregnant. He thought she was pure and set apart. How could she do this to him? The angel surprised him and told him to go through with the marriage. He then said, "You shall call His name JESUS, for He will save His people from their sins" (Matthew 1:21 NKJV).

The Name of Jesus Is Set Apart

This name—*Jesus*—is set apart in history. Those who needed healing or deliverance called out the name on the street. The religious leaders cursed the name and plotted to erase it—and the Man who bore the name—from the earth. His name became a part of the mocking death sentence nailed above His head on the cross: "This is Jesus, the King of the Jews."

Jesus's name is also set apart from evil and sin. It is the name Christians pray to and the name of the Savior. Paul would eventually call it the name above all names. Pastor and magazine publisher A. W. Tozer marveled at Christ's holiness: "We cannot grasp the true meaning of the divine holiness by thinking of someone or something very pure and then raising the concept to the highest degree we are capable of. God's holiness is not simply the best we know infinitely bettered. We know nothing like the divine holiness. It stands apart, unique, unapproachable, incomprehensible, and unattainable. The natural man is blind to it. He may fear God's power and admire His wisdom, but His holiness he cannot even imagine." The name that we pray to is not just different or unique. It is wholly holy.

> 🍃 **Final Thought**
>
> *Jesus could've taught, "hallowed be thy character" or "thy memory." Instead, we pray, "hallowed be thy name." Songwriters Bill and Gloria Gaither created the Homecoming concert series where the audience sings along with well-known recording artists. The chorus "There's Just Something About That Name" is one of the highlights. The lyrics and emotion underline the nature of the name of Jesus. His name should be spoken in reverence, never as a punctuation mark or an expletive.*

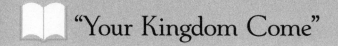

"Your Kingdom Come"

Many of Jesus's parables begin with the words "The kingdom of God is like..." His descriptions are like snapshots of remote Australia or the moon tacked upon a bulletin board. The more you look at them, the more you want to see the entirety of the landscape and experience it for yourself. When the kingdom of God is fully realized, all pain, suffering, mourning, and tears will evaporate faster than the morning dew. Theologians call this the second advent. As Israel looked forward to the coming of the Messiah, so Christians long for the coming of the kingdom of God.

The Kingdom of God Is Full of Mysteries

The disciples questioned Jesus often about His parables. They were looking at His snapshots but not understanding the panoramic picture. Jesus told them, "The secret of the kingdom of God has been given to you" (Mark 4:11 NIV). The disciples still struggled with the meanings of Jesus's teaching. Jesus was pointing to Himself as the fulfillment of the prophecies and the personification of the kingdom of God. Yet the disciples were still searching for—like many of their contemporaries—a political coup d'état.

The Kingdom of God Is Not of This World

Jesus did not come to overthrow earthly kingdoms or unseat military dictators. During His trial, Pilate questioned Him about His identity and mission. Jesus answered, "My kingdom is not of this world. If My kingdom were of this world, My servants would fight, so that I should not be delivered to the Jews; but now My kingdom is not from here" (John 18:36 NKJV).

In His longest teaching session—often referred to as the Sermon on the Mount—Jesus urged His followers to "seek first His kingdom and His righteousness" (Matthew 6:33 NASB) but didn't promise that they would fully realize it until He comes again.

When the apostle John described the second advent, his words were still full of mystery and surprise: "I saw the holy city, the new Jerusalem, coming down from God out of heaven like a bride beautifully dressed for her husband. I heard a loud shout from the throne, saying, 'Look, God's home is now among his people! He will live with them, and they will be his people. God himself will be with them'" (Revelation 21:2–3 NLT).

The Kingdom of God Is within You

The paradox of proximity exists with the presence of God—He is both infinitely above you and intimately close to you. The same paradox exists with the kingdom of God. It is not of this world and is simultaneously within you. This paradox should inspire awe and tenderness.

Fifteenth-century Catholic monk Thomas à Kempis challenged himself and his readers to "turn, then, to God with all your heart. Forsake this wretched world and your soul shall find rest." To Thomas, the kingdom of God—the gifts of peace and joy that only the Holy Spirit can give—belong exclusively to those who have learned to "despise" the external things of the world and embrace instead the inner, communal life with God.

He urged his readers to prepare a dwelling place for Christ in their hearts, a place that delights the Lord and welcomes His comfort and presence: "His visits with the inward man are frequent, His communion sweet and full of consolation, His peace great, and His intimacy wonderful indeed."

 Final Thought

Consider the thieves crucified on either side of Jesus. They represent the tension between the kingdom of this world and the kingdom of God. They both mocked Him, but one wised up and said to Jesus, "'Remember me when you come into power!' Jesus replied, 'I promise that today you will be with me in paradise'" (Luke 23:42–43 CEV). When you pray "Your kingdom come," hear Jesus's response: "You will be with Me in paradise."

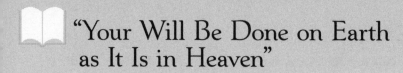

"Your Will Be Done on Earth as It Is in Heaven"

Amazon.com lists thousands of books written about how to discover God's will for your life. Christians throughout time have been frustrated trying to find the secret code or formula. A + B doesn't equal C. Jesus prayed for God's will. He also told believers that He will grant whatever is prayed according to God's will. If God's will is so important to the Christian faith, why does it feel so elusive?

Imagine yourself as the apprentice to a master painter such as Rembrandt. What if instead of applying the paint to the canvas himself, he talked you through every brushstroke in an attempt to paint his vision through your hands? How well would you do?

God's Will

God has chosen to coach us through accomplishing His will. He teaches us about His will through the examples of the heroes and heroines of the Bible. They are His masterworks.

If you travel to Paris or Rome, you'll see art students of every age and ability copying the work of the masters. They sit for hours in front of a painting at a museum to try to capture and understand what the artist was trying to accomplish. Some art students have sketchbooks full of hands as rendered by their favorite artists. They hope to capture the nuance of his or her work. In the same way, you must become a student of the will of God and sit for hours watching the lives of the men and women of the Bible.

Heroes and Heroines

Here are some questions to consider as you study the lives of Bible heroes and heroines:

- How did he handle adversity?
- How did she respond to failure?
- How did God speak to him?
- Who was her archenemy?
- How did the enemy attempt to derail him?
- How did she complain?

How Did He Worship?

When you pray for God's will, you join Jesus in His prayers. At his darkest hour, He prayed, "Not My will, but Yours be done" (Luke 22:42 NASB).

Something to Ponder

The most important aspect of pursuing the will of God is attitude. Micah 6:8 tells us that walking humbly with God is incredibly important. When frustration grows but you don't understand the will of God, pull back, take a deep breath, and remember to humble yourself before Him. Ask Him to show you His will.

 Final Thought

Think about a bottle of kids' soap bubbles. When you pull out the wand, it drips with the thick, glistening liquid, but there are no bubbles until you gently blow behind the ring. Each day is like a ring of soap bubbles. Like the original creation, you must await the breath of God. Only then can you soar. Pray for His will to be done, and get ready to fly.

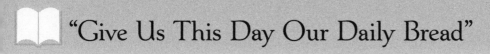

"Give Us This Day Our Daily Bread"

When the disciples heard Jesus ask for daily bread, they probably thought back on the familiar history of the exodus. While the Israelites wandered through the wilderness, God miraculously met their physical needs with a daily shower of manna. Manna was waferlike pieces of sweet bread that covered the ground every morning like fresh snow. Even though God gave them more than enough for each day, the extra couldn't be saved. God generously fed them constantly and consistently, but the people grumbled against His provision. Did Jesus want them to pray for manna again, or did He mean something else?

Another Miracle with Bread

A few weeks after Jesus taught His disciples how to pray, He performed another bread miracle: the feeding of five thousand men plus wives and children in one day. There may have been more than twenty thousand people fed on that single day. Jesus miraculously transformed five small loaves and two fish into a smorgasbord for a crowd that would overflow a high school football stadium. That puts a twist in the equation—what is daily bread?

Bread is what you need—physically, intellectually, emotionally, relationally, and spiritually. Pray for the necessities, not the niceties of life. It's too easy to be distracted from what's important.

During the Korean War, a general commissioned his staff to survey all his commanding officers about their most acute needs. His staff visited with COs leading infantry units at the front, managing MASH units a few miles back, and supervising headquarters staff. The results startled the general. Those at the front lines asked for more ammunition, more bandages, and more soldiers. Those farthest away from the fighting asked for Coca-Cola® and better movies. The general reminded everyone that they were fighting a war, not taking a vacation.

You are on the front lines, not the sidelines, of your life. When you pray, avoid the temptation to pray for daily cupcakes. Allow God to supply your needs and bless you beyond belief.

Day by Day

Someone once quipped, "Life wouldn't be so hard if it wasn't so daily." The movie *Groundhog Day* hits home because viewers feel trapped in the monotony of the daily grind. A few minutes after Jesus taught the model prayer, He coached His disciples on worry. He said, "Do not worry about tomorrow; for tomorrow will care for itself. Each day has enough trouble of its own" (Matthew 6:34 NASB).

When you pray for daily bread, ask God for what you will need for the next twenty-four hours. Prisoners of war have reported praying hour by hour or minute by minute.

Consider the Lilies

It's as if Jesus anticipated our problems with praying for His will and for daily bread. Almost in the same breath as His instructions on prayer, Jesus said, "Look at the ravens. They don't plant or harvest or store food in barns, for God feeds them. And you are far more valuable to him than any birds! Can all your worries add a single moment to your life? And if worry can't accomplish a little thing like that, what's the use of worrying over bigger things? Look at the lilies and how they grow. They don't work or make their clothing, yet Solomon in all his glory was not dressed as beautifully as they are" (Luke 12:24–27 NLT).

When you doubt His provision and pray for daily bread with a skeptical heart, look around at the majesty of creation that He holds together.

Jesus Is the Bread of Life

After Jesus fed the multitudes, the crowd became too rowdy. Jesus headed to the mountains, and the disciples headed to the water. A storm tossed the ship in the middle of the night. While they trimmed sails, they spotted Jesus walking across the lake. They invited Him into the boat and "immediately the boat was at the land to which they were going" (John 6:21 NASB). The crowds chased Jesus all the way to Capernaum. They were hunting for more food and more miracles. Jesus excited them when He said, "The bread of God is that which comes down out of heaven, and gives life to the world" (John 6:33 NASB).

The crowd only cheered for more, but He silenced them. "I am the bread of life; he who comes to Me will not hunger, and he who believes in Me will never thirst" (John 6:35

NASB). When you pray for daily bread, don't forget that the ultimate bread is Jesus Himself. Ask Him to draw close, to surprise you amid your stormy seas, and to be the provision that never leaves you hungry.

Point to Remember

Goal-setters struggle with the concept of daily bread. "Isn't it wise to think ahead?" they argue. "Doesn't the Bible say, 'Count the cost'?" It does, but the Bible also warns, "The mind of man plans his way, but the LORD directs his steps" (Proverbs 16:9 NASB). Ask God for today's dose of planning ahead, always remembering that He clothes every bird and flower.

Digging Deeper

All the requests in the Lord's Prayer—including daily bread—are plural. Bible scholar Hank Hanegraaff observed, "Not only are we praying for the needs of our immediate family, but we are praying for the needs of our extended family as well. We do not pray as mere rugged individualists but as members of a community of faith. All we need to do is turn on the television to see that our sisters and brothers around the world suffer daily from maladies ranging from droughts to deadly diseases. Yet, these images fade from our minds before the next commercial interruption."

 Final Thought

Agur, son of Jakeh, compiled the wise sayings for what is now known as Proverbs 30. He asked for daily bread in his wise prayer. "Keep falsehood and lies far from me; give me neither poverty nor riches, but give me only my daily bread. Otherwise, I may have too much and disown you and say, 'Who is the LORD?' Or I may become poor and steal, and so dishonor the name of my God" (vv. 8–9 NIV).

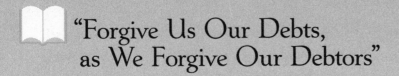

"Forgive Us Our Debts, as We Forgive Our Debtors"

Have you been in a church service or meeting where everyone joins in praying the Lord's Prayer aloud? If many backgrounds are represented, this phrase will bring chaos—and a few smiles—to the assembly. Do you use the word *debts* or *trespasses*? No matter which word you use, this phrase is special. The fifth commandment is the first with a promise, and the fifth request in the Lord's Prayer is the first with an elaboration.

Jesus used the Greek word *opheilema*: "a debt that is due today." Like the request before it, there is immediacy to this phrase—debts are current. Immediately after teaching the prayer, Jesus said, "If you forgive others for their transgressions, your heavenly Father will also forgive you. But if you do not forgive others, then your Father will not forgive your transgressions" (Matthew 6:14–15 NASB).

An Unforgiving Heart

This is not a heavenly quid pro quo. Jesus was illustrating the insidious nature of an unforgiving heart. He told His followers two parables. First, a wealthy man forgave two debts. The first debtor owed two years of wages; the second owed two months. Jesus asked, "Which of them will love the wealthy man more?" They answered, "The one forgiven more."

He also told a parable about a man who was forgiven for millions in debt but then turned around and refused to forgive a man for a tiny debt.

An Unforgiving Spirit

Pastor and author John Piper wrote, "If we hold fast to an unforgiving spirit, we will lose heaven, and gain hell. The reason is not because we can earn heaven or merit heaven by forgiving others, but because holding fast to an unforgiving spirit proves that we do not trust Christ. If we trust him, we will not be able to take forgiveness from his hand for our million-dollar debt and withhold it from our ten-dollar debtor."

When you pray, "Forgive us our debts," remind yourself of the inestimable value of his forgiveness.

- **What is forgiveness of sin?**

To forgive sin is to take away iniquity. It is a metaphor. A man carries a heavy burden, and another man comes and lifts it off. When the heavy burden of sin is on us, God in pardoning lifts it off from the conscience and lays it upon Christ.

 Final Thought

A Pharisee invited Jesus to dinner. As they dined, a woman burst into the room. She knelt at Jesus's feet and sparked incredulity and insolence from the religious leaders. Her tears dripped onto Jesus's feet. She wiped them with her hair and then poured an expensive oil onto them, anointing Jesus. Jesus told the table of slack-jawed men, "her many sins have been forgiven—as her great love has shown. But whoever has been forgiven little loves little" (Luke 7:47 NIV).

"Do Not Lead Us into Temptation, but Deliver Us from the Evil One"

Some have joked that this entreaty is the most often prayed phrase of the Lord's Prayer. Temptations seem to be around every corner. What tempts you? The bowl of chocolate candies on a coworker's desk? Clicking on the wrong link while surfing the Internet? Expanding a simple misunderstanding into an outright lie? Spending money reserved for another part of the budget? Jesus was tempted but withstood the onslaught on your behalf. His model prayer can encourage and strengthen you.

Temptation

The phrase "Do not lead us into temptation" should not be expanded to say, "Sometimes you do lead us into temptation; don't do it anymore." Pastor and author John MacArthur pointed out that this "petition reflects the believing one's desire to avoid the dangers of sin altogether."

James watched Jesus travel around Nazareth, Bethany, and other towns in Judea. He was part of the family mob that showed up at Peter's house for an intervention (Mark 3). He faced the most cunning and destructive temptation of all—disbelieving Jesus. But as Jesus's ministry continued, James came to embrace Jesus's teachings and became a leader in the early church. He saw Jesus flee from and avoid temptation. He was up close and personal.

James wrote in his epistle, "Let no one say when he is tempted, 'I am being tempted by God'; for God cannot be tempted by evil, and He Himself does not tempt anyone" (James 1:13 NASB). The devil must love to tempt a believer to believe his tempter is God Himself.

The apostle Paul had something in common with James: he disbelieved Jesus until God got his attention on the road to Damascus (Acts 9). He offered this warning and promise: "Whoever thinks he stands must be careful not to fall. No temptation has overtaken you except what is common to humanity. God is faithful, and He will not allow you to be tempted beyond what you are able, but with the temptation He will also provide a way of escape so that you are able to bear it" (1 Corinthians 10:12–13 HCSB).

God knows the way of escape and will deliver you.

The Evil One

Part of military basic training takes place in the classroom. New soldiers learn the uniform colors, insignia, silhouettes of aircraft and tanks, and the weapons used by their enemies. In the same way, Christians should understand the profile of their enemy.

The Bible calls the devil arrogant and rash. The apostle Peter, who denied Christ three times, understood the nature of the devil. In his letter, Peter wrote, "Be sober, be vigilant; because your adversary the devil walks about like a roaring lion, seeking whom he may devour" (1 Peter 5:8 NKJV).

The Bible also calls the devil crafty and deceitful. Paul often pointed to how Satan tempted Eve as an example of how he twists words. The psalmist compared Satan to a hunter: "Surely He shall deliver you from the snare of the fowler" (Psalm 91:3 NKJV). Jesus referred to him as a wolf in one of His parables (John 10:12).

"Bible Answer Man" Hank Hanegraaff warned Christians of the dangers of either overestimating or underestimating Satan's power.

He took issue with those who describe Satan using terms such as the "author of darkness"; in so doing, he said, they unwittingly draw a parallel between him and God, the Author of light. He wrote, "That, however, is far from true. God is the sovereign Author of all creation; Satan is but an angel that he has created. Satan is not the opposite of the Creator. Rather, as a fallen angel, he is the counterpart to the archangel Michael."

But underestimating Satan is also a mistake, he wrote, reminding readers that though he is malevolent, Satan also possesses a brilliant intellect. Hanegraaff quotes Charles Haddon Spurgeon: "We must not expect that a man, unaided from above, should ever be a match for an angel, especially an angel whose intellect has been sharpened by malice."

When you pray "Deliver us from evil," pray with confidence and courage that God will answer and deliver.

 Check Your Understanding

- **Will Satan be defeated? If so, when?**
  Think of Satan as a bull in a nineteenth-century bullfight. As you interact with him on

earth, remember that he is stabbed, bleeding, and near death. He is still dangerous, but already defeated. He is crushed (Genesis 3:15), and it's only a matter of time until he is destroyed (Revelation 20:14).

- **How should a person behave when tempted?**

   You should first prepare yourself for temptation. It will come. It is foolish to believe you are immune (Ephesians 6:11). When temptation comes, take your cue from Joseph. When Potiphar's wife tried to seduce him, Joseph immediately escaped and ran so fast that his tunic remained in her hand (Genesis 39).

- **If a person has given in to temptation repeatedly, how can he or she possibly pray this prayer?**

   The apostle Paul called himself the chief of sinners, yet knew great mercy and grace. God's grace is for you as well. Receive it and be refreshed (1 Timothy 1).

Something to Ponder

Some Christians who are dealing with temptation tend to focus on the sin rather than the cure. While it's important to acknowledge the specific sin you're battling, obsessing over it—or worrying about whether that sin is worse than others—won't help you conquer it. Once you confess the sin to God and resolve to turn away from it, it's time to focus on God and the power He gives you to overcome sin.

 Final Thought

Hank Hanegraaff said: "It is significant to note that Jesus was led by the Spirit into the desert 'to be tempted by the devil' (Matthew 4:1). Thus while Satan was the agent of the temptation, God was the author of the testing. Satan used the occasion to tempt Christ to sin; God used the occasion to demonstrate that he could not sin."

"For Yours Is the Kingdom and the Power and the Glory Forever"

The ending to the Lord's Prayer is controversial, and it does not appear in some of the manuscripts of the gospel of Matthew. In many Bibles, footnotes mark this fact. Biblical scholars fill in the details from history. The words echo 1 Chronicles 29:11, a psalm of thanksgiving written by David in response to the outpouring of offerings for the construction of the temple. The words became the response of God's people in the synagogue. After a prayer was offered, the people would respond, "For yours is the kingdom and the power and the glory forever." Christians carry on the tradition even today.

Praise God

Bible commentator Matthew Henry highlighted this verse. The temple was built for the glory of God, David's psalm points to the worship of God, and those who say these words are intended to be conduits of praise to God. Praise is integral to prayer. The model prayer begins by ascribing praise to God. It is appropriate that the disciples would respond with the words of praise they had been taught since childhood.

When you praise God, you magnify Him. When Mary, the mother of Jesus, discovered God's plan, she said, "My soul magnifies the Lord" (Luke 1:46 NKJV). Sherlock Holmes magnified clues with his magnifying glass, and scientists magnify cells with a microscope.

Magnify God

When you magnify God, you are not a microscope; you don't make the very small a little larger. Instead, you are like a telescope that magnifies a celestial object hundreds of light-years away and larger than our entire solar system. The naked eye can see it, but magnification sharpens the details and inspires more awe of its beauty.

God is larger than you can imagine, and your praise brings the details of His majesty into clearer focus and stirs your heart to even more worship. In prayer, step up to the telescope and become amazed with God. Don't sit on the couch and let others look through the lens.

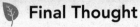 **Final Thought**

It is good to magnify the Lord and honor His great Majesty. The psalmist said in Psalm 145:11: "They shall speak of the glory of your kingdom and tell of your power." (ESV). We should in prayer speak of His glory and His power, revering Who God is.

The Importance of Prayer

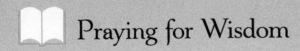

Praying for Wisdom

The Lord's Prayer is the most frequently prayed prayer in history. Second place is awarded to the Serenity Prayer. Soldiers in Europe and the Pacific during World War II heard their chaplains pray it. Now, every day, millions worldwide pray the Serenity Prayer to begin group meetings as they seek healing and restoration. The prayer appears on every surface from framed fine art and building-size murals to snow globes and ink pens. The prayer's popularity is exceeded only by its wisdom.

Reinhold Niebuhr was born at the turn of the twentieth century just as the industrial revolution was picking up steam. After graduation from Yale in 1914, he was assigned to a church in Detroit, Michigan. His church grew quickly because of his winsome preaching and the burgeoning automobile industry. In 1928, Niebuhr joined the faculty of Union Theological Seminary in New York. His teaching and writing influenced generations of students, including Dietrich Bonhoeffer, the great German writer and theologian.

Niebuhr composed the prayer when he was preaching in Heath, Massachusetts, while his family was on vacation. His daughter wrote, "It was in an ordinary Sunday morning service at the Heath Union Church in the summer of 1943 that my father first used his new prayer."

The original version of the prayer for wisdom reads, "God, give us grace to accept with serenity the things that cannot be changed, courage to change the things that should be changed, and the wisdom to distinguish the one from the other." Three requests are wrapped up in these famous words.

Serenity

Peace feels fleeting. To-do lists are long and complicated by over commitment. Interruptions add insult to injury. Visual stimuli come from LCD screens on phones, computers, televisions, and even billboards. Noises bombard our ears from every direction and source. One day ends in frustration, and another day begins owing debts to yesterday. It seems impossible to find a moment for a deep breath and a free thought.

God offers a different peace. As Jesus prepared His disciples for His death, He told them, "Peace I leave with you; my peace I give you. I do not give to you as the world gives.

Do not let your hearts be troubled and do not be afraid" (John 14:27 NIV). His peace is better than a soothing bath and can permeate the most difficult schedule.

Courage

Paul began each of his letters by bestowing God's grace on the readers. He ended every letter with a flurry of instructions. Some are common and others pointed. At the end of his first letter to the church at Corinth, Paul admonished the leaders, "Watch, stand fast in the faith, be brave, be strong. Let all *that* you *do* be done with love" (1 Corinthians 16:13–14 NKJV). The Corinthians didn't need courage to fight a battle or hold off a siege, they needed courage to confront false ideas about faith, old habits of idolatry, and a hedonistic culture.

God's courage has more steel in it than earthly courage. His courage is reinforced by His omnipotence—His all-powerful nature. When you pray for courage, remember that God encouraged Joshua, David, and Jeremiah, and the persecuted church before you.

Wisdom

Niebuhr's ultimate prayer is for wisdom. Solomon, often called the wisest man who ever lived, discussed the value of wisdom in Proverbs 4:5–9, advising his "son" to actively pursue wisdom. Wisdom, it seems, is not something that comes to people automatically, and it is something that people can forget. Not only did Solomon warn against forgetting wisdom; he also warned against abandoning it. Wisdom (which he personified in female terms) will guard over those who cling to her, he wrote, and those who place great value on her will be exalted.

By asking for wisdom, Niebuhr echoed the observation of James that those who lacked wisdom could ask God to supply it. God, in His generosity of spirit, would grant that request "without reproach" (James 1:5 NASB)—without expressing any disapproval over that lack of wisdom. Solomon, James, and Reinhold Niebuhr—three men who believed God's promise to give His people wisdom. That promise is for you as well.

Myth Buster

Some say that Reinhold Niebuhr didn't really write the Serenity Prayer, and the answer is a bit uncertain. In 2008, Fred Shapiro, the editor of *The Yale Book of Quotations*, asserted that the prayer was in circulation at least six years before it was attributed to the pastor.

Niebuhr himself was modest about his composition. He said, "Of course, it may have been spooking around for years, even centuries, but I don't think so. I honestly do believe that I wrote it myself." The prayer now reads: "God grant me the serenity to accept the things I cannot change, courage to change the things I can, and wisdom to know the difference."

Something to Ponder

Alcoholics Anonymous added another section to the prayer: "Living one day at a time; enjoying one moment at a time; accepting hardships as the pathway to peace; taking, as He did, this sinful world as it is, not as I would have it; trusting that He will make all things right if I surrender to His Will; so that I may be reasonably happy in this life and supremely happy with Him forever and ever in the next."

 Check Your Understanding

- **How does acceptance result in serenity?**

  Implied in the Serenity Prayer is the concept of relinquishment; in accepting that you cannot change a situation, you relinquish your attempt to control the situation. And with that comes peace.

- **How can a person acquire courage?**

  The Bible tells of many people who lacked courage but became bold by God's power. Each Spirit-led courageous act emboldens preparation for the next one.

 Final Thought

Solomon was given the opportunity to receive unequaled wealth or unparalleled wisdom from God. He chose wisdom, and God bestowed riches, wisdom, and honor. God then encouraged Solomon with these words: "If you walk in My ways, to keep My statutes and My commandments, as your father David walked, then I will lengthen your days" (1 Kings 3:14 NKJV). May God grant you wisdom—and much more.

The Prayer of Saint Francis of Assisi—Praying for Peace

Francesco felt caught between his parents. His mother wanted him to grow up to be a great spiritual leader. His father, a fabric salesman, wanted his son to grow up in the family business. Francesco made his own path by becoming a troubadour and poet. After a while, however, he saw the wisdom of his mom's ideas. Francesco—or Francis as he would be known in English—decided to dedicate his life to simplicity, devotion, and living out the love of Christ.

Instrument of Peace

Saint Francis founded the Franciscan order of monks but is ultimately best known for his poetic prayer:

"Lord, make me an instrument of Thy peace; where there is hatred, let me sow love; where there is injury, pardon; where there is doubt, faith; where there is despair, hope; where there is darkness, light; and where there is sadness, joy.

O Divine Master, grant that I may not so much seek to be consoled as to console; to be understood, as to understand; to be loved, as to love; for it is in giving that we receive, it is in pardoning that we are pardoned, and it is in dying that we are born to Eternal Life. Amen."

His words gather together scriptural admonitions like so many roses in a bouquet. His requests reflect the "fruit of the Spirit" (Galatians 5:22–23 NKJV) and "the Beatitudes" (Matthew 5 NKJV). Early in his life, Saint Francis was known as a flashy dresser who liked to pick a fight, spend a franc, and woo women. His narcissism gave way to humility, however, when he saw genuine poverty and need. This prayer is offered out of that humility.

Inspiration of Generations

The simplicity of his poetry belies his troubadour spirit and shines a spotlight on a code of behavior. This prayer has inspired three generations of songwriters, painters, and pastors to hone their crafts, at the same time motivating missionaries and caregivers to serve another day.

Myth Buster

Did Saint Francis really write this prayer? Scholars are divided. The prayer as it appears in English can be traced back only to 1936 when copies were distributed during World War II. A similar prayer appeared in a French Catholic journal, *La Clochette* ("The Little Bell"), in 1912 and became wildly popular when published in the official papal newspaper, *L'Osservatore Romano*. The prayer may not be from the thirteenth century, but it does reflect the ideals of Saint Francis.

 Final Thought

Rich Mullins wrote songs like "Awesome God" and "Elijah." He was fascinated by Saint Francis after seeing Brother Sun, Sister Moon, *a biography directed by Franco Zeffirelli. Mullins said, "That's really what I want to do. I mean, I really do want to live in poverty, I really do want my life to mean something. I really do want to imitate Christ and live according to the rule of the gospels."*

Praying for God's Protection

Few people in church history have as many legends attached to them as does Saint Patrick. He lived in the fifth century, and few verifiable records of his life survive from that time. The fifteen hundred years since then have provided plenty of time and opportunities for stories to be handed down—and to grow to mythic proportions. One story about him is unquestionably true, however, and it's a good one: Saint Patrick expanded the presence of Christianity in Ireland, and things were never quite the same after that.

Most of what is known about Patrick can be traced to two surviving letters, one of which told the story of his life. Much of what he wrote rings true to historians and lines up with what is known about the British Isles during that period.

Faith in Christ

Here is what is believed to be true: Patrick was born in Britain to a wealthy Roman family—his father was a not particularly religious Christian deacon—toward the end of the fourth century. At the age of sixteen, Patrick was sold into slavery by Irish kidnappers. During captivity, his faith in Christ was sealed and began to grow. Six years later—by his account, in obedience to the voice of God—he escaped and returned to his family. Soon thereafter he left for France to prepare for the priesthood. All along, his intention was to spread the gospel of Christ to the Irish.

When he returned to Ireland, he faced significant opposition from the Druids, a religious order who worshipped nature and didn't appreciate the presence of Christians. As Patrick and his followers traveled through the countryside on their way to meet with the king, a group of Druids lay in wait. Patrick learned of the planned ambush and wrote a prayer for protection that he placed on his breastplate. The prayer has come to be known as the Lorica, or the Deer's Cry; as Patrick and his twenty men passed by the Druids, all the would-be attackers saw were a doe and twenty fawns.

Saint Patrick's Prayer

These are the best-known, and most frequently prayed, words from Patrick's prayer: "Christ be with me, Christ within me, / Christ behind me, Christ before me, / Christ beside me,

Christ to win me, / Christ to comfort and restore me, / Christ beneath me, Christ above me, / Christ in quiet, Christ in danger, / Christ in hearts of all that love me, / Christ in mouth of friend and stranger."

Patrick went on to tirelessly evangelize the people of Ireland. According to his autobiographical letter, he baptized thousands of people, ordained priests, founded a number of monasteries, established church councils and dioceses, and led wealthy women and princes to Christ. Some of the women became nuns, which didn't sit well with their families.

Some of Patrick's evangelistic methods were highly criticized at the time, but many became patterns for sharing Christ that survive to this day. He was the first Christian to undertake a massive evangelistic effort, proving that believers did not need special training or advanced education to preach the gospel and make disciples of all nations.

Further Insights

Saint Patrick influenced future missions in two other ways:

- Although he came from wealth, Patrick renounced his background and lived among the poor Irish as they did, believing that they would be more inclined to listen to his message about Christ if he shared their way of living.
- Because he had little education, Patrick had difficulty communicating with those who spoke different languages. His openness in describing the challenges he faced prompted future foreign missionaries to begin learning the required languages before leaving for the mission field.

 Final Thought

Acts 17:22–29 records the apostle Paul's method for preaching Christ to pagans in Athens. Standing before a crowd of Athenians, Paul commended them for taking their religion seriously. "I even found an altar with this inscription: TO AN UNKNOWN GOD. So you are ignorant of the very thing you worship—and this is what I am going to proclaim to you," Paul told the crowd (v. 23 NIV). He then proceeded to inform the Athenians about this "unknown god"—the Creator God who is so powerful and mighty that He cannot be contained by shrines—unlike the gods the Greeks worshipped.

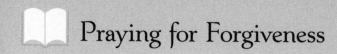

Praying for Forgiveness

Though he is occasionally edged out by George Washington in presidential popularity polls, Abraham Lincoln is the US president most often cited as the "most influential" or "most highly regarded." His wit and humility made him a man of the people, while his wisdom steered the country through one of the most difficult times in its history. In Lincoln's own words, it was prayer that saw him through: "I have been driven many times to my knees by the overwhelming conviction that I had nowhere else to go."

Prayer and Humiliation

Given his well-documented dependence on prayer, it's not surprising that Abraham Lincoln set aside a national day of "prayer and humiliation" in the spring of 1863, two years into the Civil War.

The proclamation suggested that the Civil War was God's punishment for the country's sins and a call to national reformation. After listing the many blessings of God on the United States, Lincoln wrote: "Intoxicated with unbroken success, we have become too self-sufficient to feel the necessity of redeeming and preserving grace, too proud to pray to the God that made us! It behooves us then, to humble ourselves before the offended Power, to confess our national sins, and to pray for clemency and forgiveness."

Two years later, Lincoln wrote of a different kind of forgiveness—that which everyone needed to extend to those who were their enemies during the Civil War.

"With Malice toward None"

In his second inaugural speech, Lincoln said: "With malice toward none; with charity for all; with firmness in the right, as God gives us to see the right, let us strive on to finish the work we are in; to bind up the nation's wounds; to care for him who shall have borne the battle, and for his widow, and his orphan—to do all which may achieve and cherish a just, and a lasting peace, among ourselves, and with all nations."

Prayer and forgiveness—that's what set Lincoln's presidency apart, at a time when the country needed a great deal of both.

Further Insights

Lincoln's forgiveness was legendary. In 1857, Lincoln was to assist lawyer Edwin Stanton in defending a client, but Stanton snubbed Lincoln, calling him a "long-armed creature." After Lincoln became president, Stanton remarked that Washington was in disarray because of the "painful imbecility of Lincoln." Within the year, Lincoln appointed him secretary of war, believing him to be the best person for the job. He never mentioned Stanton's poor treatment of him.

 Final Thought

- *Despite his position of power, Lincoln often realized that he had nowhere to turn but to God in prayer.*
- *Lincoln took the difficult route over the popular route in rebuking the country for its arrogance in forgetting God.*

Finding Words when You Have None

The Book of Common Prayer came out of the English Reformation. It is a compendium of written prayers, liturgies for various types of worship services, daily Bible readings, the book of Psalms, and other resources for public and private worship. It was born in 1549, revised in 1552 and 1559 and then again in 1662. Since that time it has had several major revisions, and the latest revision, the 1979 revision, is used today in the United States. *The Book of Common Prayer* has been translated into nearly forty languages, including several Native American languages.

For nearly four centuries, *The Book of Common Prayer* has been used for both public and private devotion. Its stately prayers blend Protestant interpretation with Catholic form, with many of its words and phrases becoming part of the language.

The *Book of Common Prayer* is a treasury of majestic prayers for:

- The world (for example, for peace, enemies, and "All Sorts and Conditions of Men")
- The church (for the clergy, the parish, and beyond)
- The nation (the government, elections, the military)
- The social order (cities, rural areas, the unemployed)
- The natural order (creation, conservation, the harvest)
- Family and personal life (children, the elderly, travelers, victims of addiction)
- Other prayers (preparation for mealtimes, worship services, Communion)

Although it is considered a literary masterpiece, *The Book of Common Prayer* doesn't ignore the ordinary routines of everyday life. Its readers know that after a stressful day, they can take a deep breath, turn to "Other Prayers," and find these words: "O Lord, support us all the day long, until the shadows lengthen, and the evening comes, and the busy world is hushed, and the fever of life is over, and our work is done. Then in your mercy, grant us a safe lodging, and a holy rest, and peace at the last."

In all, the personal prayer section offers seventy prayers for various situations, celebrations, demographics, and difficulties—in essence, a prayer for nearly every purpose.

Final Thought

Some Christians believe written prayers are lifeless, while others consider them to be unbiblical because Jesus didn't use written prayers. The reality is that the Psalms are the written prayers of the Bible and have served as a life-giving prayer book for Jews and Christians for centuries. And every day, all around the world, Christians pray a universal, written prayer, the Lord's Prayer, written in the gospels of Matthew and Luke.

Rejoice always, pray continually,
give thanks in all circumstances;
for this is God's will for you in
Christ Jesus.

1 THESSALONIANS 5:16–18 NIV

Contributors

Jeff Adams is an award-winning author and pastor. He lives in Arizona with his wife and daughter. He teaches what he's learned, and he learns so that he may teach.

Jan Apilado is an author and chaplain, along with her husband, for three different military organizations. They are retired pastors living in the Oregon Cascade Mountains.

James Stuart Bell is a publishing veteran and compiler of this volume and approximately forty other volumes of short stories. He has cover credit on more than one hundred books and owns Whitestone Communications.

Holly Blevins is a wife and mom living in Berryville, Virginia, where she's a youth leader at BLAZE ministries. She loves leading worship, hiking, and writing.

Laura L. Bradford is an award-winning poet and author. Her works have appeared in *Chicken Soup* and *Guideposts* books, as well as other compilations.

AnnaLee Conti, ordained minister and teacher, resides in the Mid-Hudson Valley, New York, with her pastor husband, Bob. She has published books, short stories, and articles.

Jenni Davenport is a Midwest mom who works as an editor during the day, is a freelancer at night, and has a circus of kids in her house every weekend.

Betty Johnson Dalrymple is a contributor to numerous devotional books, such as *God Allows U-Turns, Chicken Soup for the Soul,* and *Love Is a Verb.* She facilitates a grief support group.

Brenda Dillon has a horse farm in Michigan and would rather be in the barn than in the kitchen. Her love for Jesus is the pivotal point in her life.

Beth Duewel is a mother of three, trying to hit the mark with her mom's meat loaf recipe for Jerry. The paper angel still tops the Christmas tree.

Anita Estes resides in the Hudson Valley with her husband and various pets. She is in *Who's Who of American Teachers*. She is the author of *When God Speaks* and *Letters to God on a Prodigal Son*.

Virginia Rose Fairbrother has been a pastor's wife, ESL teacher, and writer. She and David have been married forty-six years. They have three children and six grandchildren.

Ellen Farrington's works are published online and in several books and magazines. She holds advanced degrees in the biological sciences and lives with her family in New England.

Anna M. Gregory and her husband are blessed with five sons and numerous grandchildren. She writes devotionals as God gives her the words to encourage others.

Dorothy J. Haire is a retired speech-language pathologist and a retired pastor who has earned four degrees. She is writing a commentary on the book of James.

Charles Earl Harrel served as a pastor for thirty years. He has more than three hundred and fifty published works.

Cassie Harris is an aspiring author who loves to watch God at work. She is attending Grace College and pursuing a degree in journalism and biblical studies.

Gail R. Helgeson continues to daily put her trust in God. She finds joy in writing, traveling, and spending time with her husband and two grown children.

Bob Hostetler is a pastor, an author, an agent with the Steve Laube Agency, and executive editor for the new Christian Writers Institute.

Charles J. Huff lives in Aurora, Illinois, with his wife of forty-plus years. He has been published at christiandevotions.us. Find his blog at chashuff.wordpress.com.

LaRose Karr enjoys speaking and ministering to God's people. Her family is her greatest blessing. She believes her writing is a gift from God and gives Him all the glory!

Donna Lee (Shane) Loomis is a wife of fifty years, mother, and grandmother. Family, children, writing, and sharing God's love are her greatest passions.

Joyce Starr Macias is a freelance writer and a retired newspaper reporter. She specializes in stories about her personal walk with God that have appeared in several magazines and books.

Marleen McDowell and her family pioneer in their solar home deep in the Oregon Cascade Mountains. Marleen enjoys the forest animals, gardening, canning, sewing, and sharing Jesus through her writings.

Marybeth Mitcham is an emerging freelance author whose writings have been published online and in the Christmas Moments #2 anthology.

Susan Allen Panzica is a speaker, Bible teacher, writer of the Eternity Cafe blog, and executive director of Justice Network, which raises awareness about human trafficking.

Marty Prudhomme is a freelance writer who has written and taught Bible studies for twenty years. She serves as Louisiana vice president of Leaders Training for Aglow International.

Janice Richardson writes Christian articles and stories focusing on how God is impacting people's lives. She resides in Calgary, Alberta, with her husband and the youngest of three sons.

Bobbie Roper is a retired pastor's wife and mother of four and has ten grandchildren. She is a women's Bible study teacher, seminar leader, and freelance writer.

Bill Shane (deceased) was a Colorado native. Bill devoted his life, from the age of eight, to God, family, and friends. He was a loving, caring family man who believed God had a special purpose for his family and supported that in the way he lived his life.

David Michael Smith is a writer of inspirational short stories, a church deacon, a faithful husband, and a loving father from Georgetown, Delaware. Email him at davidandgeri@hotmail.com.

Evelyn Rhodes Smith and her husband, Ted, live in Edgewood Summit, a retirement community in Charleston, West Virginia. Her stories appear in *A Cup of Comfort* series and volumes for Bethany House Publishers.

Ray Stenner was forced to retire because of illness but keeps busy with renovations and volunteer work with his loving wife, Rose, and enjoys time with their family.

Delores E. Topliff lives near Minneapolis. She loves Jesus, family, grandchildren, friends, writing, college teaching, mission trips, travel, and her small farm.

Faith Turnet is a North Carolina veteran educator and enjoys travel. She speaks to churches through her Devoted Diva Ministry.

Susan L. Tuttle lives in Michigan, where she's happily married to her best friend, is a home-schooling mom of three, and loves to write encouraging stories.

Elfriede Volk has been married for fifty-three years and has four children and eight grandchildren. She and her husband work as volunteer missionaries in various parts of the world.

Susan M. Watkins is featured in multiple publications and on CBN.com. Additional credits include Gloria Gaynor's "We Will Survive" and Max Lucado's HisIsMine.com.

Melinda Wright (as told to Anita Estes) is the wife of a church planter, mother of three, and grandmother of four. She loves cooking, hiking, entertaining, camping, and watching how God brings forth life.

Dr. Joshua F. Younce is a chiropractic physician in the western suburbs of Chicago. He served as team doctor for Wheaton Academy. Josh is married to Cheri, with two children, Sydney and Jackson.

Scripture Reference Index

Acts
2:42–47, 269
6, 212
7:51–52, 286
9, 302
12:3–11, 194
17:11, 186
17:22–29, 314

1 Chronicles
29:11, 305

2 Chronicles
20:6, 10

Colossians
1:3–6, 272
1:9, 177
1:9–14, 271
3:23, 222

1 Corinthians
10:12–13, 302
10:13, 207, 208

14:15, 230
16:13–14, 309

2 Corinthians
13:11, 269

Daniel
6:10, xi
9:4, 11

Deuteronomy
10:15, 261

Ecclesiastes
3:1–2, 211

Ephesians
1:15–23, 272
1:17, 191
1:18–19, 270
3:14–21, 271
3:18–19, 271
3:20, 37
3:20–21, 165, 182

4:2, 249
4:29, 249
5, 22
5:17, 199
5:22, 223
5:25, 223
6:4, 215
6:10–18, 208
6:11, 304

Exodus
4:11, 255
18, 212
33:18, 177

Galatians
4:4, 182
5:22–23, 243, 311
6:2, 227
6:4, 222

Genesis
2:24, 268
3:15, 304

22, 181
32:24–30, 194
39, 304

Habakkuk
2:20, 183
3:17–18, 218

Hebrews
4:14–15, 207
4:16, 4
10:36, 213
11:1, 29
12:1, 213

Isaiah
26:3–4, 209
40:31, 242
41:10, 230
55:8–9, 54
58:8, 246
65:24, 115

James
1:5, 141, 200, 309
1:5–6, 4
1:6, 237
1:13, 302
1:14–15, 207
1:17, 29
1:19–20, 232
2:14–17, 227
3:16, 240
4:2, 18, 29
4:8, 4
4:13–14, 211
4:13–17, 199
5:14–15, 4, 98
5:15–16, 5

Jeremiah
29:11, 199, 201
33:3, 4, 124, 185

John
3:16, 189
4:29, 263
6:21, 298
6:33, 298
6:35, 298–299
8:44, 189
10:4–5, 188
10:10, 189
10:12, 303
11, 228
11:19, 228
14:2, 289
14:13–4, 109
14:27, 309

16:13, 200
16:33, 183
17, 267
17:11, 267
17:20–23, 268
18:36, 293
20:27–29, 238

1 John
2:4–5, 199
5:14, 199

Jonah
1:2, 178
3:10, 178

Joshua
1:9, 226

Jude
7, 282
12–13, 282
24–25, 282

1 Kings
3:5–15, 194
3:7–8, 279
3:9, 279
3:11–13, 280
3:14, 310
4:29–31, 280
8:30, 289
17:21–22, xi
18:27, 275
18:36–37, 275
19, 185

Lamentations
3:22–26, 217

Luke
1:32–33, 292
1:46, 305
4:18–19, 247
7:47, 301
11:1, 14
11:2, 11
11:3, 11
11:4, 11
11:9–10, 11–12
12:24–27, 298
15:8–9, 165
18:1, 12
18:16, 133
22:42, 296
23:42–43, 294

Malachi
4:2, 244

Mark
2:27, 242
3, 302
4:11, 293
6, 212
9:23–24, 236
9:24, 237
11:24, x
14:35, 93

Matthew
1:19–25, 194
1:21, 292

4:1, 304
5, 311
5:10–12, 205
6:8, 29
6:9, 11
6:9–10, 291
6:13, 11
6:14–15, 300
6:27–29, 251
6:33, 293
6:34, 298
11:28–30, 242
13:57–58, 18
14:15–21, 212
18:10, 39
18:20, xiii
21:12–13, 232
26:39, xi, 181, 182
27:46, 238
28:18–20, 225

Micah
6:8, 296

Nehemiah
1:4, 273
1:6, 273
1:7, 273
1:8–9, 273

1 Peter
3:8, 269
5:7, 4, 40, 252
5:8, 303

Philippians
1:3–11, 272
2:1–4, 269
4:6, 252
4:6–7, 4, 157, 251
4:9, 157
4:19, 143, 247, 248

Proverbs
3:5–6, 180, 199
3:7–8, 244
4:5–9, 309
12:15, 200
16:9, 299
30:8–9, 299

Psalms
1:1–3, 226
3:4, 114
5:1–3, 176
7, 233
13, 233
18:2, 235
23, 149

23:1, 177
23:4, 5
27, 278
27:1, 230
27:5, 278
29:11, 210
31, 264
31:14, 162, 264
31:15, 220
32:7, 219, 220
32:8, 220
33:20, 220
34:18, 217, 289
35, 254
37:4, 142
37:7, 183
37:8–9, 232
46:1–3, 209
51:1, 10
55, 233
57:1, 277
64:2–3, 277
64:8, 277
91:1–2, 4

91:3, 303
91:11–12, 40
121:7–8, 219
139:23–24, 283
143:10, 199
145:11, 306
147:3, 189
149:4, 280

Revelation
12:10, 189
20:14, 304
21:2–3, 293

Romans
8:26–27, 182
8:34, 261
8:38–39, 234
12:2, 199
12:15, 227
13:13, 240
15:30, 176

1 Samuel
1:11, 10, 284, 285
1:15–17, 284
1:16–17, xi
2:1, 284
3:10, 193
18:7, 114
25, 250

1 Thessalonians
5:16–18, 319

2 Thessalonians
1:11–12, 272

1 Timothy
1, 304
2:3–4, 199
4:12, 225

Zechariah
4:6, 72

Topical Index

A

Aaron, 178–179
ability to pray. *see also* learning to pray
   barriers to prayer, 195–196
   guide for prayer, 171–319
Abraham, 175
accidents, 19–22, 31–34, 71–73. *see also* car accidents
   falls, 38–40, 115–118
   sports, 26–30
Adam and Eve, 175, 176
Adams, Jeff
   "A Heavenly Code Blue," 83–85
   "He Opened My Eyes," 26–30
"Against All Odds"
   (Marybeth Mitcham), 54–57
Agur, 299
Alcoholics Anonymous, 310
Alcorn, Randy, 289
all-knowing God, 263
"Amazing Grace," 189
Ambrose, 262
Amen, 37
aneurysms, 51, 86–90
"The Angel Holdup" (Susan Allen Panzica), 38–40
angelic intervention
   comfort and healing, 41–44
   family's and friends' prayers, 38–40, 71–73
   finding your way, 124
   grieving, 148–151
   hospitals, 41–44, 54–57
   people in need, 77–79
"An Angel Named Grace" (Bill Shane, Donna Lee
   Loomis), 41–44

anger, 62–66, 232–233
answers to prayer, 13–170
anticipation, praying with, 201
Apilado, Jan, 67–70
appearances by God, 43. *see also* presence of God;
   voice of God
   accident, comfort following, 31–34
   dreams, 74–76, 81–82
appreciation to God for revealing his will, 201
armed forces. *see* military service
arthritis, 7
attitude of the heart in prayer, 11, 296
audience for prayer, 289

B

Baal, 275
barriers to prayer, 195–197, 261
basics of prayer, 10–12
Beatitudes, 311
beauty, presence of God, 4
bedtime prayers, 258–260
"Before the Snow Flies" (LaRose Karr), 119–121
Bell, James Stuart, 100–103
Benson, Herbert, 6, 8
Bible. *see also Scripture Reference Index*
   effective prayer, as guide to, 175–177
   heroes and heroines, 295
   looking for God's message in, 186–187
   parenting, 216
   prayers of, 266–287
   promises of prayer, 3–5
   scripture reading as prayer, 184, 200
birth defects, 54–57

Blevins, Holly, 74–76
blindness, 26–30, 261–262
Boardman, William E., 4
The Book of Common Prayer, 317–318
Bradford, Laura L., 80–82
bread, 297–299
"Breaking Selfish Pride" (Faith Turnet), 91–94
"A Bright New World" (Joyce Starr Macias), 152–156
Brown, Ty'Ann A., x–xiii
Bruce Almighty (film), 187
busyness, as barrier to prayer, 195

C

cancer, 130–132, 152–156, 166–170
car accidents, 19–22, 31–34, 112–114, 157–160
cars
    praying while driving, 185, 196
    as sanctuary, 185
certainty in God, 239
change and new paths, 45–49
Chapman, Steven Curtis, 184
Child of God, 25
children
    birth defects, 54–57
    endurance while raising, 213–214
    faith in prayer, 122–124
    infertility, 133–135, 217–218
    injuries to, 71–73
    parents' troubles, 58–61, 62–66
Christmas trees, 133–135
chronic illnesses
    birth defects, 54–57
    praying during, 244–246
    survival, 23–25, 50–53
Civil War, 315–316
college graduation, 225–226
comfort, 5, 231
    accident, presence of God, 31–34, 157
    angelic intervention, 41–44
    sympathy for grief, 228–229
competition, parenting and, 214
complaining to God, 197, 234
comprehension of God's word, 191–192
condolences, 227–229
confidence in purpose, 219–220, 221–222
confirmation of God's voice, 186

Conlon, Tom and Roseann, 133–135
conscience, forgiveness and, 5
consistency of God, 179–180
Conti, AnnaLee, 125–129
conviction in prayer, 12
courage, 309, 310
crèche, 133–135
cures. *see* healing and rehabilitation

D

"Dad, Let's Pray!" (Bobbie Roper), 122–124
daily bread, 297–299
Dalrymple, Betty Johnson, 130–132
dating and courtship, 89–90
Davenport, Jenni, 136–140
David, 175, 264
    prayer of protection, 277–278
deadlines, waiting to know God's will, 200–201
death, 35–37
    of a parent, 58–61, 148–151, 152–156
    of a spouse, 80–82, 108–111, 125–129
    sympathy, praying in, 227–229
    visions of God, 286
debts, 300–301
decisions, discovering God's will, 199–201
Deer's Cry (Prayer of St. Patrick), 313
delegation of responsibilities, 212
denominations of Christianity, 267–268
depression and anxiety, 42, 234–235
    healing, 7–8
    physical disability and, 87–88
    survival, 3
determination, praying with, 205–206
devil. *see* Satan
Dillon, Brenda, 16–18
disability, 86–90
the disciples, 14–15, 225. *see also specific disciples by name*
    fulfillment of God's promise to, 191
discovering God's will, 199–201
distractions
    internal and external, 196
    listening for God's voice, 193, 194
    prayer and, 185, 186, 195–196
    serenity and, 308
    as springboard to prayer, 195–196, 197
divorce, 86–90. *see also* marital discord

doubting God, 236–239, 263, 298

Doxology ("Praise God from Whom All Blessings Flow"), 282

dreams
  appearances by God, 74–76, 81–82
  bedtime prayers and, 259, 260
  parenting, 138–139
  Solomon's, 280

Duewel, Beth, 148–151

E

"An Earthquake Full of Blessings" (AnnaLee Conti), 125–129

effective prayer, Bible as guide to, 175–177

Elijah (the Tishbite), 185, 275–276

emotions, control of, 233

employment. *see also* unemployment
  new jobs, 221–222
  problems, 91–94, 119–121

end-of-life, 35–37, 148–151. *see also* death

end times and rapture, 137, 138–139

endurance
  child-rearing, 213–214
  Paul's prayers, 271

enemies, 254

engagement (marriage), 223–224

English Reformation, 317

epidemic illness, 95–99

epilepsy, 23–25

errors while praying, 184

escapes from temptation, 208, 302–303

Estes, Anita, 157–160

exhaustion, 242–243

expectations for prayer, 11, 223–224

external distractions, 196

"external secular meditation," 7

eye injuries and conditions, 26–30, 86–90

F

"Face-to-Face with Jesus" (Delores E. Topliff), 19–22

facial injuries, 31–34, 71–73

Fairbrother, Virginia Rose, 50–53

faith and trust in God, 37, 98, 115–118, 121, 131–132, 161–165, 199
  financial distress and, 247
  forgiveness, 300
  gift of, 29

infertility and, 217–218

Paul's prayers, 270–272, 271

unemployment and, 210

worrying, 251–252

falls and falling, 38–40, 115–118

family problems, 249–250. *see also* marital discord; parenting

Farrington, Ellen, 62–66

"Father Knows Best" (Dorothy J. Haire), 108–111

fatigue
  as barrier to prayer, 196
  child-rearing and, 215

favoritism, 240

fear, 230–231, 263
  bedtime prayers and, 258–259
  illness and, 246

Fellowship of Christian Athletes, 195

female and male roles in public worship, 255

de Fénelon, François, 197

"The Final Authority" (Elfriede Volk), 95–99

financial troubles, 247–248. *see also* unemployment
  husband and wife, 45–49, 145–147
  planning for marriage, 223

food, 77–79

forgiveness, 5, 286–287, 300–301
  Lincoln and, 315–316

Franciscan order of monks, 311

Frank, Janet, 8

friends, 71–73, 86–90, 261

frustration
  depression and, 234
  prayer and, 296

G

Gaither, Bill and Gloria, 292

gift card, 77–79

gift of faith, 29

giving thanks to God
  avoiding temptation, 208
  healing and survival, 34
  infertility, dealing with, 218
  observing the Sabbath, 243
  starting a new job, 221, 222
  while discovering God's will, 201

"Glory Be to the Father" (Gloria Patri), 282

glory of God, 305–306

"God's Intrusion" (Brenda Dillon), 16–18

God's voice
  how God speaks, 191–192
  listening, 185–187, 193–194
  qualities of, 188–189
  recognizing, 188–189
God's will, discovering, 199–201
God's Word, 95, 158. *see also* Bible; voice of God
  comprehension of, 191–192
  content of, 189–190
  interpretation of, 185–186, 188–189
grace, 4
graduation from college, 225–226
gratitude. *see* giving thanks
Greek gods, 314
Gregory, Anna M., 45–49
grief and grieving, 148–151, 264
  infertility and, 217–218
  job loss, 209–210
  sympathy for, 227–229
groceries, 77–79
group prayer, 202–204, 210, 254–255
Grudem, Wayne, 178
guide for prayer, 171–319
Guthrie, David and Nancy, 205

H

Haire, Dorothy J., 108–111
hand holding during mealtime prayers, 256–257
Hanegraaff, Hank, 299, 303, 304
Hannah's prayers, 284–285
happiness, optimism and, 8
Harrel, Charles Earl, 35–37
Harris, Cassie, 23–25
headaches, 7, 104–107. *see also* migraine headaches
"The Healer She Could Only Imagine" (Charles Earl Harrel), 35–37
healing and rehabilitation, 4, 83–85, 166–170, 244–246
  after life support decisions, 35–37
  birth defects, 54–57
  chronic illness, 50–53
  headaches, 104–107
  marriage, 62–66
  neurological damage, 87–88
  reasons for praying, 6–7
  research, 6–9
  typhus, 95–99

health. *see* illness
health care staff, 41–44, 50–53, 54–57, 86–90, 246
hearing God, 185–187. *see also* voice of God
heart ailments, 16–18, 41–44, 83–85
heaven, 289–290
Heaven (Alcorn), 289
"A Heavenly Code Blue" (Jeff Adams), 83–85
"He Gives His Angels Charge over Us" (Delores E. Topliff), 71–73
Helgeson, Gail R., 161–165
helplessness, 273
Henry, Matthew, 183–184, 305
"He Opened My Eyes" (Jeff Adams), 26–30
heroes and heroines of the Bible, 295
high blood pressure, 7
High Priestly Prayer, 175, 267–269
hiking, 115–118
holidays, 77–79, 133–135
holiness, 291–292
Holy Spirit
  God's Word, help in understanding, 191–192
  intercession by, 183–184
  understanding, 192
"Home Is Where the Heart Is" (James Stuart Bell), 100–103
homes, 45–49, 100–103
  retirement, 141–144
hope, 29, 37, 166–170
hospitals, 41–44, 50–53, 54–57, 58–61, 83–85, 86–90
Hostetler, Bob, 2–6
Huff, Charles J., 112–114
humility in prayer, 11
  The Prayer of Saint Francis of Assisi, 311–312
  Solomon's, 279–281, 289
hunting, 122–124
husband and wife
  death and widowhood, 108–111
  divorce, 86–90
  expectation when getting married, 223–224
  financial trouble, 145–147
  infertility, 217–218
  marital discord, 42, 62–66, 86–90, 104–105
  mid-life change of direction, 67–70
  widowhood, 80–82, 108–111, 125–129
Hybels, Bill, 195

I

illness, 3–4
  chronic illnesses, 50–53
  fears, 246
  heart ailments, 16–18, 41–44, 83–85
  how to pray during, 244–246
  mental illness, 58–61
  parents, 152–156
  prayer group requests, 203
  typhus epidemic, 95–99
importance of prayer, 307–318
impossibility, 264–265. *see also* miracles
imprecatory prayers, 254
inadequacy, as barrier to prayer, 196
indecision, 77–79
infertility, 133–135
  grief and, 217–218
insignificant events, prayer for, 38–40
insomnia, 8
intercession by Holy Spirit, 183–184
internal distractions, 196
"internal secular meditation," 7
interpretation of God's Word, 185–186, 188–189
interruptions. *see* distractions
"An Intimate Look at Prayer" (Bob Hostetler), 2–5
intuition, understanding God's will, 201
Ireland, 313
Isaiah (prophet), 179

J

Jacob, 240
Jacobs, Gregg D., 8
jealousy, 240–241
Jennings, Ken, 263
"Jesus Loves Me, This I Know," 189
Job, 205
job loss. *see* unemployment
Jonah, 178, 179
Joshua, 264
journals, prayer groups, 202
joy, 138–139
Jude's prayers, 282–283

K

Karr, LaRose, 119–121
kingdom of God, 293–294, 305–306

kneeling for bedtime prayers, 258–260
Knight, Ellen, 77–79
knowledge, Paul's prayers, 272
Koenig, Harold, 7
Kreeft, Peter, 212

L

La Clochette (journal), 312
LaFontaine, Don, 188–189
Laird, S. P., 7
the Last Supper, 191
Lazarus' death, 264
learning to pray, 172–173. *see also* understanding
"Leaving the God of Money" (Marleen McDowell), 145–147
Lewis, C. S., 258
life support decisions, 35–37
lilies, 251, 298
Lincoln, Abraham, 315–316
listening by God, 261–262
listening to God, 185–187, 193–194. *see also* voice of God
loneliness, 42
longing, praying with, 199–201
Loomis, Donna Lee, 41–44
The Lord's Prayer, 11, 175, 288–306
  "Our Father in Heaven," 289–290
  "Hallowed Be Your Name," 291–292
  "Your Kingdom Come," 293–294
  "Your Will Be Done on Earth as It Is in Heaven," 295–296
  "Give Us This Day Our Daily Bread," 297–299
  "Forgive Us Our Debts, as We Forgive Our Debtors," 300–301
  "Do Not Lead Us into Temptation, but Deliver Us from the Evil One," 302–304
  "For Yours Is the Kingdom and the Power and the Glory Forever," 305–306
Lord, Teach Us to Pray, 172
Lorica (Prayer of St. Patrick), 313
loss, 45–49
L'Osservatore Romano, 312
lost belongings, 161–165
"Loving My Soldier" (Ellen Farrington), 62–66
Lucado, Max, 247, 261
Luther, Martin, 212, 238

M

MacArthur, John, 302
Macias, Joyce Starr, 152–156
magnification of God, 305–306
making time for prayer, 195
male and female roles in public worship, 255
manna, 297
marital discord, 42, 62–66, 86–90, 104–105
martyrdom, 287
Matheson, George, 261–262
McDowell, Marleen, 145–147
mealtime prayers, hand holding during, 256–257
medication, depression and, 235
meditation, 7. *see also* silence
mental illness, 58–61, 62–66
mercy of God, 4, 273–274
"The Message from Heaven" (Betty Johnson
    Dalrymple), 130–132
methods for praying, 10–12
mid-life change of direction, 67–70
migraine headaches, 7, 86–90, 104–107
military service
    marital problems after, 62–66
    praying with confidence concerning, 219–220
Miller, Lisa, 7–8
"Miracle Boy" (Melinda Wright, Anita Estes), 157–160
miracles, 161–165
    healing and cures, 16–18, 28–30, 35–37, 54–57,
        58–61, 157–160, 166–170
    pregnancy, 133–135
    survival, 19–22, 23–25, 31–34, 50–53
"The Miraculous Ride" (Jenni Davenport), 136–140
missionaries, St. Patrick's influence, 314
mistakes while praying, 184
Mitcham, Marybeth, 54–57
money, 145–147. *see also* financial troubles
Montgomery, James, 10
Moses, 175, 177, 178–179, 193, 212, 261, 273
Mother Teresa, 236, 237
mountain climbing, 115–118
mourning, 227–229
movement to prayer, 178–182
Mullins, Rich, 312
Murray, Andrew, 3–4, 172
"My Dream Husband" (Laura L. Bradford), 80–82
"My Emmanuel Moment" (Holly Blevins), 74–76
"My Only True Security" (Anna M. Gregory), 45–49

mysteries, parables and, 293
"The Mysterious Comforter" (Joshua F. Younce),
    31–34

N

names
    Child of God, 24–25
    Jesus, 292
national day of "prayer and humiliation," 315
"The Nativity Baby" (David Michael Smith), 133–135
nativity scene, 133–135
near death experiences, 41–44, 83–85, 86–87
needs and wants, 297–299
Nehemiah, 273–274
nervous system, effects of prayer on, 8
neurological conditions, 23–25, 86–90
Newberg, Andrew, 8
New Testament prayers, 176, 270–272, 282. *See also*
    Scripture Index
    mealtime prayers, 256
Nichols, Fern, 202
Niebuhr, Reinhold, 308, 309–310
Noah, 176
"No More Headaches" (Marty Prudhomme), 104–107
"Nowhere to Call Home" (Bobbie Roper), 141–144
nurses, 86–90

O

Old Testament, 178. *see also Scripture Reference Index*
    mealtime prayers, 256
    name for God, 291
omniscient God, 263
opheilema, 300
organ transplants, 50–53
"Our Father …." *see* The Lord's Prayer
overcommitment, 243, 308
overwhelming situations, 183

P

Panzica, Susan Allen, 38–40
"Paper Angels" (Beth Duewel), 148–151
parables, 293–294, 300, 303
parenting, 136–140
    accidents and, 112–114, 157–160
    bedtime prayers, 258–260
    birth defects, 54–57
    disabilities and, 88–90

endurance, 213–216
faith of a child, 122–124
favoritism, 240
illness and, 95–99, 104
marital problems, 62–66
mealtime prayers, 256
protecting children, 19–22, 38–40, 71–73, 258
security, 45–49
teenagers, 2–3, 136–140
parents, caring for, 58–61, 152–156, 166–170
Pargament, Kenneth, 7
patience, waiting for God's will, 200–201
Paul, the apostle, 175, 176–177, 183, 186, 188–189, 191, 261
on an "unknown god," 314
prayers for the churches, 270–272
temptation, 302, 303, 304
peace and sense of peace, 110, 124, 132, 157–160
life decisions and choices, 101
perfect peace, 4
The Prayer of Saint Francis of Assisi, 311–312
Serenity Prayer, 308–310
unemployment, 209–210
widowhood, 80–82
worrying and, 252
peace of God, 4
persecution, praying with determination during, 205–206
persistence in prayer, 11–12, 197
Peterson, Eugene, 193, 194
Piper, John, 300
planning, 299
post-traumatic stress disorder, 62–66
poverty, 45–49
practicality and practical matters, 11, 228, 253–265
"Praise God from Whom All Blessings Flow" (Doxology), 282
praising God, 305. *see also* giving thanks to God
prayer groups and meetings, 202–204, 210, 254–255
Prayer of Saint Francis of Assisi, 311–312
Prayer of Saint Patrick, 313–314
prayer requests, 202–203
"The Prayer Stone" (Ray Stenner, Janice Richardson), 86–90
praying aloud, 254–255
"A Precise Prayer for Healing" (Susan L. Tuttle), 166–170

pregnancy, 133–135
presence of God, 4, 43. *see also* voice of God
acceptance of God, 154, 155
accidents, comfort following, 31–34, 157
dreams, 74–76, 81–82
protection by, 21–22
survival and healing, 52
widowhood, 110
pride, 91–94
private requests for prayer, 202–203, 204
productivity, 211–212
protection
of children, 19–22, 38–40, 71–73, 258
David's prayer of, 277–278
Prayer of St. Patrick, 313–314
Prudhomme, Marty, 104–107
psalmists, 175, 176–177
Psalms, as written prayer, 318. *see also Scripture Reference Index*
public worship, 254–255
mealtime prayers, 256
prayer groups and meetings, 202–204, 210, 254–255
purity, Paul's prayers, 272

Q
questioning God, 236–239

R
"A Race to the Bottom" (Susan M. Watkins), 115–118
racquetball, 26–30
reasons for praying, 6–9
recognizing God's voice, 188–189
Redmond, Derek, 191
relational prayer, 11
relaxation
techniques, 7
while waiting for God's will, 200–201
relinquishment, 310
reminding God of truths learned from Bible, 179
reputation, 91–94
requests for prayer, 202–203
research, healing aspect of prayer, 6–9
resisting temptation, 208
restaurant mealtime prayers, 256
results of prayer, 1–12, 13–170
resuscitation, 83–85, 86–87

retirement, 141–144, 147
"A Return to Sanity" (Evelyn Rhodes Smith), 58–61
Richardson, Janice, 86–90
Roper, Bobbie
  "Dad, Let's Pray!," 122–124
  "Nowhere to Call Home," 141–144

S

Sabbath, 242–243
sacrificial love, 224
safety, 5
Saint Francis of Assisi, 311–312
Saint Patrick, 313–314
Samuel, 193
sanity, 58–61
Satan
  temptation, 303–304
  voice of, 189, 190
Scripture. *see also Scripture Reference Index*
  praying the Scriptures, 184, 199
security, 45–49
  presence of God, 4
seminary, 67–70
serenity, 84–85, 308–310. *see also* peace and sense of
    peace
Serenity Prayer, 308–310
Sermon on the Mount, 293
sexual temptation and sin, 207–208, 282
Shane, Bill, 41–44
Shane, Donna Lee Loomis, 41–44
Shapiro, Fred, 309–310
"Shortest, Biggest Prayer" (Charles J. Huff), 112–114
signs from God, xii, 52, 102, 187
silence. *see also* distractions
  meditation, 7
  prayer and, 184, 185, 187, 196
sin. *see also* temptation
  forgiveness, 300–301
singing
  as aid to praying, 184
  mealtime prayers, 256
skepticism, 236–239, 263, 298
sleep difficulties, 8
Smith, David Michael
  "An Unexpected Gift," 77–79
  "The Nativity Baby," 133–135

Smith, Evelyn Rhodes, 58–61
Solomon
    humility in prayer, 279–281, 289
    on wisdom, 309, 310
"A Sparkling Miracle" (Gail R. Helgeson), 161–165
speech, loss of ability, 3–4
sports injury, 26–30
Sproul, R. C., 291
Spurgeon, Charles Haddon, 262, 303
stamina, child-rearing, 214–215
Stanton, Edwin, 316
starting to pray, 176–177
Stenner, Ray, 86–90
Stephen's prayers, 286–287
stepping out in faith, 121
steps for prayer, 10–12
strength, 5. *see also* endurance
    Paul's prayers, 271
suffering. *see also* illness
    depression and, 234–235
    illness and, 244–246
    praying with determination during, 205–206
suicide attempt, 88
surgery, 50–53, 87, 166–170
survival. *see also* accidents; healing and rehabilitation;
      miracles
    depression and anxiety, 3
    suffering and, 205–206
    unemployment, 210
    violent crimes, 231
sympathy, 227–229
synantilambanetai, 183

T

techniques, 200–201
techniques for praying, 10–12
technology. *see also* distractions
    prayer groups and, 204
teenagers, 2–3, 136–140
television, prayer and, 185, 186
temptation, 207–208, 302–304
testing, 304. *see also* temptation
Thanking God. *see* giving thanks to God
Thanksgiving, 77–79, 256–257
"Three Days to Live" (Virginia Rose Fairbrother),
      50–53

time
as barrier to prayer, 195
exhaustion, 242–243
management, 211–212
prayer groups, 203–204
waiting for God's will, 200–201
Timeless Healing: The Power and Biology of Belief
(Benson), 6, 8
time management, 211–212
topical Bibles, 186–187
Topliff, Delores E.
"Face-to-Face with Jesus," 19–22
"He Gives His Angels Charge over Us," 71–73
Tozer, A. W., 292
travelling, 161–165
trespasses, 300–301
Trinity, 268
trust in God. *see* faith and trust in God
Turkey, xii–xiii
Turnet, Faith, 91–94
Tuttle, Susan L., 166–170
"The Two-Percent Life Experience" (Jan Apilado),
67–70

U

uncertainty about what to pray for, 183–184
understanding
bedtime prayers, 260
doubting God, 239
Elijah's prayers, 276
forgiveness, 301
God's will, 201
Holy Spirit, 192
how to be moved to pray, 179–182
parenting, 215–216
Paul's prayers, 272
Satan and temptation, 303–304
serenity, 310
unity, 268
unemployment, 45–49
how to pray with peace, 209–210
"An Unexpected Gift" (David Michael Smith), 77–79
unity, Christian, 267–269
University of Rochester, 6

V

vision of Jesus, 21–22, 74–76, 286
visits from God, 43. *see also* presence of God
accident, comfort following, 31–34, 157
dreams, 74–76, 81–82
voice of God, 23–25, 43, 67–70, 110, 193–194
how to hear, 185–187
"The Voice of My Maker" (Cassie Harris), 23–25
Volk, Elfriede, 95–99
volunteering, after loss of job, 210

W

waiting for God's will, 200–201
walking and exercise, 243
Walsh, Sheila, 235
warnings and fear, 231
wartime, prayers during, 309, 312
Watkins, Susan M., 115–118
weakness. *see also* temptation
help from Holy Spirit during, 191
wedding, 31–34, 223–224
widowhood, 80–82, 108–111, 125–129
will of God, 183, 295–296
winter, 121, 122–124
wisdom, 4, 142, 263, 308–310
Paul's prayers, 272
Solomon's prayer, 279–281
worldliness, 195
worrying, 251–252, 298. *see also* fear
Wright, Melinda, 157–160
written prayers, 184, 200. *see also* Bible; The Lord's
Prayer
The Book of Common Prayer, 317–318
Prayer of Saint Francis (of Assisi), 311–312
Prayer of Saint Patrick, 313–314
Psalms, 318 (*see also Scripture Reference Index*)

Y

The Yale Book of Quotations, 309–310
Younce, Joshua F., 31–34
youth. *see also* children; parenting
graduation from college, 225–226

Note from the Editors

We hope you enjoyed *What Prayer Can Do,* published by the Books and Inspirational Media Division of Guideposts, a nonprofit organization that touches millions of lives every day through products and services that inspire, encourage, help you grow in your faith, and celebrate God's love.

Thank you for making a difference with your purchase of this book, which helps fund our many outreach programs to military personnel, prisons, hospitals, nursing homes, and educational institutions.

We also create many useful and uplifting online resources. Visit Guideposts.org to read true stories of hope and inspiration, sign up for free newsletters, download free e-books, join our Facebook community, and follow our stimulating blogs. We also encourage you to become a prayer partner by visiting us at Ourprayer.org or on the OurPrayer Facebook page.

To learn about other Guideposts publications, including the best-selling devotional *Daily Guideposts,* go to Guideposts.org/Shop, call (800) 932-2145, or write to Guideposts, PO Box 5815, Harlan, Iowa 51593.